Church and Society in County Kildare, c.1470–1547

Church and Society in County Kildare, *c.*1470–1547

MARY ANN LYONS

FOUR COURTS PRESS

Set in 10.5 on 13 point Times for
FOUR COURTS PRESS LTD
Fumbally Lane, Dublin 8, Ireland
e-mail: info@four-courts-press.ie
and in North America
FOUR COURTS PRESS LTD
c/o ISBS, 5804 N.E. Hassalo Street, Portland, OR 97213.

© Mary Ann Lyons 2000

A catalogue record for this title
is available from the British Library.

ISBN 1–85182–459–6

Printed in England
by MPG Books, Bodmin, Cornwall

Contents

To my parents

Maynooth Historical Studies

GENERAL EDITOR: RAYMOND GILLESPIE

Over the last three generations the study of Irish history has been transformed almost out of recognition. The work of scholars such as J.C. Beckett, R. Dudley Edwards, R.B. McDowell, T.W. Moody and D.B. Quinn established scholarly standards within which the study of Irish history could proceed and, with their students, demonstrated in their writing how those standards could be applied. In the main these writings concentrated on the traditional historical themes, dealing with the political and constitutional problems which Ireland encountered in the past. More recently a new generation of scholars have built on these insights but have also looked again at the traditional canon of Irish history. Some have re-examined older problems in the light of fresh evidence or new conceptual models. Others have broadened the range of the debate on the Irish past by insisting on the importance of economic, social, local or cultural factors in shaping the Irish historical experience.

The result of this expansion in historical research has been a dramatic growth in publications dealing with the whole range of Irish history and hence a series of lively debates on the nature of the study of the Irish past. Maynooth Historical Studies is part of that new phenomenon. The series contributes to the debate on the interpretation of the Irish past by presenting the results of new research which either looks again at old problems or casts light into hitherto dark corners of the historical landscape. Both the individual volumes, and the series as a whole, reflect the complexity of understanding the evolution of Irish society and in so doing presents the study of Irish history as the vibrant and challenging discipline that it is.

List of Abbreviations

Cal. Carew MSS, 1515-74	*Calendar of the Carew manuscripts preserved in the archiepiscopal library at Lambeth, 1515-1624.* 6 vols London, 1867-73.
Cal. pat. rolls, Ire., Hen. VIII-Eliz.	*Calendar of the patent and close rolls of chancery in Ireland in the reigns of Henry VIII, Edward VI, Mary, and Elizabeth.* Ed. James Morrin. i (1514-75); ii (1576-1603). Dublin, 1861-63.
Cal. S.P. Ire.	*Calendar of state papers relating to Ireland, 1509-1625.* 16 vols London, 1860-61.
Fiants Ire.	Calendar of fiants, Henry VIII to Elizabeth. In *Report of the Deputy Keeper of the Public Records of Ireland.* 7-22. Dublin, 1875-90.
L. & P. Hen. VIII	*Letters and papers, foreign and domestic, Henry VIII.* 21 vols London, 1862-1932.
N.A.I.	National Archives of Ireland
S.P. Hen. VIII	*State papers, Henry VIII.* 11 vols. London, 1830-52.

Sums of money which are not followed by (sterling) are in Irish value. The exchange rate in the sixteenth century was £1 sterling = IR £1 10*s*. 0*d*.

Preface

This study is based upon a Master's dissertation entitled 'Church and society in early sixteenth-century Kildare' which I completed under the direction of Colm Lennon in the Department of Modern History, N.U.I. Maynooth in 1991. For several years, as both an undergraduate and postgraduate student, I have benefited greatly from Dr Lennon's tutelage and exemplary scholarship as well as his constant support, confidence and interest, all of which I greatly appreciate. My thanks to Raymond Gillespie, series editor, for his encouragement and advice in the preparation of this work and to Professor Vincent Comerford and all the members of the Department of Modern History, N.U.I. Maynooth for their support and assistance. Vincent Carey, Enda Delaney and Pauline Mooney each read drafts of the work and made helpful suggestions for which I am very grateful. My thanks to Professor Steven Ellis for his continued interest in and support of my research in this area. I also wish to thank Mr Jim Keenan for his cartography, and Helen Litton for her work in preparing the text for publication. My thanks to my colleagues in the Department of Government and Society in the University of Limerick for their encouragement and support, especially John Logan, Bernadette Whelan, Padráig Lenihan and Ruán O'Donnell. The Revd Sean Lyons and the Revd James Brennan both translated documents for which I am grateful. Finally, I am indebted to my immediate family for their unfailing support and gentle encouragement.

List of Illustrations

Introduction

The history of late medieval Kildare is inevitably intertwined with that of the earls of Kildare since the Fitzgerald dynasty's influence permeated and dominated the county's political, social, economic and ecclesiastical life, particularly during the period of their political ascendancy (c.1470 to 1534). Not surprisingly therefore the treatment to date of the county's history at this time has tended to be completely overshadowed by a concentration on its chief magnates. However, the population of county Kildare in their own right experienced an interesting and turbulent phase in their history during this period, especially in the 1530s, when they not only witnessed first hand the abrupt and violent end to the Kildare ascendancy, but also experienced further dislocation with the suppression of the county's monastic houses. This study therefore aims to present an insight into county society in the period from 1470 down to the end of King Henry VIII's reign in 1547.

It begins with a mosaic of Kildare, setting the county within the context of the contracted English colony in the late medieval lordship when the Kildare ascendancy was in its infancy. Various districts throughout the county are described in detail, providing vignettes on the lives of tenants and members of the gentry in their local contexts and highlighting variations between areas within Kildare. The ascent of the earls of Kildare to their position of dominance in the latter half of the fifteenth century is discussed in relation to their role in staying the advance of Gaelic elements on the Pale marches, and as a prelude to the study of the Kildares' county estate in the early sixteenth century. The ninth earl's administration of his county estate and the ramifications at local level of his coordination of the county's defences are explored. The historical context for the restoration of the shire's liberty in the 1510s is examined, as are the reasons for the controversy which surrounded the earl's liberty in the 1530s. The hybrid character of the familial, social, cultural, economic, legal, ecclesiastical and military spheres of life in county Kildare in this period is then discussed, highlighting the inappropriateness of attempting to construct a mutually exclusive dichotomy between English and Gaelic elements within that society.

Church organization, and the involvement of the county's laity in the life of the church in the pre-Reformation and early Reformation eras, is afforded detailed treatment as a subject which has heretofore received no unified scholarly assessment. Set within the context of an examination of the state of the church in the lordship in the late medieval period, this study outlines the structures and jurisdictions of church organization in the county as a whole. James Murray has presented a comprehensive study of the archdiocese of Dublin in the Tudor period and, as a result, greater attention is focused on the diocese of Kildare in the present work.[1] The diocese's episcopal succession is traced from the early fifteenth century and the state of the county's monasteries, its diocesan finances, the circumstances in which its clergy lived and ministered, and instances of clerical abuse in the early sixteenth century are discussed.

Lay piety and patronage of the church were very vibrant in county Kildare as elsewhere in the lordship in the pre-Reformation period. The involvement of the county gentry in church affairs is therefore examined. By virtue of the unrivalled munificence of the patronage of the Kildares, particular emphasis is placed on their involvement in local church affairs and especially their establishment in 1518 of a chantry college adjacent to their castle at Maynooth. Following the death of Bishop Edmund Lane in the early 1520s, episcopal succession to Kildare diocese became complicated by the factional politics of the time. This development is examined in conjunction with tracing incursions made on the ninth earl's landed interests by successive archbishops of Dublin in the 1510s and 1520s which were intensified by Archbishop John Alen in the early 1530s. At that time, mounting opposition from senior prelates including Alen and Walter Wellesley, bishop of Kildare, was, as we shall see, bitterly resented by the ninth earl of Kildare who himself threatened Wellesley's life and whose supporters killed Alen in 1534.

The Geraldine rebellion in 1534-5 and the subsequent execution of Gearóid Óg's son Thomas, Lord Offaly and tenth earl of Kildare, along with the leaders of the family's senior collateral branches had a resounding impact throughout the lordship, nowhere more so than in Kildare itself. Although government officials exaggerated the degree of devastation caused by the disturbances, property in areas of the county borderlands certainly suffered widespread and outright destruction both during the rebellion and as a result of raids mounted by the neighbouring Gaelic septs in the late 1530s. In addition, the county was stripped of its liberty status in 1534 and was laid open to the untrammelled

---

1 James Murray, 'The Tudor diocese of Dublin: episcopal government, ecclesiastical politics and enforcement of the Reformation, c.1534-1590' (Ph.D. thesis, University of Dublin, 1997) (hereafter Murray, 'The Tudor diocese of Dublin'). I wish to thank James Murray for allowing me to cite material from his doctoral thesis for the purpose of this study.

influence of the Dublin administration. Two of the government's leading officials at this time, Sir John Alen and Sir Gerald Aylmer, had family estates in Kildare and they sought to engender a sense of urgency in Henry VIII, advising him to seize this momentary opportunity to take immediate steps towards the establishment of order in Leinster.

Coming as it did in the immediate wake of the suppression of the Kildare revolt and the abolition of the county's liberty, the campaign for the dissolution of the county's monasteries proved particularly opportune. Consequently, as this study shows, it was explicitly adapted to facilitate the strengthening of the county borderlands' existing defences and the extension of the administration's effective authority throughout and beyond the county. As such it helped to lay the foundations for the implementation of Anthony St Leger's political programme for establishing order in Leinster in the early 1540s. The second half of this work therefore concentrates upon the political and social impact of the dissolution of Kildare's religious houses in the 1530s and early 1540s and the subsequent distribution of their properties, the most tangible impact of the Henrician Reformation in the shire.

Like the other shires of the Pale, county Kildare had a solid lesser aristocracy and gentry establishment with families such as the Wogans, the Eustaces and the Aylmers originally being of Anglo-Norman stock. To complement the discussion of the political dimension to the suppression campaign, the impact of the distribution of the monastic properties on the composition of these upper strata of county society and on the fortunes of individual lesser aristocracy and gentry families is examined. Through an analysis of Kildare's prominent, old-stock families and some of the more recent *arrivistes*, this study presents an insight into the fabric of county society prior to and during the Henrician Reformation period. Small families such as the Kerdiffs, the Sherlocks and the Flatisburys who owned relatively modest holdings and who had limited influence, if any, in the Dublin administration are shown to have had minimal involvement in or returns from the suppression of the monasteries in their immediate vicinity. In the keen competition for these properties, these families lost out to members of more prominent families who had political connections and influence, notably the Suttons and the Eustaces.

The degree to which the acquisition of monastic property served to consolidate or in certain instances augment the holdings of individual members of the county's lesser aristocracy and gentry families is also examined. Cases of individuals such as Martin Pelles of Athy, whose receipt of grants of monastic holdings facilitated his social advancement, are also isolated for study. There are relatively few records indicating the transfer of ownership of the ninth earl of Kildare's confiscated estates during the Henrician period. However, in so far as it is relevant, the impact of this piecemeal distribution of parcels of the earl's lands on the county's aristocracy and gentry will be discussed at appropriate junctures and in particular in the fourth section of this study. Finally, evidence of survivalism among these strata of county society during and after the reign of Henry VIII is brought to light, and its role in perpetuating the old religion within immediate family and community circles is discussed. By the end of the reign of Henry VIII, Kildare had survived the loss of its principal dynasty and the closure of its monasteries. As such, the county to which Gerald, the restored eleventh earl of Kildare, returned in the early 1550s had been fundamentally altered since the era of his father and grandfather.

1

Life in Late Medieval Kildare

> All the king's subjects of the ... four shires [of Meath, Louth,
> Dublin and Kildare] be near hand Irish, and wear their habits and
> use their tongue, so as they are clean gone and decayed; and there
> is not eight of the lords, knights, esquires, and gentlemen of the
> four shires but be in debt, and their land be made waste; and with-
> out brief remedy be had they must sell their lands, or else depart
> them and go to some other land
>
> Sir William Darcy, 'Decay of Ireland', 24 June 1515
> (*Cal. Carew Mss*, 1515-74, p. 8)

Until recently, our perception of the state of the English Pale in the late medieval period has been strongly coloured by an uncritical reliance upon contemporary reports such as that penned by Sir William Darcy on the 'degenerate' state of the colony. Contemporaries invariably exaggerated the degree of Gaelic 'infiltration' of the colony in an effort to spur the crown on to halt the incursions on the periphery of the marches of the Pale. Darcy's fatalistic account of the Palesmen 'falling to Irish order and Irish habits' was amplified in the summations of a later generation of commentators including Edmund Spenser and Edmund Campion. Spenser blamed the Old English for having 'degenerated from their ancient dignities' through 'licentious conversing with the Irish or worrying or fostering with them, or lack of meet nurture, or other such unhappy occasions'.[1] By contrast, Campion attributed the decline of the colony to a Gaelic revival whereby 'the Irish had raised continuous tumults against the English planted here with conquest, ... [and] ... coursed them into a narrow circuit of certain skies in Leinster ... "their pale", as whereabouts they durst not peep'.[2] Other contemporary writers reporting on the state of the

---

1 Edmund Spenser, *A view of the present state of Ireland* (Dublin, 1763 ed.), p. 102. 2 Edmund Campion, *History of Ireland* (1571), chap.1; quoted in 'A statute of the fortieth year of King Edward III', in *Tracts relating to Ireland*, ed. James Hardiman (Dublin, 1843), ii, pp xxv, xxviii.

Pale in the late medieval era tended to draw artificially sharp distinctions between areas where the population adhered to English law, customs and language and outlying districts where, with the exception of walled towns, English people did not observe the king's laws, but spoke Gaelic and dressed after the Irish fashion.[3] Such accounts echoed Polydore Vergil's description of medieval Ireland wherein he distinguished between two categories of inhabitants: 'one is gentle and cultured', living an English manner of life, obedient to the king and understanding the English language, 'the other type of islander is savage, rude and uncouth ... wild men in the woods'.[4]

Recent research, however, has challenged the accuracy of these contemporary accounts of the state of the Pale in this era and in the process has exposed the inadequacy of these simplistic accounts. The suggestion that a Gaelic revival caused the contraction in the crown's sphere of influence in the second half of the fifteenth century has been refuted. Steven Ellis acknowledges that the late medieval period witnessed the English colony in a defensive stance, what with the easing of royal control, territorial expansion on the part of the Gaelic clans and simultaneous cultural assimilation among the Englishry. Nevertheless he views these changes as stemming from the colony's associated weaknesses of royal neglect, misgovernment and poor provision for defence of English areas, rather than the result of any concerted initiative by Gaelic septs to challenge the crown.[5] The extent of Gaelic incursions on the Pale and the perceived gravity of the Gaelic threat have also been questioned, thus undermining the credibility of extremist accounts such as that written by Darcy in 1515. That the Dublin administration was concerned with making provision for the defence of the four counties of Dublin, Louth, Meath and Kildare in the last quarter of the fifteenth century is undisputed. However, Ellis has shown that most of the marches of the Pale were generally amenable to government control and that there is no substantial evidence to support the widely-held view that the English Pale was gradually shrinking under the Yorkists and early Tudors.[6] Moreover, Darcy's alarmism is exposed by the fact that in the 1520s, the maghery or heartland of the Pale was so peaceful that there were complaints about its lords' abandoning fortified dwellings for stately houses similar to those which were in vogue in England. By living in these 'little ordinary houses, as [if] they were in a land of peace', the Palesmen were accused of leaving the task of providing defence to the marchers.[7]

---

3 'State of Ireland', 1515 (*S.P. Hen. VIII*, ii, p. 22).   4 Polydor Vergil, *Anglica historia*, ed. and trans. Denys Hay (London, 1950), p. 79.   5 S.G. Ellis, *Tudor Ireland: crown, community and the conflict of cultures, 1470-1603* (London, 1985), p. 29 (hereafter Ellis, *Tudor Ireland*).   6 Ibid., pp 57-8.   7 Ibid., p. 57.

The inappropriateness of contemporaries' clear-cut distinctions between 'English' and 'Irish' areas has also been highlighted by evidence which indicates that the proportion of customary tenants with Gaelic names employed on manors in the maghery of Dublin and Meath numbered between a quarter and a half of the total recorded. In the case of Kildare, especially in the marches, that proportion rose to almost two-thirds.[8] This coexistence of English landowners and Gaelic tenants and the consequent interface of both cultures rendered any attempts to maintain these cultural divisions impractical and futile.[9]

I

The landscape of county Kildare in the late medieval period was marked by evidence that it formed part of the maghery (heartland) and marches (outlying areas) of the English Pale. The Pale maghery boundary was distinguished by a rampart which stretched from Dundalk, to Ardee, to Kells, south to Kilcock, Clane, Naas and the bridge of Kilcullen and finally eastwards to Ballymore Eustace, Rathmore, and Dalkey, and the marchlands were dotted with towers, castles and cultivated manorial estates. As in the case of each of the other three counties, only a small area of Kildare therefore fell within the maghery. This northeastern and eastern section of the county incorporated the districts of Maynooth, Ravensdale, Confey, Leixlip, Castletown, Donaghcomper, Kildrought (now Celbridge), Stacumney, Lyons, Oughterard, Castlewarden, Kill and Rathmore. The region was characterised by an undulating to rolling topography with generally fertile loam soil mainly used for arable farming, with a small proportion of land being used for pasture.

In the northeast, the village of Maynooth was the seat of the Fitzgeralds, earls of Kildare, whose political influence was at its height for the greater part of the period presently under review. The village had grown up around the Geraldine castle which had been established there in the early thirteenth century. A chapel had been constructed by the mid-thirteenth century and in 1286, a patent was issued for a weekly market and a three-day annual fair. A mill also existed in the village by the early fourteenth century. However, Maynooth was always a very small settlement, having had no burgesses, and no medieval

---

8 S.G. Ellis, *Tudor frontiers and noble power: the making of the British state* (Oxford, 1995), p. 29 (hereafter Ellis, *Tudor frontiers and noble power*). **9** Vincent Carey, *Surviving the Tudors* (forthcoming). For the purposes of this study, a distinction is made between English (English persons born in Ireland) and English-born (English persons born in England).

religious houses to elevate it to the status of a town.[10] In the early sixteenth century, there were approximately sixty cottages in Maynooth.[11] The lower and middling ranks of the population were predominantly Gaelic though several English names appear among the ninth earl's tenants and among jurors in the surveying of monastic and crown lands in 1540-1.[12] A number of women, presumably widows for the most part, were named occupants of valuable houses in the village in the late 1510s, notably Margery Brennan whose rent was 6s. 8d., and Margaret White who paid 3s. 4d. rent, while others such as Margaret Hussey and Catherine Moran lived in more modest cottages. Some tenants paid their rent in kind to the earls of Kildare: for instance, Thomas Kerd held his cottage free of rent in return for mending the earl's gear. In the barony of Salt, Owen O'Coigle presented the ninth earl with two gallons of aqua vitae in lieu of rent for his cottage. The majority of the local population worked the earl's manorial estate of Maynooth, which extended over much of the village's hinterland into the districts of Carton, Laraghbryan, Taghadoe, Jigginstown, Painstown, and Clonshambo.[13] They mainly engaged in arable farming with small parcels of land being given over to meadow and pasture. They grew wheat and oats and many kept chickens. Tenants were expected to pay their rent and dues on the feast of the Nativity. In general their holdings were modest, the largest individual holdings being in the region of eighty to ninety acres.[14] Some local residents presumably worked in Maynooth Castle as farm hands, stable boys, keepers of the earl's hounds and as kitchen staff. However, not unusually, the more senior positions such as lady-in-waiting to the countess were reserved to members of the county's English families particularly the Eustaces, with whom the Kildares had close familial ties in this period.[15]

Local Gaelic men worked in the village as tanners, shoemakers, millers and carpenters. Like the earls of Ormond, the Kildares rented out their mills to local individuals: for example, in 1518, Thomas Miagh was the ninth earl's master miller. He was also the village carpenter, and he lived in a better class of house for which he paid 2s. 6d. rent. He was assisted by an under-miller who was likewise employed by the earl.[16] The names of occupants of cottages

---

10 Anngret Simms and J.H. Andrews (ed.), *Irish country towns* (Cork, 1994), p. 62. **11** *Crown surveys of lands, 1540-41 with the Kildare rental begun in 1518*, ed. Gearóid MacNiocaill (Dublin, 1992), pp 133-4, 279-82 (hereafter *Crown surveys*). **12** See *Crown surveys* and *Extents of Irish monastic possessions, 1540-1541, from manuscripts in the Public Record Office, London*, ed. N.B. White (Dublin, 1943) (hereafter *Extents Ir. mon. possessions*). **13** *Crown surveys*, pp 133-44. **14** Ibid., pp 139-42. **15** See C.W. Fitzgerald, *The earls of Kildare and their ancestors from 1057 to 1773* (Dublin, 1858), p. 147 (hereafter Fitzgerald, *The earls of Kildare*). **16** *Crown surveys*, pp 247, 280. See also *Calendar of Ormond deeds, 1172-1350* [etc.], ed. Edmund Curtis (6 vols, Dublin, 1932-43), iii (1413-1509), p. 338 (hereafter *Ormond deeds*).

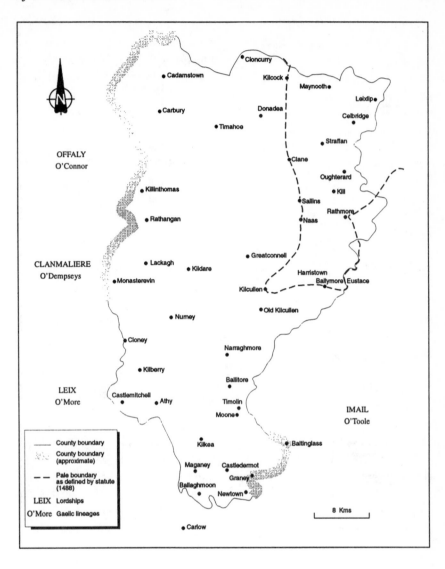

Map 1 The County of Kildare (*c.*1540)

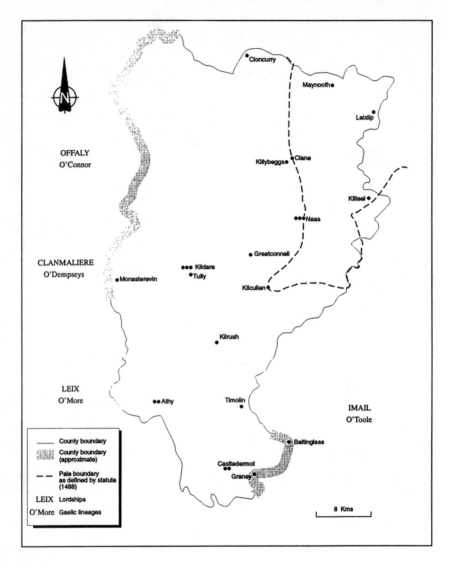

Map 2 Religious houses in the County of Kildare (*c.*1530)

in Maynooth and the vicinity which appear in the Kildare rental in 1518 seem to suggest that certain family names including Fowler, Carter, Tanner, Baker, Gunner, Glover, and Carpenter stemmed from traditional associations with specific trades.[17] The parish vicar resided in the village in a cottage with three acres attached. The villagers attended Mass in their parish church of Laraghbryan.[18] Because it was the home of the earls of Kildare, Maynooth witnessed visits from royal dignitaries, including Sir Richard Edgecombe in 1488. While Edgecombe was entertained at the Geraldine castle, the trail of less distinguished messengers dispatched to the ninth earl of Kildare could find accommodation in one of his cottages which was reserved 'for lodgings to messengers' and which was occupied free of rent in 1518 by Fenlagh Albanagh.[19] While the village was spared the attacks of Gaelic clans in the late medieval period, it undoubtedly incurred severe damages as a result of the rebellion in 1534-5 and the subsequent removal of the earls from Maynooth.

Leixlip village, which lay southeast of Maynooth, also had close ties with the Fitzgeralds. During his lifetime, the eighth earl had received a grant from Henry VII of the manor, castle and lands of Leixlip. His son, the ninth earl, rented the castle and land to Robert Usher of Dublin. By the late 1520s, the property had passed to Thomas Fitzgerald. In 1534 Sir James Fitzgerald owned Leixlip Castle and manor which was confiscated because he was accused of involvement in the rebellion. In 1538, following the surrender of the manor and castle by its occupant, Matthew King of Dublin, the property was leased to Sir John Alen of St Wolstan's. The local population seem to have been more homogeneous than was the case in Maynooth since in Leixlip, English names such as Harrold, Foster, Golding and Peppard frequently feature among both tenants and juror lists, though of course Irish names such as Ryan and Wollaghan still appear.[20] Land was generally used for arable purposes and trees were grown at St Catherine's near Leixlip. Like Maynooth, Leixlip had its own mill and a local miller. In 1518, Richard Tressy secured the rights from the ninth earl of Kildare to operate the mill which ground wheat and malt, a portion of which was reserved for payment of the rent of the mill in kind.[21] Leixlip had several parks and gardens along with two weirs on the river Liffey and the villagers were served by three rectors based at Castledillon, Confey and Leixlip village.[22]

17 *Crown surveys*, pp 180-1. 18 Ibid., p. 179. 19 Ibid., pp 280-1. 20 Ibid., pp 203-4. See also Walter Fitzgerald, 'Leixlip Castle', in *Kildare Arch. Soc. Jn.*, ii (1896-9), pp 393-406 (hereafter *Kildare Arch. Soc. Jn.*). 21 *Crown surveys*, p. 249. 22 Ibid., pp 203, 234, 283; *Extents Ir. mon. possessions*, pp 22, 28.

The districts of Kildrought, Donacomper, Stacumney and Castletown also lay under the direct influence of the earls of Kildare, particularly Castletown, which had been a possession of the Fitzgeralds since the late fourteenth century. Kildrought had grown up around a bridge and in the early sixteenth century the village had a castle and a mill that belonged to the ninth earl of Kildare and which he set to three Gaelic men.[23] As in Maynooth, the local population appears to have been a mix of Gaelic Irish and English with the Irish being in the majority. In 1535 Sir John Fitzgerald was seized of the manor of Kildrought and was unable to pass the property to his son, Edward, since the latter was implicated in the Geraldine rebellion. The manor, which consisted of 180 acres, therefore reverted to the crown and was subsequently granted to William Alen, a kinsman of Sir John Alen of St Wolstan's nearby.[24]

Much of the land in this district belonged to the priory of St Wolstan's, situated on the southern bank of the river Liffey. This monastic estate was dotted with around twenty-four cottages along with four mills which were located on the river Liffey. Arable farming dominated with some pockets of land being reserved for orchards, pasture and meadowland. The prior of the monastery reared his own herd of cattle on the commonage of pasture of the manor of Donaghcomper which was also at the disposal of his tenants. Although a considerable proportion of the land in the vicinity was covered by wood, brushwood and underwood, comparatively little was waste. The local population was served by four rectors based at Stacumney, Killadoon, Donaghcomper and Donaghmore.[25]

Further south, in the districts of Lyons, Oughterard, Castlewarden, Kill and Rathmore, the earls of Kildare were again dominant, but the Aylmers of Lyons were also of considerable standing in the immediate vicinity. The ninth earl's manor of Rathmore encompassed the village and hinterlands of Lady Castle, Oughterard, Timahoe, Ballenegyll, Garvoge, Dyromohon, Cohrcossan, Calen and Kepok as well as property in the vicinity of the towns of Rathmore, Oughterard, Naas and several villages in northwest Wicklow. At this time Rathmore was a town of some standing, having burgesses and portreeves.[26] In 1518, the demesne of Rathmore was leased by the ninth earl to Walter Hussey of Mulhussey in Meath.[27] In 1540, Nicholas Eustace was the principal leaseholder of Kildare's estate in Rathmore and lesser-ranking occupants were a

---

23 *Crown surveys*, p. 278. 24 Ibid., p. 284. 25 Mervyn Archdall, *Monasticon Hibernicum: or, a history of the abbeys, priories, and other religious houses in Ireland* (incomplete revised ed., 2 vols, Dublin, 1873-6), ii, pp 292-5 (hereafter Archdall, *Mon. Hib.*). 26 Geoffrey Martin, 'Plantation boroughs in medieval Ireland, with a handlist of boroughs to *c.*1500', in David Harkness and Mary O'Dowd (eds), *The town in Ireland, Historical Studies XIII* (Belfast, 1981), p. 49 (hereafter Martin, 'Plantation boroughs'). 27 *Crown surveys*, p. 253.

mix of Gaelic and English. Indeed in the district as a whole the population was of a similar composition to that of Maynooth with Alens, Westons, Baileys, Vales, Langs and Trotts living alongside Roddies, Laghnans, O'Ferralls and Lalors.[28]

Agriculture was generally arable, with wheat and oats being the district's principal crops. In the late 1530s the tenants on the Rathmore estate generally paid their rent in money. In addition they were obliged to pay customs, which in the case of Taghadoe tenants consisted of four carting days, four plough days, two hook days, one weeding day and two hens, all provided at their own expense in the service of the earl.[29] The local mill at Rathmore to which farmers brought their corn to be ground belonged to the earl of Kildare, and in the late 1510s and early 1520s Thomas Miagh of Maynooth, the earl's master miller, oversaw its operation.[30] The population of certain districts within this region was particularly hard hit by the Geraldine revolt and the ensuing disorder in the Pale. The earl of Kildare's manorial lands of Rathmore suffered severe damage and holdings were vacated, particularly the Wicklow properties and those in Rathmore itself, in Evellston and Goddamendy, Timahoe, Ballenegyll, Dyrmohon and Clane.[31] The local people were served by vicars based in Kill, Oughterard, Castlewarden and Rathmore and there were churches in Oughterard and Castlewarden, though both lay in a dishevelled state and their clergy tended to be absent for long spells in the 1540s.[32]

Further south, Ballymore Eustace, which lay on the border of the maghery of the Pale, came within the ambit of the Eustace family estates and in the 1530s it formed part of the estate of Christopher Eustace of Coghlanstown. This district was particularly important for the defence of the Pale and for five generations, down to the 1530s, the Eustaces had manned the castle there. As a result of its strategic importance, Ballymore was the target of attack by Gaelic septs who sought to undermine the Eustaces' hold on that corner of the Pale maghery during the Geraldine revolt. In the late 1530s, the castle was in the possession of George Browne, archbishop of Dublin. At that time, the local population was decidedly more Gaelic in composition than in the more northerly districts of the county. This is evidenced by the fact that apart from the Eustaces, all of those who served as jurors in the valuation of crown lands in 1540-1 in the area were of Gaelic origin.[33]Again the land was used for

28 Ibid., pp 144-5; *Extents Ir. mon. possessions*, pp 22, 91, 94.   **29** *Crown surveys*, p. 147.   **30** Ibid., p. 247.   **31** Ibid., pp 144-8.   **32** Ibid., pp 133, 142, 160, 223; *Extents Ir. mon. possessions*, pp 39, 41, 91; *Calendar of inquisitions formerly in the office of the chief remembrancer of the exchequer prepared for the MSS of the Irish Record Commission*, ed. Margaret Griffith (Dublin, 1991), pp 97, 110, 120-21, 126 (hereafter *Calendar of inquisitions*).   **33** *Crown surveys*, p. 222.

arable farming and rents and customs were paid to Eustace by the traditional means of money and in kind payments.[34] The owner of this property, Christopher Eustace, was executed for his implication in the Geraldine rebellion and in 1540, his kinsman, John Eustace, occupied a substantial portion of Christopher's confiscated estate at Ballymore.

The Pale maghery boundary skirted the villages of Kilcock and Clane and the towns of Kilcullen and Naas, the latter being the most important urban centre in northeast Kildare. Kilcock was a small village in which the ninth earl of Kildare leased his land to Sir Thomas Eustace.[35] South of Kilcock lay Rathcoffey, the seat of the Wogan family. The nearby village of Clane was also subject to the authority of the earls. As already mentioned, the ninth earl held lands in Kepok which were occupied in the early 1540s by Nicholas Wogan and Richard Penkiston, members of two long-standing county families. Kildare also leased land in the village from Sir John Rawson, prior of St John's in Kilmainham. The village's location on the border of the Pale meant that the local population also bore the burden of cess, payable to the earl, as well as being obliged to pay for three carts and for the support of two and a half horsemen. Some of these military men resided in the vicinity for extended periods: for example, in 1524, a galloglas named Owen Beady received a lease for three years of the tithes of Ballenegyll in Clane from the earl. The local jurors in the valuation of the village's priory in 1540 were almost exclusively Gaelic and two of the occupants of Kildare's land in the village in 1540 were also Gaelic. However, there was also a strong English presence at the upper stratum of local society. The entire barony of Clane was divided between Roger Penkiston, Sir David Wogan and his wife, Anastasia Stanton, and John St Michael, all of whom held their property by a knight's fee. Men of more modest means including John Russell occupied property at Blackcastle and held land in the village from the earl. Gerald and David Sutton occupied the lands of the priory in the 1530s and 1540s.[36] Local tithes were paid to the earl in the traditional form of wheat and malt, which had to be delivered to the earl's castle in Maynooth before Easter or Candlemas every year.[37] Apart from the priory in the village, the people of Clane were served by vicars resident in Clane and in nearby Bodenstown.[38]

The medieval town of Naas was fortified and enclosed by a circular wall and gates guarded by watchmen.[39] In the mid-fifteenth century, a levy was

---

34 Ibid., p. 223. **35** Ibid. **36** *Extents Ir. mon. possessions*, p. 164; *Crown surveys*, pp 143, 148, 241, 253, 278, 291, 351-2. **37** *Crown surveys*, pp 250-1, 253. **38** *Calendar of inquisitions*, pp 44, 103, 121; *Crown surveys*, p. 143; *Extents Ir. mon. possessions*, p. 93. **39** Avril Thomas, *The walled towns of Ireland* (2 vols, Dublin, 1992), i, p. 16.

imposed on the 'gentlemen and commons of Kildare' for the maintenance of the town walls and this levy continued to be collected throughout the sixteenth century.[40] Tolls were charged upon admission to Naas and the ninth earl of Kildare set the custom toll to local men such as Gerald and David Sutton for a fee.[41] In 1419 the town hosted a parliamentary session and had two parliamentary representatives in the sixteenth century. As this study shows, in the early sixteenth century, Naas was continually regarded as an indispensable outpost for the Dublin administration. Its inhabitants were obliged to render labour days in the service of the earl of Kildare, to fund five carts and five horsemen for the protection of this section of the maghery boundary and to pay a fee imposed on the barony.[42]

The town had three monastic houses on the eve of the Reformation, all of which were in good repair, and these owned several of the town's cottages and tenements. They also owned two water mills and numerous gardens in the town centre. The largest house, St John's Hospital, had an orchard and a small plantation of ash trees in its precincts. The community evidently kept horses as they had a stable and a barn, also in the precincts. In the surrounding fields in Johnstown, the monks owned 177 acres of arable land and fourteen of pasture, broom and heath. Tenants in the cottages belonging to St John's Hospital paid their rent in money and were liable to pay customs which consisted of two days of autumn reaping in the demesne of the monastery.[43] Apart from the churches in each of these monasteries and the nearby rectory of Whitechurch which was affiliated to St John's Hospital, Naas had at least one parish church, that of St David, whose feast day was celebrated every year by the townspeople 'with gluttony and idolatry as far as they dare'.[44]

A weekly market and court sessions were held in Naas.[45] The town's cottages were thatched and we get some notion of the size of Naas from Lord Deputy Sidney's description of an attack by Rory O'More and Cormack McCormack O'Connor on the town in 1577. Somewhere in the region of 700 or 800 houses were burned, and there were said to have been over 500 men in the town.[46] In the early sixteenth century Naas had an abundant supply of tradesmen, the majority of whom were Gaelic, and several shoemakers and tanners worked there in the late 1530s and early 1540s.[47] However, a very substantial proportion of the town's population appears to have been of English

---

40 Ibid., pp 113, 126. **41** *Crown surveys*, p. 253. **42** Ibid., pp 278, 284, 351-2. **43** *Extents Ir. mon. possessions*, pp 155-7, 165-6. **44** Ibid., p. 156; Archdall, *Mon. Hib.*, ii, p. 288; T.J. De Burgh, 'Ancient Naas', in *Kildare Arch. Soc. Jn.*, i (1891-95), pp 190-1 (hereafter De Burgh, 'Ancient Naas'). **45** *Extents Ir. mon. possessions*, p. 155; Martin, 'Plantation boroughs', p. 46. **46** De Burgh, 'Ancient Naas', pp 190-1. **47** *Calendar of inquisitions*, pp 55, 101.

origin. Among the occupants of monastic and Geraldine land in the town and in its hinterland in the 1530s and 1540s, Gaelic names are comparatively rare. This was true not only of the upper stratum of society but also of the town's humbler residents. Down to the mid-1530s it was the crown, the ninth earl of Kildare, Christopher Eustace of Coghlanstown, Sir Christopher Preston, Philip Brune, Patrick Flatisbury and Robert Power who held the greater part of the land in the barony and general vicinity of Naas.[48] Equally, the occupants of the cottages in the town appear to have been English for the most part with names such as Ashe, Lewis, Robbins, Walker and Rawchester recorded.[49]

South of Naas lay the town of Kilcullen, situated southwest of the border of the maghery. Prior to 1319, this town was surrounded by strong walls and defended by seven gates, but in that year Maurice Jacques built a bridge over the river Liffey at a spot to the east of Kilcullen. The town of Kilcullen-Bridge (more commonly called Kilcullen) rapidly developed there and caused the decline of the ancient settlement which subsequently became known as Old Kilcullen. Kilcullen's location on the margins of the maghery is evident in the strongly Gaelic composition of the population in the locality in the early sixteenth century, the Eustaces being the only Englishmen to serve as jurors in 1540-1.[50] The ninth earl of Kildare subjected the population of the barony of Kilcullen to cess payments, with one horseman being cessed upon local inhabitants who were also obliged to pay for one cart. In addition, the earl exacted an annual fee of 20s. from local residents.[51] Sir Thomas Eustace, lord of Kilcullen and later Viscount Baltinglass, was the most important individual in this area during the 1530s and 1540s. Eustace was in charge of a very substantial army whom he quartered on the local people and he was patron and the eventual occupant of the Franciscan house of New Abbey in Kilcullen.[52] Connall Priory also held a castle and eighty acres of land in the district which was primarily used for arable farming.[53]

Great Connall lay to the northeast of Kilcullen. Although situated well beyond the maghery boundary and in an area which was almost exclusively Gaelic, the monastic community of Connall was largely English.[54] The local people attended Mass in the priory church which had served as the parish church from time immemorial, or in the parish church at nearby Old Connall. In 1540 the house and all its buildings were still standing and its manorial holdings flanked both sides of the river Liffey. These were comprised of over 229 acres of arable land and forty-two cottages. The monks also grew fir trees

---

48 *Crown surveys*, pp 146, 219, 291.   **49** Archdall, *Mon. Hib.*, ii, pp 287-8.   **50** *Extents Ir. mon. possessions*, p. 173; *Crown surveys*, pp 19, 157, 162.   **51** *Crown surveys*, pp 292, 351-2.   **52** *Extents Ir. mon. possessions*, p. 173.   **53** Ibid., pp 159, 173.   **54** Ibid., pp 157, 163.

and operated a mill on their manor. Tenants paid their rent in money and their customs in kind, each giving two Hookdays annually. Those who reared cattle were obliged to present the prior with one hen for every cow which they owned every year and in the late 1530s there were approximately sixty cows on the manorial estate alone. The surrounding landscape was dotted with cottages and messuages, the homes of tenants of the monastic estate, and the land was mainly used for arable farming, particularly grain cultivation. The ninth earl of Kildare had several substantial holdings in this vicinity, notably in Milltown and Morristownbiller, along with having leases of parcels of the priory's property in Kildare town. He also owned the mill at Milltown in the barony of Connall. Furthermore he impressed his authority on the local inhabitants by imposing an annual fee of 125*s.* on the barony of Connall; by subjecting them to labour exactions, and by obliging them to provide funding for three carts.[55] As we shall see at a later point in this study, the ninth earl also visited Connall priory and exerted strong personal influence over Walter Wellesley in his capacity as prior.

Travelling southwards along the southeastern boundary of county Kildare, one passes through the village of Timolin and the small town of Moone.[56] Timolin was the site for a nunnery which existed until 1530. The land was mainly used for arable farming with wheat and oats being the main crops. Tenants also kept hens and some local people brewed and sold beer. In addition to paying their rents the convent's tenants paid customs by plough days in spring and by wagon and cart days in autumn. They were expected to complete two days weeding, two days reaping and two days digging turf every year without payment. Tenants were also obliged to present the prioress with a hen at Christmas and a gallon of beer in relevant cases.[57] Further south, the monastic estate of Baltinglass Abbey straddled the shifting boundary between Kildare, Wicklow and Carlow. The population of this district was almost exclusively Gaelic, the Husseys being the only English gentry resident there in the early 1500s. Apart from the labourers who worked the abbey's land, its tenants in 1540 also included a Gaelic rhymer, Ludovick McKeogh, who occupied a messuage and five acres at Kilmorith near Baltinglass. In the areas of Carken, Tenebran, Newhouse, and Knowyrk, four horsemen, three of whom were members of the Sex family, occupied small holdings belonging to the abbey.[58] Another horseman, Faly O'Dempsey, had a more substantial holding in Grangerosnalvan near Kilkea, which was comprised of a castle, two mes-

55 Ibid., pp 157-63; *Crown surveys*, pp 278, 290, 352. **56** Martin, 'Plantation boroughs', p. 46. **57** *Extents Ir. mon. possessions*, p. 171. **58** Ibid., pp 127, 129, 130; see also *Crown surveys*, p. 168.

suages, four cottages and fifty acres. Unlike the holdings in Wicklow and Carlow, those in Kildare were of a substantial size, ranging from fifty to 320 acres.

These lands in Kildare were largely given over to arable farming, with wheat and oats being the principal crops. However, the borderland character of Baltinglass is evident in the practice of pastoral farming in the district; tenants of the abbey's manorial estate reared bullocks, milk cows, sheep and pigs from which they had a supply of meat, milk and butter. They also kept hens and brewed their own beer and they used their animals and produce to pay their customs to the abbot in the usual manner. The tenants generally lived in cottages, except for one, Robert Hussey, who resided in a castle in Gilltown where he held 174 acres of the abbey's land in 1540. Labourers and farmers in this southeastern district had access to three mills on the estate, at Baltinglass, Gilltown and Newhouse. Following the suppression of the abbey, local farmers availed of the buildings on the site by driving their animals into a curtilage built of stone walls where they were housed overnight. The parishioners of Baltinglass attended Mass in the parish church and the community at Gilltown also had recourse to a local church.[59] As we shall discover at a later stage in this study, down to the mid-1530s the monastery at Baltinglass and its estate was a viable, functioning concern. However, as a result of its being neglected following its suppression in 1537, the estate was partly overrun by neighbouring Gaelic septs and quickly fell into a state of poor repair. Travelling further south from the Baltinglass estate, one passed through Graney where the nunnery had formed the centre of a medieval settlement which in 1539 was comprised of the convent manor, 100 messuages and a church.[60] The southern extreme of county Kildare was dotted with small villages such as Levitstown and Newtown. However, it was Castledermot which provided a focal point for this region in terms of its defence and its commercial activity.

As a result of its borderland location, Castledermot was walled and had four gates.[61] St John's Hospital which was run by the Crutched Friars lay outside the town walls while the town's second monastery, the Franciscan friary, lay within its precincts. Castledermot was regarded by the Kildares, the Ormonds and the Dublin administration as a key defence outpost of the Pale during this period. A Geraldine castle was constructed there in the late fifteenth century and the eighth earl convened parliamentary sessions in the town

---

59 *Extents Ir. mon. possessions*, pp 125-33. 60 Ibid., pp 123-5; Archdall, *Mon. Hib.*, ii, pp 258-61. 61 Archdall, *Mon. Hib.*, ii, p. 251. See Michael Comerford, 'Castledermot: its history and antiquities', in *Kildare Arch. Soc. Jn.*, i (1891-5), pp 361-78.

in 1496 and again in 1499.[62] The ninth earl also owned a manor at Castledermot.[63] The durability of the Geraldine association with the town, which dated back to the thirteenth century, was evident when Geraldine supporters garrisoned Castledermot during the rebellion in 1534-5. However, the inhabitants of the town enjoyed an uneasy relationship with the ninth earl of Kildare who proved himself capable of launching surprise and occasionally savage punitive attacks on them.[64] Both the hospital and the earl's manorial lands were used for arable farming. Tenants on the Franciscan friary's land also engaged in some pastoral farming, rearing sheep, goats and pigs and keeping hens, as a result of which they had their own supplies of butter and eggs. Like their counterparts in Baltinglass and Timolin, the inhabitants of Castledermot brewed their own beer.[65] They had access to two mills in the immediate vicinity, one on Kildare's manor and one on the site of the Franciscan friary.[66] Apart from the churches on the two monastic sites, the inhabitants of the town also had at least one other church and a rector and a vicar were stationed there in the 1530s.[67]

North of Castledermot lay Kilkea, another Geraldine stronghold. The population of this Kilkea-Castledermot region was predominantly Gaelic with the Eustaces being the only resident English gentry family of standing in Kilkea in the late 1530s.[68] Again the land was largely used for arable farming and the tenants brought their corn to the earl of Kildare's mill on his manorial estate.[69] The inhabitants of Kilkea were obliged to maintain three horsemen and to pay for four carts per year.[70] By virtue of its location and its being a recognised outpost of the Kildares, Kilkea was subjected to successive punitive raids mounted by the earl of Ossory during the course of the Kildare rebellion. As a result, substantial areas of the earl's former manor were left in a devastated condition in the late 1530s.[71] Following the capture of Silken Thomas, Ossory secured possession of Kilkea Castle and eventually had himself appointed constable of both Kilkea and Carlow Castles.[72]

Further north, on the banks of the river Barrow, the town of Athy served as another traditional Geraldine outpost. The earls of Kildare had inherited Woodstock Castle from the baron de Rheban and in 1500, the eighth earl had this fortress thoroughly repaired. He is also said to have built a second castle

62 Anonymous, *Residences and castles of the duke of Leinster and of his ancestors* (Dublin, 1878), p. 97 (hereafter *Residences and castles of the duke of Leinster*). **63** *Crown surveys*, pp 173-4. **64** *Residences and castles of the duke of Leinster*, pp 97-8. **65** *Extents Ir. mon. possessions*, p. 170. **66** Ibid., p. 170; *Crown surveys*, p. 173. **67** Archdall, *Mon. Hib.*, ii, p. 261; *Calendar of inquisitions*, p. 44. **68** *Extents Ir. mon. possessions*, pp 168-70; *Crown surveys*, p. 206. **69** *Crown surveys*, p. 278. **70** Ibid., pp 351-2. **71** Ibid., pp 162-71. **72** *Residences and castles of the duke of Leinster*, pp 45-6.

on the opposite or east bank of the river in order to protect the bridge at Athy. The ninth earl's manorial lands stretched west of the river into the district of Castlemitchell.[73] Several members of the extended Fitzgerald family also lived in the vicinity of Athy in the early sixteenth century. The St Michaels, barons of Rheban, were the most prominent dynasty in the locality whose inhabitants were otherwise predominantly Gaelic. Athy was a borough with its own sovereign and portreeves and in 1515, along with Kildare town, it received a royal charter from Henry VIII, who conferred special judicial and administrative privileges on its senior officials. The town had two monastic houses; a hospital run by the Crutched Friars which lay beyond the bridge and a Dominican priory situated on the east side of the bridge. The land in the vicinity of the town which belonged to the monasteries and to the earl of Kildare's manorial estate was used for mixed farming, mostly arable cultivation, with some cattle being reared on the land owned by the Dominican friars.[74] Like most tenants throughout the rest of the county, those in Athy were expected to set aside service days when they worked without payment on the property of the earl or on that of either of the monasteries. Indeed Athy was, as we shall see, one of the earl's centres for co-ordinating the maintenance of the county's marchland defences. Local people brewed beer, made bread from their corn, and kept chickens, presenting their produce as custom payments to the earl and to the priors of the monasteries. Tenants on the property of the priory had recourse to two water mills and the friars also had two fishing weirs on the river Barrow. Apart from the churches in the precincts of the monasteries, Athy also had a parish church and a resident rector.[75] As we shall see later, the town was garrisoned by Geraldine supporters during the Kildare revolt; consequently, it suffered very heavy damages during the rebellion, particularly arising from the attacks by the earl of Ossory's forces and the ongoing raids by the O'Mores and the Kavanaghs. The monasteries and substantial areas of the earl's manorial estate were burned and laid to waste.[76] After the removal of the Kildares in 1537, Athy continued to be earmarked by the Dublin administration as a strategic outpost and consequently a soldier was installed there as constable and was invested with confiscated Geraldine and monastic property.

73 Ibid., pp 85-6; James Carroll, 'Remains in Athy and neighbourhood', in *Kildare Arch. Soc. Jn.*, i (1891-99), pp 102-12; Michael Comerford, '"The ford of Ae": some historical notes on the town of Athy' in *Kildare Arch. Soc. Jn.*, i (1891-95), pp 57-70 (hereafter Comerford, '"The ford of Ae"'); OMurithi [pseudonym of Walter Fitzgerald], 'The white castle of Athy and its sculptured stones', in *Kildare Arch. Soc. Jn.*, iv (1903-5), pp 47-62 (hereafter OMurithi, 'The white castle of Athy'). 74 *Extents Ir. mon. possessions*, pp 172-3; *Crown surveys*, pp 152-5; Archdall, *Mon. Hib.*, ii, p. 251. 75 *Extents Ir. mon. possessions*, p. 124. 76 Ibid., pp 172-3; *Crown surveys*, pp 152-5.

To the north of Athy, the flat, central plain of Kildare was dotted with small settlements in places such as Kilberry, Cloney and Kildangan in the west and Narraghmore, Fontstown, Calverstown, Kilrush, Davidstown, Nurney, Tully and Ballysax in the central and eastern quarters. The population of these areas was predominantly Gaelic. The ninth earl of Kildare held land in Narragh, Burtown, and Davidstown and collateral branches of the Fitzgerald family had seats based at Ballyshannon, Belan, Burtown, Fontstown, Brownstown, Mullaghmast, Kilmeed and Glassealy (near Narraghmore), Kilrush, and Narraghbeg.[77] The Wellesley family occupied extensive property in the area of Narraghmore and Walter Delahide held land at Nurney. The land was generally used for arable farming. Kildare town lay at the heart of the county, west of the Curragh and its location beyond the Pale maghery resulted in its being bypassed by the main highways connecting Dublin with the Ormond lordship and with the towns of Munster. Those travelling southwards preferred to pass through the Pale towns of Naas and Kilcullen. The prevailing threat of raids from Gaelic septs in Leix and north Kilkenny prevented the development of any permanent route across the Barrow and southwards into the Ormond lordship. As a result, Kildare town lost its administrative functions as the shire town to Naas.

In the late fifteenth century, the diocesan cathedral, three monastic houses and the Geraldine castle formed the core of the town. St Brigid's Cathedral had been built in the 1220s in a very severe architectural style. It was partially restored in the fifteenth century at which time a small underground cell is thought to have been added. It was a cruciform church with no aisles and it had a chapel projecting from each transept arm. All of its windows were lancets which were inserted in groups of threes in the gables and singly or doubly elsewhere. The cathedral also had a massive tower.[78] In the churchyard there was a firehouse wherein a fire was said to have been continuously kept alight since the time of St Brigid down to the early thirteenth century. This attracted visitors to the town, including the chronicler, Richard Stanihurst. He described how:

> there was in Kildare an ancient monument named the firehouse, wherein Cambrensis says there was a continual fire kept night and day, and yet the ashes never increased. I travelled of set purpose to the town … to see the place, where I did see such a monument like a vault.[79]

---

77 See *Extents Ir. mon. possessions*, pp 71, 96, 159-60, 177; *Crown surveys*, pp 19, 149, 153, 187, 223, 240. **78** Harold Leask, *Irish churches and monastic buildings, ii. Gothic architecture* (Dundalk, 1958), p. 89. **79** Quoted in Denis Murphy, 'Kildare: its history and antiquities', in

From the late fifteenth century the dean and chapter of Kildare lived as a community in a college house. Nearby the cathedral stood the Brigittine nunnery, founded by St Brigid in the fifth century. The nuns held a small amount of land and two cottages in the town. Two communities of Carmelite and Franciscan friars also resided in Kildare where the Franciscans in particular had more substantial property in land, messuages and cottages. All three houses were of very modest value. Kildare was a borough with a sovereign and portreeves and in 1515 was granted a royal charter which invested exceptional judicial rights in the town officials. They were expected to levy customs on the townspeople in order to raise finance to build town walls and to maintain the pavements. Kildare hosted a weekly market and an annual fair. It also had a court house which the ninth earl of Kildare held by fee-farm from the prior of Connall.[80]

The Fitzgeralds had very strong ties with Kildare town where a succession of earls of Kildare had been buried.[81] In 1316 the first earl had been granted the castle and manor of Kildare and both remained in the dynasty's possession during the period under review. Their manorial estate enveloped the town and in the early sixteenth century it was almost exclusively reserved for arable farming.[82] The inhabitants of the town were Gaelic. In addition to growing corn, they kept hens, brewed their own beer and baked cakes which they presented as payment of customs to the monasteries' superiors and to the earl of Kildare in the usual manner. None of the monasteries had a mill but the ninth earl had a horse mill in the town which he leased to a Gaelic man named James O'Doyn in 1524.[83] Kildare served as a centre for coordinating work schemes for the repair and maintenance of defences and the town's inhabitants were obliged to render days of unpaid service to the earl or to the monasteries.

The ninth earl of Kildare had regular dealings with both the secular and regular clergy of the town. During the 1520s, the dean and chapter of the diocese leased all of the profits from the town's tithes to him and when the disturbances broke out in the 1530s, a substantial amount of the family's plate collection was entrusted to the custody of the Carmelite friars of Kildare.[84] However, being a Geraldine base, and because of its exposed location beyond the Pale rampart, Kildare, like Athy and Castledermot, was the target of attacks by the earls' opponents: in 1492, Sir James of Ormond and his ally, O'Brien, burned the town. Kildare was heavily involved in the rebellion, the castle being captured by the king's forces on 1 December 1534. Six days later it was regained by Geraldine supporters. The following year it was lost and

Kildare Arch. Soc. Jn., ii (1896-9), p. 293 (hereafter Murphy, 'Kildare: its history and antiquities'). **80** *Extents Ir. mon. possessions*, p. 159. **81** Murphy, 'Kildare: its history and antiquities', pp 301-2. **82** *Crown surveys*, pp 148-50. **83** Ibid., pp 234, 255. **84** Ibid., pp 241, 305, 317; *Residences and castles of the duke of Leinster*, p. 69.

regained once more by the Irish who then burned it in the month of July. In May 1540 O'Connor Faly took what remained of the castle and burned the town.[85] As a result, at the time of their being surveyed by extents jurors in 1540, Kildare's monasteries were found to be in a very sorry state, the Franciscan and Carmelite houses having been almost completely burned down by the O'Connors. Similarly, crown surveyors found that the earl of Kildare's former manorial estate had been badly damaged, largely as a result of O'Connor Faly's raid.[86]

To the west of Kildare and on the fringes of O'Connor country lay Monasterevin with its large manor situated on the banks of the river Barrow. The abbey's estate was immense: within the immediate vicinity of the town of Evin alone, the monks owned three messuages, six cottages and 280 acres. The population of the area appears to have been exclusively Gaelic. The monastic community lived under the supervision of a Gaelic cleric named Hugh Dempsey certainly from the early 1520s down to its suppression, and it appears that the abbey continued to function throughout the reign of Henry VIII. During that time, over half of its manorial land was used for arable farming while the remainder was in pasture and meadow. The monks also kept horses and had their own watermill on the river Barrow.[87] This monastic estate was viewed by the ninth earl of Kildare and by the Dublin administration as being of indispensable strategic value, serving as the county's most westerly outpost amidst the Irishry.

Travelling northwards through the Geraldine estate at Lackagh in west Kildare, one reached the town of Rathangan which was also the site of a fortress of the earls of Kildare. The inhabitants of the town and its hinterland appear to have been Gaelic in the main and they had a parish church and a vicar in residence in 1540.[88] The ninth earl's manorial estate of Rathangan was mainly used for arable farming, though 260 acres of his land in the vicinity of the town were under pasture. Rathangan served as a base from which the earls of Kildare coordinated their cess of works in the baronies of Connall, Clane and Carbury, and they imposed galloglas, kerne and horsemen on certain of their tenants in order to bolster the defences of this border area.[89] During the Kildare rebellion, Sir John Alen, master of the rolls, urged that Rathangan Castle be taken from the Geraldines as soon as possible and in April 1535 the

85 *Residences and castles of the duke of Leinster*, pp 68-9. **86** *Extents Ir. mon. possessions*, pp 163-4, 166-9; *Crown surveys*, pp 149-50. **87** Walter Fitzgerald, 'The house and demesne of Monasterevin', in *Kildare Arch. Soc. Jn.*, iv (1903-05), pp 256-7 (hereafter Fitzgerald, 'The house and demesne of Monasterevin'); idem, 'Miscellanea: the proprietors of the manor of Monasterevin in the sixteenth century' in *Kildare Arch. Soc. Jn.*, ix (1918-21), pp 80-2. **88** *Extents Ir. mon. possessions*, pp 42, 62. **89** *Crown surveys*, pp 157-8.

king's forces captured the fortress. Rathangan witnessed some of the most dramatic episodes in the rebellion. In 1535, while the castle lay in English hands, Silken Thomas caused a herd of cattle to be driven past the town early one morning. Duped into thinking that this was booty for confiscation, the king's soldiers came out of the castle and were surprised by Thomas's forces who killed many of them. In July of that year the castle was regained by the earl's forces but, having secured the help of Thomas's uncle, Sir James Fitzgerald, the English forces soon after regained it.

Officials in Dublin were clearly nervous of the support for the Kildares which was forthcoming in Rathangan, particularly given its proximity to O'Connor's territory. They were determined to evacuate all of Thomas's hiding places in the district. In August 1535, using Cahir O'Connor as their guide, Lord Deputy Skeffington and his forces made their way through the woods nearby. There they found Thomas's former refuge – a 'strong house, made all of earth, and so ditched, watered, and of such force, as men of experience said, that being manned, ordnanced, and vitalled, it had not been pregnable'. The deputy burned the house and in doing so, hoped to ensure that 'O'Connor shall not long trouble us'.[90] In the late 1530s, several government officials expressed their concern that Rathangan Castle ought to be entrusted to loyal Englishmen who would ensure the defence of this section of the western marches of Kildare.

North of Rathangan lay the territory of the Bermingham family. Prior to their acquisition of Carbury in Kildare in the early fourteenth century, the original Bermingham country (Clann Fheorais) lay west of Carbury, roughly comprising the present baronies of Warrenstown and Collestown.[91] In the 1360s Robert Preston, chief baron of the exchequer, successfully asserted his right of possession of Carbury Castle. In reprisal, the Berminghams abandoned their loyalty to the English crown preferring to pursue dynastic interests, and united with their traditional Gaelic enemies, the O'Connors, in attacking the Pale and ravaging Preston's estate in Meath.[92] However, Carbury Castle remained an English outpost certainly until 1475 when it was destroyed by Hugh O'Donnell at the invitation of O'Connor. By that stage the Berminghams had become Gaelicised: they dropped their English name and instead adopted the Gaelic name MacPheorais. The seriousness with which the Dublin administration viewed the threat posed by the disaffected Berminghams to the secu-

---

90 Sir Gerald Aylmer and Sir John Alen to Thomas Cromwell, 21 Aug. 1535 (*S.P. Hen. VIII*, ii, p. 266). **91** D.B. Quinn and K.W. Nicholls, 'Ireland in 1534', in T.W. Moody, F.X. Martin and F.J. Byrne (eds), *A new history of Ireland, iii. Early modern Ireland, 1534-1691*, p. 6. **92** Michael Devitt, 'Carbury and the Birminghams' country', in *Kildare Arch. Soc. Jn.*, ii (1896-9), p. 103 (hereafter, Devitt, 'Carbury').

rity of the Pale is highlighted in the passage of an act of parliament at Naas in 1480. It stipulated that 'it is very necessary, beneficial, and expedient that a tower or pile of the new fashion should be built at Kishawanny, on the extreme frontier of the old march, not only in resistance of O'Connor, but also for the chastisement of the Berminghams'.[93]

Right down to the 1530s many members of the extended Bermingham family remained staunch antagonists of the Dublin government and of the colony. At that time William Bermingham was the principal lord in the district. He was looked upon with contempt by his fellow Kildareman, David Sutton, who criticised Bermingham for his oppressive treatment of gentlemen and tenants within his jurisdiction. Sutton alleged that Bermingham imposed a variety of exactions, including coign and livery, on the king's land and on that of local gentlemen to an even more excessive degree than the earl of Kildare. He is also said to have demanded works from his tenants at their own expense. They were allegedly obliged to present him with sixteenth quarters to the gallon of ale or butter in payment of their rent. He exacted a levy of a gallon of butter on every cow in his lordship and he supposedly established a law within the barony of Carbury that no man was permitted to bring any of his produce to a market; instead, he was to present his goods to Bermingham's wife who would decide upon a fit price for them. Sutton claimed that Bermingham habitually captured thieves and then released them in order that he might receive payment of *caina* or fines which his assailants paid to secure their release.[94]

This northwestern area of the county was not, however, the exclusive preserve of the Berminghams. Several of the ninth earl of Kildare's allies had holdings there, including Walter Delahide who had a manor at Castle Carbury, Richard Walshe who had a manor at Tecroan and Killard, and Peter Walshe and Walter Fitzgerald who also held land in the area.[95] While some individual Englishmen such as Richard Eustace resided as tenants on these estates, the overwhelming majority of tenants and notables in the region were of Gaelic origin. Farming was mixed, with land being used for arable cultivation and for grazing and, as already noted, tenants paid customs in kind. This district was gradually penetrated by the earls of Kildare in the early sixteenth century and was targeted by the Dublin administration as a valuable strategic outpost in the late 1530s and early 1540s. To the east of Carbury lay Donadea which in the

---

93 Quoted in Devitt, 'Carbury', p. 105. 94 H.F. Hore and James Graves (eds), *The social state of the southern and eastern counties of Ireland in the sixteenth century* (Dublin, 1870), pp 163-5 (hereafter Hore and Graves (eds), *Southern and eastern counties*). 95 *Crown surveys*, pp 183-6, 201-2.

early sixteenth century formed part of Christopher Eustace's estate. The inhabitants of the locality appear to have been almost exclusively Gaelic and
Eustace's land was mainly used for arable farming.[96] Southwest of Donadea
was Timahoe. This is the last locality for discussion, since it formed part of the
earl of Kildare's manor of Rathmore. The earl owned 200 acres in this district
and the property were divided between Maurice FitzRichard, Donald O'Grady
and Edmund O'Lenon in the late 1530s. In line with the standard practice,
these tenants were obliged to render service days as part of the terms of their
tenure and engaged in arable farming. Some of the earl's property in Timahoe
was held by him on lease from the prior of St John's Hospital in Kilmainham
and the local community were ministered to by a resident rector.[97]

II

It is clear that while each district had its own distinctive historical experience,
few were impervious to the influence of the earls of Kildare who are shown to
have permeated the political, economic and ecclesiastical affairs of the county,
particularly in the period 1470 to 1534. That hegemony necessarily set county
Kildare apart from the other three shires of the Pale. It is therefore appropriate
at this point to briefly investigate the ascent of the Kildare dynasty to their
position of unrivalled authority in the county as at once overlords and captains
of the shire's defences. In the thirteenth century, the Fitzgeralds had been subtenants of the Kildare fifth of the old liberty of Leinster. Although the earldom
of Kildare was created in 1316, and in spite of receiving a grant of the entire
county as a palatinate the following year, the Fitzgeralds still only remained
important at local level. In the fourteenth century, successive earls of Kildare
occasionally acted as substitute governors of Ireland for short spells.[98]

In the early fourteenth century their estates comprised four large manors at
Maynooth, Rathmore, Rathangan in county Kildare as well as the manors of
Lea and Geashill which they had recovered from the Gaelic Irish, and the
smaller manors of Kildare town, Rathbride and Kilcock. Following the death
of the fifth earl of Kildare, James Butler, the fourth earl of Ormond, gained
possession of the Kildare estates through his wife's claim. As a result of the

---

96 *Extents Ir. mon. possessions*, p. 173; *Crown surveys*, pp 221-2.   **97** *Extents Ir. mon. possessions*, p. 93; *Crown surveys*, pp 99, 146-7, 241.   **98** See Fitzgerald, *The earls of Kildare*; A.J.
Otway-Ruthven, 'The medieval county of Kildare', in *Irish Historical Studies*, xi, no. 43 (Mar.
1959), pp 181-99; Ellis, *Tudor frontiers and noble power*, p. 168.

Fitzgeralds' abeyance during the period 1432-*c*.1453, the county suffered gradual intrusions by neighbouring Gaelic septs, particularly in the Barrow valley region. In the southeast, on the Kildare-Carlow-Wicklow border, Baltinglass Abbey and Carlow Castle were the only surviving defence fortresses to guard that entire flank of the Pale marchland. The Kavanaghs had managed to secure a passage into the south of the county with their capture of Tullow Castle after 1435 and their destruction of Castledermot *c*.1443. In the northwest, the O'Connors of Offaly had captured Rathangan and on the Kildare-Meath border, as we have seen, the Berminghams of Carbury had long since enjoyed semi-autonomous status and were closely allied with the O'Connors during the fifteenth century. These difficulties were further compounded by 'misrule and misgovernance' which is said to have stemmed from a long-running dispute between the Ormond earl of Wiltshire and Thomas Fitzmaurice Fitzgerald concerning possession of the manors of Maynooth and Rathmore.[99]

If the medieval shire of Kildare had not been exceptional in succumbing to Gaelic incursions prior to the fifteenth century, the same cannot be said of its reclamation. Under the Yorkists and early Tudors, this erosion of the colony's marchlands in Kildare was arrested and reversed, initially by Geraldine expansion southwards and later by the Butlers' extension of their lordship northwards from Kilkenny. Even during the Kildares' eclipse, Sir Edward FitzEustace had already set about effecting the military re-organization of county Kildare. He tabled statutes for the construction of castles throughout the county and made arrangements for teams of labourers and workmen to be made available to dig trenches and build fortresses in the county marches. In particular he identified the key border castle at Ballymore Eustace for immediate repair. In a further attempt to strengthen the Pale defences there, the hereditary constable, Sir Robert Eustace, was instructed to maintain a company of Englishmen in the district in order to ensure the defence of Ballymore manor against the raids of the neighbouring O'Toole and O'Byrne septs. After Sir Edward's death his son Roland, later Baron Portlester, became a close ally of the Kildares and they co-operated in devising and implementing schemes aimed at recovering lands lost to the Gaelic Irish and strengthening the county's fortifications.

From the time of his appointment as justiciar in 1454 Thomas, seventh earl of Kildare and grand-nephew of the fifth earl, set about creating the basis for the Kildare ascendancy and the recovery of the English colony by furthering the work already instigated by his predecessor. Ellis has emphasised

---

99 Ellis, *Tudor frontiers and noble power*, p. 111.

the similarity between Thomas and Lord Dacre in the west marches of England, since both noblemen's occupancy of the governorship undoubtedly bolstered their efforts to restore the administration and defence of their wasted inheritance.[100] Thomas and his son Gearóid Mór, the eighth earl, with the assistance of Baron Portlester, succeeded in re-establishing effective control on this western periphery of the Pale by erecting a chain of fortifications in strategic locations. In 1456, by grant of parliament, FitzEustace received £10 for building a tower in his town of Kilcullen. Twelve years later, he super-vised the construction of a castle there and in 1478, he had the town enclosed by a wall.[101] By *c.*1459, Thomas had recovered Rathangan. The ford of Kinnegad, O'Connor's path of entry into Meath, was blocked. A tower was built at Kilmahuke in Allen by a member of the collateral branch of the Fitzgerald family. In 1468 the castles at Cloncurry, Ataghtyn, Coransford, Ballivor and Ballycor were secured against O'Connor and another tower was built at Agane.[102]

By 1500 the O'Connors had been forced to retreat and the castles and manors of Lea and Morett to the west were regained from Gaelic possession. These manors were valuable acquisitions for strategic rather than financial purposes; Lea was adopted by the earls as their principal base for campaigns in this western extreme of the Pale marchlands. Leighlin Castle was in Geraldine hands by 1480. Defence towers were constructed in the county at Narraghmore and Ballynagappagh in 1465, near Windgates in 1472, at Galmorestown in 1477, at Bolablught in 1480 and at Lackagh in the west in 1494.[103] In 1478 Calverstown was walled and six years later Kildare Castle was fortified. The earls of Kildare also held castles at Rathnulty, Clonmore and Clonogan in county Carlow. An act of parliament of 1483 entrusted to the eighth earl all waste land which lay between Calverstown and Leighlinbridge in south Kildare and north Carlow whose absentee owners failed to occupy these properties within a period of six years thence. In 1485 the eighth earl had begun the construction of a castle at Castledermot in the south with the pur-pose of ensuring 'the true re-adaption of all the waste lands in the county of Carlow'. Portlester was also actively involved, and, Ellis tentatively suggests, possibly pioneered the resettling of county Kildare marchlands. In the 1470s he built anew a town with a castle at Galmorestown near Baltinglass where he is said to have intended to reside. Galmorestown had contained 120 acres of land which had long since lain waste but which Portlester had set about culti-vating with his own ploughs and which was worked by his tenants, half of whom had Gaelic names.[104]

100 Ibid., p. 113.   **101** Ibid., p. 114.   **102** Ibid., p. 115.   **103** Ibid., p. 114.   **104** Ibid., pp 114-15.

Hence, by the mid-1480s, the earls of Kildare had effectively forced the Gaelic septs to retreat from the regions of south Kildare and north Carlow and had established a foothold in the southeastern marches of Dublin, having recovered the districts of Fassaroe and Castlekevin. In addition, Thomas and Gearóid Mór used their senior positions in the Dublin administration to secure legislative backing for their efforts to assert a claim on some of the estates of the attainted earl of Ormond which had been confiscated by the crown in 1468. The Fitzgeralds retained possession of these manors in 1486 and eventually established title to them. The properties in question were the manors of Oughterany, Oughterard, Castlewarden, and Clintonscourt in county Kildare. They also secured possession of the manors of Kildrought, Donadea and both Cartons in county Kildare as well as the manor of Lucan in county Dublin.[105] The eighth earl adopted a similar strategy in relation to the autonomous territory of the Berminghams in Carbury in the northwest. From 1483 onwards, he was engaged in buying up titles to land there and by 1519 the region had been infiltrated to the point of admitting the ninth earl's justices to hold court sessions at Carbury Castle.

The earls' estates in county Kildare were also expanded through marital endowments. Although the eighth earl already enjoyed a life grant of the manor of Leixlip from Richard III, through his marriage to Elizabeth St John, a kinswoman of Henry VII, he acquired ownership of Leixlip among other properties. His son received several grants of land in England and in Ireland upon the occasion of his marriage in 1503 to Elizabeth Zouche, who was also a relative of the king. In Kildare, the future ninth earl received the manor of Rathangan. The main phase in Geraldine expansion occurred during the lifetime of the eighth earl and in particular during the 1480s and after 1496. This aggrandisement involved the expropriation of Gaelic landowners and their being replaced by the earl's tenants who in some cases were the same individuals. The earls bought up the common-law titles to those estates, usually by the authority of commissions which invested in them any crown lands which they managed to recover from Gaelic septs. By 1550, Gaelic inhabitants were in the majority in most parts of Kildare and Meath, which suggests that the Kildares' expansion during their ascendancy had been achieved largely by recruiting Gaelic peasants.[106] The defence of Dublin and Meath borderlands

---

105 A.J. Otway-Ruthven, *A history of medieval Ireland* (2nd ed., London, 1980), p. 400 (hereafter Otway-Ruthven, *A history of medieval Ireland*); K.W. Nicholls, *Gaelic and gaelicised Ireland in the middle ages* (Dublin, 1972), pp 174-5; Steven Ellis, *Reform and revival: English government in Ireland, 1470-1534* (London, 1984), pp 59-60 (hereafter Ellis, *Reform and revival*); idem, *Tudor Ireland*, p. 65; idem, *Tudor frontiers and noble power*, pp 108-13. 106 Ellis, *Tudor Ireland*, p. 35.

adjacent to the county was inextricably linked with the defence of county Kildare and hence the earls extended their holdings in these neighbouring counties at the same time. This 'colonial expansion' highlights an important and (as far as the Kildares were concerned), fortuitous ambiguity in their governance of the lordship. Moreover, it left them open to allegations made by their critics in the Pale that their campaigns against the Gaelic septs in Leinster and elsewhere were primarily motivated by a desire to advance Geraldine interests at the expense of those of the crown.[107]

Much of the development of the marchlands can be attributed to the ninth earl (1513-34) and this is evident in his reputation among his contemporaries as being 'the greatest improver of his lands in this land'.[108] The extent and strength of the ninth earl's influence throughout the county was bolstered by the fact that other members of his immediate family owned substantial estates in county Kildare, though their interests could occasionally be at variance with those of their senior kinsman. Maurice Fitzgerald was based at Lackagh in the west; Sir Thomas and Sir James held the manor of Leixlip in the 1520s and 1530s. Gerald's brother, Walter, was based in the Dublin-Kildare marches. Thomas FitzMaurice Fitzgerald, the ninth earl's cousin, held 1,700 acres of land in the county, chiefly in the manors of Kildare town and Kilkea further south. James Fitzgerald of Osberstown had a lease of the earl's manor of Morett and Sir Gerald Shanesson held the manor of Cloncurry, bordering on Bermingham country.[109]

Right down to the 1530s the ninth earl's most valuable properties were his twenty manors in county Kildare which were worth £709 annually. By that time, according to Ellis, the Kildares' landed influence had gravitated towards the east and south of the county. Their holdings at Lea, Morett and Geashill to the west were essentially only valuable in military terms. By contrast, their manors at Maynooth and Kildare town were thriving and were valued respectively at £237 annually and £140 annually. In south Kildare the earls had also acquired the manors of Kilkea, Woodstock, Athy and Castledermot; Kilkea, which was worth £112, ranked as their third most valuable property.[110] Curiously the ninth earl owned little land in the Pale maghery, even though he could charge a rent of 2s. or even 3s. an acre per year for his demesne land in Maynooth as compared with a mere 12d. per acre in the marches, or even a meagre 2d. or 1d. an acre in particularly exposed border regions.[111]

---

107 Ibid., pp 65-6; idem, *Tudor frontiers and noble power*, p. 121. **108** Lord Ossory &c. to Thomas Cromwell, 2 Jan. 1536 (*S.P. Hen. VIII*, ii, p. 300). See also Ellis, *Tudor frontiers and noble power*, p. 119. **109** Ellis, *Tudor frontiers and noble power*, pp 132-4. **110** Ibid., p. 124. **111** Ibid., p. 128.

III

This, therefore, was the vast estate over which the ninth earl presided in the early sixteenth century and his influence percolated down to local level throughout virtually the entire county. The earls' dual roles as lords of this estate and as defenders of the Pale were inextricably connected, as is evidenced by the levies and fees, duties, and exactions which they imposed on their tenants. All of these undoubtedly contributed to a heightened sense of cohesion in the Kildare lordship, and served as a constant reinforcement of the earls' authority as overlords and as military captains over their tenants, particularly in Kildare. In spite of Gearóid Mór's undertaking to exempt the county's freeholders from scutage payments, this levy was collected on eight occasions during the period 1450-1531, and the ninth earl was entitled to £145 per proclamation. The greatest burden of scutage payment fell on Kildare, where nine and a half baronies paid £102 and he also received £43 from subtenants in his manors of Rathmore and Kilkea. In addition, military tenants in Kildare were obliged to pay wardships, fines and liveries to the earl. Members of the gentry and clergy of Meath, Westmeath, Dublin, Louth, Waterford, the archdeacon of Kildare, the prior of St Thomas's in Athy, the parson of Geashill and the vicar of Oregan collectively paid a total of £112 annually in annuities to the earl of Kildare.[112]

The earls' tenants were expected to attend hostings upon being summoned. Thomas Fitzgerald of Dollardstown in south Kildare pledged to be in attendance 'at every royal service when the king's banner shall be displayed and also he shall true and faithfully serve the said Gerald and his heirs when it shall be required'.[113] They were also obliged to accommodate the earls' standing defence force, whose purpose was to discourage raiding Gaelic septs. From the turn of the century, the eighth earl maintained a retinue comprised of 120 galloglas and 120 kerne for the defence of his own estates and that of the English colony, and the ninth earl transferred the burden of the cost of maintaining his troops onto Gaelic lords. Tenants in counties Kildare and Meath occasionally had their rents reduced or remitted in return for tolerating coign and livery or other military impositions.[114] As we saw in the case of Rathangan, for example, the ninth earl's tenants were permitted to hold 260 acres of pasture, three acres of wood, a turbary and an area of common pasture rent-free because they maintained galloglas and kerne who were employed in the defence of the western marches of the Pale.[115] A similar situation obtained on his manorial estate in

112 *Crown surveys*, pp 234-5, 257-8; Ellis, *Tudor frontiers and noble power*, p. 125. Gaelic septs also paid annuities to the ninth earl. 113 Ellis, *Tudor frontiers and noble power*, p. 128. 114 Ibid., pp 128-9; Carey, *Surviving the Tudors*. 115 *Crown surveys*, pp 157-8.

Kilkea. Moreover, at least twenty rent-free holdings of approximately sixty acres each in Rathangan and in the manors of Kildare and Kilkea were designated for the maintenance of horsemen. These tenants were required to pay for horses and harness and the ninth earl distributed between sixty and 100 horses a year from his own stables among his horsemen.[116] This special arrangement was an apparent acknowledgement that the tenants of these areas were entrusted with the specific task of defending particular stretches of the county marches, as opposed to the standard obligation on tenants to render military service in the defence of the country on behalf of the crown.

The earls made further provision for the defence of the Pale by levying annual tributes on virtually all of the Gaelic chieftains in Leinster and on some in the midlands and in the northeast of Connacht, thereby binding the Gaelic lords to them in return for their protection. These tributes were made either in money payments or in undertakings to maintain the earls' galloglas or to supply the earls with an agreed number of kerne.[117] In those areas of Kildare and Carlow which did not maintain galloglas, the ninth earl is said to have imposed kerne and boys who were 'to have their meat continually' in the homes of tenants.[118] In adopting these arrangements the Kildares were not unique. According to David Sutton, the earl's receiver, Sir Thomas Eustace, lord of Kilcullen and later Viscount Baltinglass, 'set coign and livery upon the king's tenants as well as upon other gentlemen's lands', as did Sir William Bermingham of Carbury.[119] Similarly, in 1540 it was found that the Gaelic tenants of the manor of Grangeford in Carlow, a possession of Baltinglass Abbey, were exempt from paying all customs except 'coign and livery'. The same was true of the tenants who occupied an area of common pasture land which belonged to the preceptory of Killybeggs near Clane.[120] This forced provision of food and quarters for Kildare's men and their horses was regarded by contemporaries as excessive to the point of causing the depopulation of English tenants from the marchlands which in turn caused an influx of Gaelic husbandmen and a decline in English social custom in the Pale.[121]

In terms of the administration of their estate, the eighth and ninth earls appear to have been loath to grant long leases, life tenures or freeholds except in the case of close relations or a handful of senior estate officials. The majority of their tenants held their land at the earls' will. As already noted, tenants

---

116 Ibid., pp 319-50; Ellis, *Tudor frontiers and noble power*, p. 129. 117 *Crown surveys*, pp 264-77; Colm Lennon, *Sixteenth-century Ireland: the incomplete conquest* (Dublin, 1994), p. 74; Ellis, *Tudor frontiers and noble power*, p. 126; Mary Ann Lyons, *Gearóid Óg, ninth earl of Kildare* (Dundalk, 1998), pp 15-16. 118 Hore and Graves (eds), *Southern and eastern counties*, p. 161. 119 Ibid., pp 161-2. See also *Crown surveys*, pp 113, 128, 207. 120 *Extents Ir. mon. possessions*, pp 92, 128. 121 Carey, *Surviving the Tudors*.

were expected to meet the earls' exactions of labour services on their manors. Like their counterparts on monastic estates and those resident on the estates of gentlemen such as Walter Delahide, James Fitzgerald and Christopher Eustace, Kildare's tenants were obliged as part of their customary tenure to make themselves available for an average of six or seven days' work every year. These included some or all of the following: plough days, boon days, weeding days, hook days, cart days, reaping days and turf days in spring and autumn. Many were also required to present a hen at Christmas time.[122] The ninth earl lived up to his reputation as a progressive overlord, as David Sutton acknowledged in 1537 describing how the earl habitually instructed his tenants that in the event of their needing to carry out repairs on 'any house of office, as hall, kitchen, barn or stable', they were to supply the materials at their own charge and he would provide masons and carpenters.[123] In certain cases, the earl granted leases on condition that the tenant would carry out structural repairs. In 1517, for example, he leased property in Painestown near Rathcoffey in north Kildare to William Eustace of Clongowes Wood for a period of twenty years, during which time Eustace was to 'build and repair well and competently' the buildings on the property at his own expense. The earl undertook to 'find timber for the reparation of the same' and the terms of the indenture stated that Eustace was to leave the property in a state of sound repair at the end of his twenty-year tenure.[124] Once a year, every group of three tenants was expected to provide one labourer who would serve as an axeman for either two or four days 'to cut passages upon the borders of Irishmen'. The local gentlemen and horsemen of the locality were instructed to accompany these labourers in order to defend them while they worked, and their horses and boys were to be maintained by the local population.[125] Tenants were also required to dig 'ditches and fastnes' and to carry stones to castles in the county's marchlands 'upon their own meat and drink and wages'.[126]

These repair and maintenance operations were coordinated from four strategic centres throughout the county. The earl himself oversaw projects in the baronies of Salt, Ikeathy and Oughterany in the northeast, as well as in the west, in Offaly, and on the crown lands which he controlled as the king's deputy. In south Kildare, the Geraldine manor at Athy served as a centre for directing works in Narragh, Rheban, Naas, half of Kilcullen barony, and the

---

122 See *Crown surveys*, pp 143, 147, 149-51,153-4 for examples; Ellis, *Tudor frontiers and noble power*, p. 131. For instances of similar customs imposed on tenants of the county's monastic estates and on Eustace's estate see *Extents Ir. mon. possessions*, pp 126-9, 155, 158-9, 163-4, 166-8, 170-2, 174-5 and *Crown surveys*, pp 184-5, 205-10, 215-23. **123** Hore and Graves (eds), *Southern and eastern counties*, pp 161-62. **124** *Crown surveys*, pp 244-5. **125** Hore and Graves (eds), *Southern and eastern counties*, p. 162. **126** Ibid., pp 161-2.

areas of Kilkea, Carlow and Rathvilly. In the northwest, the earl's manor at Rathagan provided the focal point for supervising operation in the baronies of Carbury, Clane and Connall. It has been suggested that Kildare's tenants tolerated these draining exactions since they contributed to the maintenance of some degree of stability and peace in the county's border regions.[127]

The earl had enormous stud farms in Maynooth, Fercullen, Annaly, Fassaghbantry and also in Ulster. In 1534 he owned an estimated 1,000 horses and mares. He spent around £800 annually on gifts of sixty-five horses, thirty-three hackneys and about twelve sets of harness. These he distributed amongst the local Englishry (including some of the county gentry), as well as among Gaelic men, his servants, certain courtiers and other notable personages in England, and members of his own family. Many of these gifts were apparently designed to serve a military purpose: the earl donated them as part payment of his fee to his retainers and household servants, in particular his horsemen.[128] Kildare was said to have given these horses so that the recipient would be obliged to receive him for the duration of two days and two nights.[129] Furthermore, the men who kept his stud farms were allegedly billeted on the people of counties Kildare and Carlow.

David Sutton provides a revealing insight into the perception of at least one county gentleman of the earl of Kildare as the shire's overlord. He portrayed the ninth earl as self-indulgent in his abuse of not only his tenants but the entire population of counties Kildare and Carlow. His aristocratic lifestyle exerted real strains on both counties' tenants. For instance, Kildare held a hunt within the two counties and Sutton alleges that 'every dog [had] to have bread and butter like a man'. Whenever the earl celebrated Easter of Christmas, he always did so in the company of a large assembly of guests who, along with him, would 'cess all their horses ... upon the country to have horsemeat and man's meat during the feast'. Sutton also claimed that while the county gentlemen appeared to be acquiescent to the Kildares, they did so reluctantly as they had little option.[130]

IV

As the heartland of the Fitzgerald territories, the county of Kildare had enjoyed liberty status since William de Vescy was lord of Kildare in the 1290s.

127 Carey, *Surviving the Tudors*. 128 Ellis, *Tudor frontiers and noble power*, pp 137-8. 129 For a detailed and original discussion of the political and social ramifications of Kildare's gift giving see Carey, *Surviving the Tudors*. 130 Hore and Graves (eds), *Southern and eastern counties*, p. 161.

This liberty was, however, withdrawn by the crown following a judgement by the justiciar's court in 1345.[131] But the conditions which had prompted the granting of greater franchises in the marchlands in Wales and Scotland were, as we have noted, replicated in the Irish context in the late medieval period. County Kildare was therefore by no means exceptional in experiencing these conditions. The extent of political autonomy enjoyed by the Kildares down to the early 1520s is illustrated in the ambiguity surrounding the historiography of the restoration of liberty status to the shire in the early sixteenth century. The re-establishment of the liberty in the 1510s has been the subject of revised study; earlier accounts of its restoration failed to distinguish between franchisal jurisdiction, which depended upon receipt of a royal grant, and the powers normally exercised by a magnate of the standing of the ninth earl of Kildare.[132] Down to the end of Henry VII's reign in 1509 at least, county Kildare was administered in a manner similar to the other shires of the Pale. Its local personnel comprised a royal sheriff, a chief sergeant, sub-sergeants, chief justices, escheators and other lesser officials, all of whom exercised their authority under the jurisdiction of the Dublin administration. Five indictments for felonies presented before the county sheriff in 1468 and 1470 were referred to the court of the king's bench for determination and were later presented to parliament for consideration. Down to 1494 the chancery frequently held sessions in county Kildare during its itinerary of the Pale, and chancery letters were attested at Maynooth, Naas and Kildare town as well as at Meath towns including Navan, Rathmore and Gormanstown. Like their counterparts in Meath and Louth, county Kildare's sheriffs made payments to the exchequer: in 1495-6 for example, the county sheriff owed £52 6s. 8d.[133]

As early as 1512 county Kildare made no proffers at the exchequer and the county's liberty status is explicitly referred to in an inquisition dated April 1514.[134] In 1515, while the ninth earl was visiting the court, Henry VIII approved a bill which was due to be tabled at a parliamentary session convened in Dublin in 1516. The king did so out of a desire to revitalise the Dublin administration's authority by securing the earl's active co-operation in law enforcement and the recovery of lands. If it were passed, this bill would confirm the earl and his male heirs in the title of earl of Kildare and in all of

---

131 Otway-Ruthven, *A history of medieval Ireland*, pp 174, 263; Steven Ellis, 'The destruction of the liberties: some further evidence', in *Bulletin of the Institute of Historical Research*, liv (1981), p. 156 (hereafter Ellis, 'The destruction of the liberties'). 132 Ellis, 'The destruction of the liberties', p. 154; D.B. Quinn, 'Anglo-Irish local government, 1485-1534', in *Irish Historical Studies*, i (1939), pp 354-81 (hereafter Quinn, 'Anglo-Irish local government'). 133 Ellis, *Reform and revival*, pp 173, 196-7. 134 The inquisition entry read *'coram escaetore libertatis comitatus sive libertatis Kildar'*. See Ellis, 'The destruction of the liberties', p. 156.

the possessions formerly owned by Maurice Fitzthomas, the fourth earl (1342-90), or any of his ancestors. The substance of the bill provides an insight into the extent of authority which the bill proposed to invest in the earl.

> Also be it enacted, ordained and established, by authority of this present parliament, that Gerald, earl of Kildare, have and enjoy all ... castles, lordships, manors, lands, tenements, rents, services, meadows, pastures, marests, forests, chases, parks, ponds, stangs [¼ acre], knights' fees, mills, liberties, franchises, customs, usages, and other commodities, advowsons, patronages of abbeys, priories, churches, vicarages, chapels, chantries, prebends, hospitals, and all other benefices ecclesiastical and presentation of the same, and all other hereditaments, with all manner [of] reversions that one Maurice Fitzthomas Fitzthomas, otherwise called Maurice Fitzgerald, some time earl of Kildare, or any other of ... Maurice's ancestors or heirs [had].[135]

However, the statute roll relating to that parliamentary session was subsequently mutilated by Kildare's opponents, and it cannot be ascertained whether the bill was in fact passed. Henry also conferred other privileges on the earl in 1515, notably a grant of two charters for the towns of Kildare and Athy.[136] These invested the sovereign and portreeves of both towns with the authority to determine all pleas and assizes within their respective jurisdictions and with the right to collect all profits and payments arising from those cases. Both towns' officials were to oversee the return of writs, a measure which effectively excluded the king's sheriff from their jurisdictions. They were also granted power to act as justices of the peace, and to administer the offices of escheator, clerk of the town's market and coroner. Furthermore they were permitted to levy customs which they were expected to spend on the walls and pavements of the towns, and they were ordered to account for the levies collected to the earl of Kildare.

As Steven Ellis has suggested, it is likely that, in addition to the bill confirming him in the earldom, Kildare received a similarly wide-ranging franchise, binding for the whole county, at the same time. Certainly throughout the late 1510s and 1520s several contemporaries referred to the county's liberty,

---

135 Duke of Leinster (ed.), 'The Kildare rental book', in Historical Manuscripts Commission, *Ninth Report, Part II, Appendix* (London, 1884), p. 273 (hereafter Leinster (ed.), 'The Kildare rental book').   136 The charter texts are published in *The red book of the earls of Kildare*, ed. Gearóid Mac Niocaill (Dublin, 1964), pp 178-85 (hereafter *Rd. Bk. Kildare*). See also D.B. Quinn, 'Henry VIII and Ireland, 1509-34', in *Irish Historical Studies*, xii (1960-1), p. 321.

and even the Ormond-led administration in 1522-4 did not question the legitimacy of Kildare's seneschal referring to the earl of Kildare as lord of the county liberty. There is also evidence to suggest that Kildare presided over his liberty as Henry had intended. In 1519, for example, the earl's justices travelled in circuits around the county, significantly holding pleas at Carbury Castle which, as we have seen, was an area which had become the preserve of the gaelicised Bermingham family.[137] It is probable, however, that in Kildare's mind, Henry VIII's charters and the bill served as nothing more than the crown's recognition of his existing rights.

A dearth of source material and conflicting contemporary opinions complicate our understanding of the extent of the earl's power as lord of the liberty. Contrary to the impression conveyed by the text of the bill and that given by the ninth earl's critics in the Pale, the county was not impervious to royal officials. In 1524 royal commissioners visited county Kildare to see that the king's laws 'and all writs and processes of the same, obeyable and current within the … county of Kildare, [were] obeyed and executed'. They also wished to ensure that the earl made appointments only to those offices to which he had nomination rights 'by reason of his liberty for the administration of justice' and that he co-operated with those officers who were appointed by the crown. Neither was county Kildare entirely isolated from the Dublin administration. Admittedly no scutage payments were forthcoming from the county and there were periodic breaks in the county sheriff's proffers to the exchequer. The names of its gentry are also conspicuously absent from the general list of the leading gentry of the Pale march who were summoned to Dublin in 1524 to enter into recognizances to keep the peace, to make restitution for crimes committed in their districts and to retain no more men than the deputy permitted.[138] Nonetheless, during the period 1522-4 the county seneschal appeared in the Dublin exchequer to make proffer at Easter 1523 and he enrolled his patent of office, dated 5 January 1517. He was also subject to the censure of the Dublin administration for failing to return writs.[139] Boundaries were imposed on the earl's exercise of judicial authority in the county. He was entitled to make restitution 'of all manner of thefts, robberies, trespasses, extortions, riots, oppressions, and for all other offences' amerceable or fineable 'not being determinable within the … liberty'. However, his authority fell short of that enjoyed by palatinate lords and resembled the powers invested in the officials of Kildare and Athy in 1515, since he was obliged to deliver those charged with treason, murder, homicide, rape or

---

137 Devitt, 'Carbury', pp 85-110; Ellis, *Reform and revival*, p. 185; idem, *Tudor Ireland*, p. 65.
138 'Recognisance for the English and Irish marchers, Bermingham, Ormond, and Kildare', 12 July 1524 (*S.P. Hen. VIII*, ii, pp 108-11).   139 Ellis, 'The destruction of the liberties', p. 157.

any other felony to the king's gaol in Dublin, there 'to suffer according to the king's laws'.[140]

As a result of the uncertainty surrounding the restoration of the earl's liberty in the mid-1510s and the ambiguity which shrouded its status as a franchise, controversy arose in the 1530s concerning the legal validity of the liberty and, more importantly, the ninth earl's alleged abuse of his powers as lord of that liberty. Those issues which were particularly disputed related to his power of appointment of officials, his admission of Gaelic customs and fines for felonies and the confusion concerning the observance of the king's writs within the jurisdiction. Ellis suggests that although the liberty of Kildare did not amount to palatinate status, the earl might have argued that he was entitled to this in accordance with the terms of the original charter of 1317. In 1533-4 Gearóid Óg was accused of allowing all pleas to be heard before his seneschal in his name. He was also said to have granted pardons of felonies under his seal and attestation and was alleged to have appointed sheriffs, coroners and other county officials, thereby going beyond his entitlements.[141]

Cardinal Wolsey had sought to reduce the liberties of Kildare and Tipperary in 1527-8, when the feud between Kildare and Ormond was at its most intense, but it was Wolsey's successor, Thomas Cromwell, who effected the suppression of the liberty of Kildare as part of his wider programme for the consolidation of royal authority in the marchlands of the Tudor state. By 1533, Cromwell had collected information to support his case for suppressing the liberties in the lordship and especially that of the earl of Kildare. Robert Cowley, sometimes master of the rolls, lent added weight to the chief secretary's policy by accusing the earl of committing abuses 'under colour and pretence of a liberty'. Hence in his programme for the reform of the government of the lordship entitled 'Ordinances for the government of Ireland' (1534) Cromwell denied the legality of Kildare's liberty, terming it 'the pretended liberty of Kildare', and ordered that it 'shall cease from henceforth'. This, combined with the fact that the Butler liberty was reprieved, contributed to the earl of Kildare's gradually adopting a stance of outright opposition to Cromwell's reforms and eventually to the crown.[142]

v

A salient feature of life in county Kildare during the fifteenth and early sixteenth centuries was the hybrid nature of its familial, social, cultural, eco-

---

140 'Recognisance for Kildare', Aug. 1524 (*S.P. Hen. VIII*, ii, pp 113-14).   141 Ellis, 'The destruction of the liberties', p. 157.   142 Quinn, 'Anglo-Irish local government', p. 380.

nomic, legal, ecclesiastical and military organization, which distorts symmetrical distinctions between the Englishry and the Irishry. In spite of their being Englishmen and the king's principal representatives in Ireland, the eighth and ninth earls of Kildare harnessed the Gaelic military system to suit their own ends. However, two other county peers, Sir Thomas Eustace of Kilcullen and Sir William Bermingham of Carbury, also regarded it as legitimate practice to impose coign and livery on their own tenants and on the crown's subjects throughout the county. Furthermore, the earls displayed a genuine fondness for certain features of Gaelic culture, and they were noted patrons of Gaelic bards and *seanchai*. Alison FitzEustace, the wife of the eighth earl, was renowned by the Gaelic annalists as a great patron of Gaelic poets.[143]

An act was passed in 1475 ordering the seizure of the 'goods of the rhymers and hermits who came into the county of Kildare, and [who] remain in the English land without licence, and succour the Irish enemies with victuals'.[144] In spite of this, the ninth earl retained rhymers and harpers amongst his entourage. One of his harpers was Owen Keynan of Cappervarget near Rathangan in the west of Kildare, who, in 1540 was pardoned for his implication in inciting Lord Offaly to revolt, in a manner similar to the Gaelic *fili* and bards' practice of encouraging their Gaelic patrons to undertake campaigns.[145] The earls continued to retain Gaelic harpers right down to the late sixteenth century at which time Connor O'Spellan was in the eleventh earl's pay.[146] The ninth earl also rented parcels of his estate to Gaelic rhymers: a messuage in Crumlin in county Dublin and a holding in Ballysallagh in Westmeath were occupied by Tege O'Rono and Dermot O'Coffy, respectively, both of whom were rhymers. The clan McWard who were rhymers in county Louth, also paid annual tribute to the ninth earl.[147] However, these Gaelic performers drew on a much broader base of support and patronage in the Pale than the earls of Kildare; in the late 1540s rhymers continued to itinerate around the Pale, including Dublin. In 1549, for example, a man of that profession named Toll O'Molmore M'Keighe from Rathtorkill in county Kildare was indicted for stealing a pig which belonged to another rhymer named Patrick M'Hwe from the same district.[148] Gaelic poets and rhymers also resided in the Ormond lordship in the early sixteenth century.[149]

---

143 Donough Bryan, *Gerald Fitzgerald, the great earl of Kildare, 1456-1513* (Dublin, 1933), p. 91 (hereafter Bryan, *The great earl*).   **144** *Tracts relating to Ireland*, ed. James Hardiman (Dublin, 1843), ii, p. 57.   **145** *Cal. pat. rolls Ire., Hen. VIII-Eliz.*, p. 69; Fitzgerald, *The earls of Kildare*, pp 195-6; Ellis, *Tudor Ireland*, p. 94.   **146** K.W. Nicholls, 'The Geraldines of Allen', in *The Irish Genealogist*, iv, no. 3 (1970), p. 200 (hereafter Nicholls, 'The Geraldines of Allen'). **147** *Crown surveys*, pp 234, 253, 256, 258.   **148** *Fiants Ire., Edw. VI*, nos. 279, 293.   **149** *Ormond deeds*, iii (1413-1509), p. 300; iv (1509-1547), p. 149.

Other members of the Gaelic *ollaimh* were welcomed and employed in Kildare during this period. In 1512, for example, the Tallons received Maoileachlain Mac an Leagha, a member of the acclaimed family of physicians, into their home in Herbertstown which lay in the territory of the English Eustace family.[150] The ninth earl of Kildare's 'doctor of physic' was a Gaelic man named O'Doyll to whom the earl donated a hackney in 1513.[151] The ninth earl also occasionally enlisted the services of Gaelic *ollaimh* to assist him in his administration of his estate. In 1530 he employed Maoilin Óg, son of Maoilin, *ollamh* of Siol Muireadhaigh in Abbeyderg in Longford, to draft an indenture in Irish on his behalf with MacRannal, and the Kildare rental also contains a second agreement in Gaelic.[152]

Like many of their contemporaries such as Sir Thomas Cusack and Sir Thomas Luttrell, the earls of Kildare were conversant in Gaelic. They had to be in order to effectively administer their estates, to supervise the county's military forces and to engage with the Gaelic elements over whom they asserted their dominion. Their library at Maynooth also housed twenty works, mainly devotional and history books, which were written in Irish.[153] The earls employed Gaelic judges, the ninth earl retaining three brehons.[154] As a result, he was accused by his critics in the Pale of using two legal codes, the 'prince's laws and brehon law', according as he thought best suited his own interests. David Sutton alleged that Kildare adopted brehon law in order to reap the profits of fines and ransom payments and to secure possession of forfeited land 'whereby there fell many gentlemen's lands to him'.[155] While the earl's alleged abuse of the law under the guise of adopting the brehon code may have been exceptional, his availing of the services of Gaelic judges was by no means unique in the context of the English areas of the lordship in the early sixteenth century. In 1545 two members of the Mc Clanncaidh clan of brehons were employed in the Ormond lordship, and in the late 1540s, several resident brehons still practised their profession in Kildare.[156]

Kildare society was characterised by a cultural continuum. The county boundary encompassed areas in the west and south which were virtually the

---

150 Colm Ó Lochlainn (ed.), *Irish men of learning: studies by Fr Paul Walsh* (Dublin, 1947), p. 206; Augustine Valkenburg, 'Walter Wellesley, bishop of Kildare, 147?-1539', in *Kildare Arch. Soc. Jn.*, xiv, no. 3 (1968), pp 524-5 (hereafter Valkenburg, 'Walter Wellesley'). 151 *Crown surveys*, p. 329. 152 Leinster (ed.), 'The Kildare rental book', p. 265; C.W. Russell, 'On an agreement, in Irish, between Gerald, ninth earl of Kildare and the MacRannals, executed at Maynooth', in *Proceedings of the Royal Irish Academy*, x (1869), pp 480-89; *Crown surveys*, pp 272-3. 153 *Crown surveys*, p. 356. 154 Carey, *Surviving the Tudors*. 155 Hore and Graves (eds), *Southern and eastern counties*, pp 162-3. 156 *Ormond deeds*, iv (1509-1547), pp 282-3; *Cal. pat. rolls, Ire., Hen. VIII-Eliz.*, p. 162; *Fiants Ire., Edw. VI*, no. 180.

exclusive preserve of the Gaelic Irish, while areas of the central plain and the southeast of the county were marked by a mixture in the composition of their inhabitants. Connall Priory, reputed by contemporaries to have been a virtually impenetrable bastion of English culture while lying amongst the 'wild Irish' is a case in point. Even within the Pale maghery in the northeast of the county, we find the English-born Sir John Alen at Alenscourt surrounded by Gaelic tenants, and less than forty per cent of the cottiers on the nearby earl of Kildare's manorial estate in Maynooth in 1518 were English or deemed anglicised.[157] As we shall see in our discussion of the county gentry, members of the extended Fitzgerald, Wogan and Eustace families intermarried with Gaelic neighbours. The earls of Kildare had their children fostered by Gaelic chieftains and the Kildares' kinsmen, the Fitzgeralds of Allen, adhered to the Gaelic system of inheritance in the late medieval period.[158] On a purely social level, Gaelic and English inhabitants collectively celebrated certain annual festivals, as we saw in the case of the townspeople of Naas.

The hybrid of cultures which existed in late fifteenth and early sixteenth-century Kildare is also discernible in the agricultural practices of various districts within the county. While the ninth earl's estates were in the main given over to arable farming and therefore resembled the agricultural practices of lowland England, a limited amount of pastoral farming (generally associated with the Gaelic Irish) was practised on the fringes of the county in districts including Baltinglass, Castledermot, Rathangan and Carbury.[159] In areas such as Graney in the south, out of sheer pragmatism, local communities had long since reached a *modus vivendi* with their Gaelic neighbours, partly appeasing the latter by allowing them to sell their produce in their villages and throughout the countryside.[160]

As we shall see in the following discussion of church organization, Kildare resembled Louth and Meath in that the mixed composition of its population was also manifest in the county's ecclesiastical structures and personnel. While the *ecclesia inter Anglicos* in the east and south of county was under the jurisdiction of the dean and chapter of St Patrick's Cathedral in Dublin, some of the incumbents of benefices within the Pale maghery were of Gaelic origin. The diocese of Kildare lay largely within the territory of the Gaelic Irish where parochial clergy were almost exclusively Gaelic. However, bishops of Kildare such as Walter Wellesley and William Miaghe were also obliged to appoint Gaelic clerics to vicarages and rectories which lay in *inter Anglicos* districts

157 Ellis, *Reform and revival*, p. 6; idem, *Tudor Ireland*, p. 35. **158** Nicholls, 'The Geraldines of Allen', in *The Irish Genealogist*, iv, no. 2 (1969), p. 94. **159** Carey, *Surviving the Tudors*. **160** Archdall, *Mon. Hib.*, ii, pp 259-60.

of their diocese in the 1530s and 1540s. Hence pragmatic adaptation to local circumstances and to the availability of clerical personnel dictated a degree of compromise in clerical appointments, fudging the distinctions between the *inter Anglicos* and *inter Hibernicos* orders.

The nature of Kildare society in this period was therefore coloured by this coexistence of English landowners and Gaelic tenants; by the imposition of coign and livery; by the sponsorship of Gaelic poets and rhymers and the use of Gaelic by Englishmen; by the interchange between brehon and common law; and by the appointment of Gaelic clerics to benefices in the ecclesia *inter Anglicos*. When viewed in their totality, these factors prove that complex and pragmatic concerns which governed everyday life in the county in this era combined to render attempts to maintain sharp cultural divisions between Englishry and Irishry wholly impractical.

2

The Church and the Laity in County Kildare

The fifteenth century is conventionally regarded as the era of decadence in the church throughout Christendom generally, and the church in Ireland is thought to have been in a worse state than its continental counterpart by virtue of its remoteness and resultant intellectual isolation.[1] Early sixteenth-century commentators reporting on the state of the church in Ireland also relate how

> the prelates of the church and clergy is much cause of all the misorder of the land; for there is no archbishop, ne bishops, ne prior, parson, ne vicar, ne any other person of the church, high or low, great or small, English or Irish, that useth to preach the word of God, saving the poor friars beggars; and where the word of God do cease, there can be no grace, and without the special grace of God, the land may never be reformed; and by teaching and preaching of prelates of the church and by prayer or orison of the devout persons in the same, God useth always to grant his abundant grace; ergo, the church, not using the premises is much cause of all the said misorder of this land.[2]

Contemporary accounts emanating from English-occupied areas also convey an impression of widespread disorder and dilapidation in the *Ecclesia inter Anglicos* at diocesan level, and indifference and negligence on the part of both clergy and laity. Hugh Inge, bishop of Meath (1523-8), bemoaned 'the sorrowful decay in good Christianity' in his own diocese which, by contemporary standards, was regarded as well organised and well administered. Inge alleged that this demise 'hath grown for lack of good prelates and curates in the church'. He therefore urged Cardinal Wolsey to apply himself to ensuring

1 J.A. Watt, *The church in medieval Ireland* (Dublin, 1972), pp 216-17 (hereafter Watt, *Church in medieval Ireland*); F.X. Martin, 'Confusion abounding: Bernard O'Higgins, OSA, bishop of Elphin, 1542-1561', in Art Cosgrove and Donal McCartney (eds), *Studies in Irish history presented to R. Dudley Edwards* (Dublin, 1979), p. 53; Ellis, *Tudor Ireland*, p. 185. 2 'State of Ireland', 1515 (*S.P. Hen. VIII*, ii, p. 15); Watt, *Church in medieval Ireland*, p. 182; Ellis, *Tudor Ireland*, p. 185.

that suitable clerics be promoted to bishoprics so that 'their manner of living may be [an] example of goodness and virtue'.[3] In an effort to provoke Henry VIII into taking remedial steps to halt the decline of the church in Ireland, Gerald, the ninth earl of Kildare, ominously prophesied that 'if the king do not provide a remedy there will be no more Christianity [in Tipperary and Kilkenny] than in the middle of Turkey'.[4]

However, recent work by Henry Jefferies on the archdiocese of Armagh has challenged the traditional image of the church in Ireland in the pre-Reformation period which had been so heavily coloured by insufficiently critical interpretations of such contemporary commentaries. He discards the notion that the church was a decaying institution which was 'not far from total breakdown', pointing instead to evidence of wide-scale church building and extension in county Louth. Jefferies also identifies a laity who were sufficiently committed to invest very heavily in their parish churches in Louth on the eve of the Reformation. In the case of Armagh, church courts operated quite effectively in monitoring the ministries of the priesthood and the religious lives of the faithful in the *inter Anglicos* region of the archdiocese in the pre-Reformation era. Evidence has also been uncovered by Jefferies which points to the formation of new parishes in that region in the late medieval period and suggests considerable dynamism in church life in Louth.[5]

Yet, a considerable body of evidence points to serious organizational and morale problems at all levels in the church in both *inter Anglicos* and *inter Hibernicos* areas on the eve of the Reformation. Abuses such as clerical concubinage and pluralism were common, and churches had been allowed to fall into a ruinous state throughout the lordship well before the sixteenth century. In the monastic sphere, too, serious abuses were manifest. Communities had

3 Archbishop Inge and Lord Chief Justice Bermingham to Wolsey, 23 Feb. 1528 (*S.P. Hen. VIII*, ii, p. 126); Watt, *Church in medieval Ireland*, p. 182.   **4** 'Kildare's articles against Ormond', 1525 (*S.P. Hen. VIII*, p. 123; *Cal. Carew MSS, 1515-74*, p. 34); M.V. Ronan, *The Reformation in Dublin, 1536-58* (London, 1926), p. xxiv (hereafter Ronan, *The Reformation in Dublin*); Watt, *Church in medieval Ireland*, pp 182-3; Ellis, *Tudor Ireland*, p. 184.   **5** Henry Jefferies, 'The church courts of Armagh on the eve of the Reformation', in *Seanchas Ardmhacha*, xv (1993), pp 131-32; idem, 'Diocesan synods and convocation in Armagh on the eve of the Tudor Reformations', in *Seanchas Ardmhacha*, xvi (1995), pp 120-32 (hereafter Jefferies, 'Diocesan synods and convocations in Armagh'); idem, 'The laity in the parishes of Armagh *inter Anglicos* on the eve of the Reformation', in *Archivium Hibernicum*, lii (1998), pp 73-84; idem, *Priests and prelates of Armagh in the age of Reformations, 1518-1558* (Dublin, 1997) (hereafter Jefferies, *Priests and prelates of Armagh*). For earlier accounts of the church in Armagh in the late medieval period see Anthony Lynch, 'Religion in late medieval Ireland', in *Archivium Hibernicum*, xxxvi (1981), pp 3-15 (hereafter Lynch, 'Religion in late medieval Ireland'); John Watt, 'The church and two nations in late medieval Armagh', in W.J. Sheils and Diana Wood (eds), *The churches, Ireland and the Irish* (Oxford, 1989), pp 37-54.

grown steadily smaller, with several of the lordship's lesser houses having closed before the monastic suppressions in the late 1530s. Lynch argues that monasteries had become lax and worldly as a result of which the fabric of monastic buildings fell into decay.[6] However, it cannot be said that comprehensive reform of the church in Ireland was not implemented in the pre-Reformation period, owing to a failure by the hierarchy to acknowledge the need for reform or a general reluctance to tackle the problems facing the church.

In 1496, the prospect of implementing a comprehensive reform programme was mooted on the initiative of Henry VII. A petition was dispatched to Pope Alexander VI on the king's behalf, stressing that it was 'urgently desirable, for the guidance and good government of the metropolitan and cathedral churches, that some suitable remedy should be found' and particularly so in the more remote areas of the island. In response to this petition, the pope issued a bull in October 1496 which legislated for the appointment a cohort of English bishops, namely Morton, archbishop of Canterbury, Fox, bishop of Durham, King, bishop of Bath and Wells, and Savage, bishop of London, to oversee the implementation of such a reform programme in Ireland. These prelates were directed to summon a council of all archbishops and bishops in Ireland together with their diocesan clergy and members of the laity. The brief of the council was to treat of 'all things that concern the good estate and prosperous government of the churches, clergy, and people' in the charge of these Irish-based prelates and to provide canonical sanctions in respect of these issues. The English bishops were also invested with authority to nominate individuals who should have power to pursue ecclesiastical censures against those who opposed their decrees. The purpose of this papal initiative appears to have been the subordination of the entire Irish hierarchy to this convocation. However, the fact that leading figures such as the eighth earl of Kildare made no attempt to oppose it would seem to indicate a widespread belief that this whole scheme was impracticable, and that such an authoritarian imposition was bound to meet with strong resistance from Armagh and Dublin.[7] In the end, the grand scheme came to nothing.

However, not all prelates and clerics were negligent or indifferent in their ministry. Recent scholarship based on the state of diocesan clerics in both Ireland and England in the pre-Reformation era has shed light on the difficult circumstances in which bishops and more especially priests and clerks were forced to work. The shared problems of the difficulties in securing a benefice, the small size of livings, the paltry and uncertain nature of clerical income,

6 Lynch, 'Religion in late medieval Ireland', p. 9.   7 Watt, *Church in medieval Ireland*, pp 37-9.

poor living conditions and the handicap of poor education were magnified for clerics in Ireland, as Steven Ellis and James Murray have shown.[8] Moreover, those problems were compounded by the language barrier, cultural divisions and by the separate ecclesiastical organizational frameworks which reflected those divisions.

Increasingly, the endeavours of individual clerics to adopt measures which would improve pastoral ministry at diocesan level are coming to light. For example, during his tenure as archbishop of Dublin (1484-1511), Walter Fitzsimons exhibited his progressive approach in his efforts to establish a university in Dublin.[9] He also sought to tackle the language problem within his metropolitan see by petitioning the crown to be permitted to grant certain benefices under his jurisdiction to Irish clerks. His near contemporary, William Sherwood, bishop of Meath (1460-82), had appointed Gaelic clerics to benefices *inter Hibernicos* prior to 1472, when the king was forced to recognise the inevitability of this *de facto* arrangement. By act of parliament of 1472, Sherwood was allowed to present a Gaelic cleric to 'every church being among the King's enemies, or in any other place where no Englishman of English condition can securely inhabit or dwell, of which church the said bishop is true patron'.[10] However, Dublin was different since it was the only see in the lordship in which the standards of religious life as laid down by the papal bull of *Laudabiliter* were still reasonably intact on the eve of the Reformation.[11] Fitzsimons's outlook was a minority one, as it necessarily involved compromising the English monopoly on benefices in the archdiocese. This proposal was vehemently resisted by the archdiocesan chapters who 'felt the strongest impulse to defend and preserve English ecclesiastical order and canonical rectitude where it still had some lifeblood'.[12] Sherwood's pragmatism and Fitzsimons's frustrated efforts exhibited their consciousness of the need to redress two fundamental problems facing the church in the pre-Reformation era, namely the language barrier, and the reluctance and short supply of English clerks to minister in march areas of the see.

Not all of the lordship's clergy were indifferent to their religious obligations.[13] The cathedral chapters of Dublin archdiocese, and especially that of St

8 See S.G. Ellis, 'Economic problems of the church: why the Reformation failed in Ireland', in *Journal of Ecclesiastical History*, xli (1990), pp 239-65 (hereafter Ellis, 'Economic problems'); James Murray, 'The sources of clerical income in the Tudor diocese of Dublin, *c.*1530-1600', in *Archivium Hibernicum*, xlv (1990), pp 139-60 (hereafter Murray, 'Sources of clerical income'). 9 Murray, 'The Tudor diocese of Dublin', p. 73. 10 John Brady, 'The medieval diocese of Meath', in *Ríocht na Midhe*, i, no. 3 (1957), p. 38 (hereafter Brady, 'The medieval diocese of Meath'). 11 Murray, 'The Tudor diocese of Dublin', p. 83. 12 Ibid. 13 Jefferies, *Priests and prelates of Armagh*, p. 131.

Patrick's Cathedral, were said to have been very assiduous in performing the liturgy and in structurally maintaining their cathedrals.[14] Likewise, all of the archbishops of Armagh in the immediate pre-Reformation period, namely Octavian de Palatio, John Kite and George Cromer, were extremely conscientious and hardworking. Each incumbent was resident in the archdiocese of Armagh for the full duration of his term of office and exhibited zeal in administering his pastoral duties of metropolitan visitation, regularly convening provincial councils. These primates also worked hard to ensure the general observation of conciliar decrees, and constantly sought to maintain high standards among their bishops, clergy and laity. They were engaged in ongoing correction and supervision of their bishops and they vigorously sought to stamp out clerical concubinage. In spite of their best efforts, they were constantly faced with opposition, and from an unexpected quarter. The archbishops' endeavours to eradicate concubinage were negated by the papacy which undermined the prelates by granting dispensations with great ease to offending clerics and their families. Indeed, in his study of late medieval religion Lynch argues that the papacy tolerated and even encouraged the abuses which the primates sought to suppress, thereby robbing the latters' work of its effectiveness and urgency.[15]

Other reforming bishops such as Maurice Doran, bishop of Leighlin in the 1520s, encountered even more stern opposition to their endeavours. Doran was a scrupulous prelate: when he was advised to impose double subsidies on his clergy in order to reimburse himself for the costs he incurred while seeking election, he replied that he would have his flock shorn, but not fleeced. In an extreme case, Doran paid with his life for endeavouring to impose strict standards on his diocesan subordinates; in 1525 he was murdered on the high road near Glen Renold by his archdeacon, Maurice Kavanagh, for having reproved Kavanagh for his insolent obstinacy and other crimes and for having threatened him with further censure.[16]

Recognition of the need for reform, therefore, certainly existed at all levels from the papacy and the crown down to diocesan level in the lordship. The outcome of the endeavours of Archbishop Fitzsimons and those of the archbishops of Armagh and of Bishop Doran point to the manner in which individually-instituted reforms could be blocked by personal animosities, local hostility, cultural divisions and papal indifference. These factors combined with

14 Murray, 'The Tudor diocese of Dublin', p. 49. 15 Lynch, 'Religion in late medieval Ireland', p. 8. 16 'Kildare's articles against Ormond', 1525 (*S.P. Hen. VIII*, ii, p. 122; *Cal. Carew MSS, 1515-74*, p. 33); Fitzgerald, *The earls of Kildare*, p. 98; Michael Comerford, *Collections relating to the diocese of Kildare and Leighlin* (3 vols, Dublin, 1883-6), i, p. 55 (hereafter Comerford, *Collections*); Ellis, *Tudor Ireland*, p. 187. Maurice Kavanagh was the abbot of Duiske's son. The abbot is said to have hoped that he would be appointed as bishop of Leighlin.

a lack of the requisite personnel and resources, organizational divisions between *inter Anglicos* and *inter Hibernicos*, and resultant conservative inertia to present the most formidable obstacles to the implementation of spontaneous reforms in the pre-Reformation period. That said, some bishops did actually manage to introduce modest reforms at local level on their own initiative.

I

This is the broad context in which we approach this study of the church in county Kildare in the pre-Reformation and early Reformation eras. While the church in Kildare suffered the familiar ills of financial depravity and structural decay in common with the rest of the country, there is evidence of spontaneous reform and rejuvenation both at the level of the two diocesan hierarchies and at the level of the county's laity. In order to gain an understanding of the context in which these reforms and initiatives occurred, this study begins with a general survey of church organization obtaining in the county as a whole.

The church in late medieval county Kildare was split in terms of its ecclesiastical organization into the usual division of the monastic orders and the secular and regular order. The county boundary encompassed the greater part of the diocese of Kildare, a small part of the western section of the archdiocese of Dublin and a minute division of the archdeaconry of Glendalough.[17] In the extreme periphery of the border areas of the north, west and southwest, it incorporated districts within the dioceses of Leighlin, Meath and Ossory. The state of the monastic order in the county on the eve of the Reformation is discussed and attention is then focused on the jurisdictions and institutions of the archdiocese of Dublin and the diocese of Kildare, which are treated separately. Particular emphasis is placed on the episcopacy of Edmund (sometimes Edward) Lane (1482- c.1522/3), set within the broader context of ecclesiastical developments in the county as a whole rather than strictly within his diocese of Kildare. Following Lane's death, the episcopal succession of Kildare diocese became complicated by political patrons nominating their favourite candidates for appointment. This development, along with the revival of the prerogatives of the archbishopric of Dublin from 1514 onwards, is discussed while tracing the gradual curbing of the ninth earl of Kildare's influence in church affairs which is reflective of a similar trend in the political sphere. The last section focuses on the early 1530s when these separate processes intensified and merged, especially in the actions of Archbishop John Alen.

17 Murray, 'The Tudor diocese of Dublin', pp 78-9.

Anthony Lynch paints a very bleak picture of the state of monasticism in Ireland in the late medieval period. He claims that abuses including drunkenness and the keeping of concubines were rife; the monastic buildings were allowed to fall into a decrepit state and the income of the houses was said to have been frittered away by dissolute monks. The friars alone are said to have exhibited signs of renewed fervour and zeal, epitomised in the Observant movement.[18] County Kildare had over twenty monastic houses in the early sixteenth century and some of these certainly conformed to Lynch's pathetic portrayal. The nunnery of Timolin was dissolved by Archbishop John Alen in 1530 as a result of its derelict state; only one of its houses was considered sufficiently worthy to be nominated by the lord deputy and Irish council for exemption from suppression. There is anecdotal evidence of illicit sexual relationships involving the personnel of Kildare monasteries, though they merely reflect those abuses which were common throughout the lordship at this time. There is also evidence to support Lynch's observation that the religious of Kildare's monasteries had become very worldly in their interests. That the heads of the county's monastic houses enjoyed the comforts of the gentry from whom several of them were drawn is evident in the generous conditions and pensions which they received following the suppression of their houses. Richard Weston, late prior of St Wolstan's, evidently enjoyed a very comfortable living during his term as prior of that house, as reflected in the arrangements made for him subsequent to the dissolution of that priory.[19] Robert Wellesley, the last prior of Connall Priory and a kinsman of Walter, the bishop of Kildare, received a pension of over £13, which is indicative of the comfortable standard of living to which he was accustomed. The fact that the prior at Connall could on occasion host up to 300 guests at one sitting also testifies to the immense wealth at his disposal.

The worldliness of these superiors of the county's houses is evident in their resort to preemptive measures designed to circumvent the wholescale confiscation of their monastic estates. Aegidia Wale, the last abbess of Graney nunnery, and Sir John Rawson, the last prior of St John the Baptist Priory in Kilmainham and superior of the preceptories at Tully and Kilteel in Kildare, were both masters in granting leases of their lands to favoured members of the

---

18 Lynch, 'Religion in late medieval Ireland', p. 9.   19 Archdall, *Mon. Hib.*, ii, p. 295; W.T. Kirkpatrick, 'St Wolstan's' in *Kildare Arch. Soc. Jn.*, ii (1896-9), p. 285 (hereafter Kirkpatrick, 'St Wolstan's'); Aubrey Gwynn and R.N. Hadcock, *Medieval religious houses: Ireland with an appendix to early sites* (reprint, Dublin, 1988), p. 193 (hereafter Gwynn and Hadcock, *Medieval religious houses: Ireland*).

laity prior to the suppression of their houses. In this way they secured large entry fines and sought to ensure that members of the laity would ultimately have the strongest claim to the monastic properties which they occupied when the floodgates in the property market opened with the wide scale suppression campaign in 1539-41. That worldliness was, however, entirely necessary given their roles as administrators of large estates. The degree to which monastic incomes were wasted by dissolute monks in county Kildare is, unfortunately, impossible to ascertain but recklessness on the part of the monks alone cannot explain the poverty of several of county Kildare's houses on the eve of the Reformation. Rather, houses such as New Abbey in Kilcullen, the Augustinian friary in Naas, the Dominican priory in Athy, the Franciscan friary in Castle-dermot and the Brigittine nunnery, the Franciscan friary and the Carmelite house in Kildare town were all modest monastic settlements in the first instance. Their paltry resources therefore necessarily limited their capacity for the provision of hospitality, care for the sick and education. However, while these houses might be excused for lapsed observation of monastic duties, monasteries such as Baltinglass, Monasterevin, Graney, St Wolstan's, and the three Hospitals of St John in Naas, Athy and Castledermot had the resources to provide at least some of these services to the local communities, though there is no evidence to suggest that any of them in fact did so.

While Lynch's generalizations regarding the poor quality of monastic life in Ireland have considerable application to the case of Kildare, his emphasis on the widespread ruinous physical state of monastic buildings in the pre-Reformation era is not entirely accurate in this instance. Those monasteries which lay within the Pale maghery in the east of the county were in a com-paratively sound state on the eve of their dissolution. Saint John's Hospital in Naas still had its old house, a hall with chamber and rooms, an old tiled tower, a thatched barn and a stable intact at the time of its closure. The buildings of the Augustinian friary at Naas were all standing in 1540 and the dormitory, which had glazed windows, had only recently been demolished. Likewise, the church and chancel and all buildings belonging to the Dominican priory of St Eustace in Naas were found to be standing in 1540.[20] In nearby Clane, the church, chancel and dormitory along with other buildings belonging to the Franciscan priory were still in such a good state of structural repair in 1537 that Lord Leonard Grey had them demolished in order to repair Maynooth Castle.[21] The sound state of the buildings and the estate of St Wolstan's Priory at the time of its dissolution also belies the truism that monasteries were in a state of chronic physical decline.[22] The Franciscan house of New Abbey in

20 *Extents Ir. mon. possessions*, pp 154-5, 165-6. **21** Ibid., p. 164. **22** Archdall, *Mon. Hib.*, ii,

Kilcullen was only established in 1486 and hence its buildings, which consisted of a church, a belfry, a dormitory and a hall, were in a very good state of repair in 1540.[23]

Beyond the Pale boundary the priory of Connall appears to have been a functioning monastery right down to its suppression. Lord Deputy Grey and the Irish council had recommended that it ought to be exempted from closure since its personnel provided hospitality to the lord deputy, to crown officials and soldiers and also to Irishmen. Moreover, they are said to have educated the children of gentlemen and members of the lower strata of society, teaching both men and women to be 'brought up in virtue, learning, and in the English tongue and behaviour'. Connall Priory also served the crown by raising troops to serve in the deputy's forces.[24] Again, all of the priory's buildings were found to be standing, though the chancel and the chapel were fit for demolition. The substantial value of the property (in excess of £168) disproves the notion that all monasteries were dissolute on the eve of the Reformation. Connall was a viable monastic estate, as is evident from the accounts of its properties which appear to have been inhabited and cultivated right down to 1540, and its tenants apparently paid rents, tithes, customs and altarages until its suppression.[25] Even in the march areas of the county, in Monasterevin, Athy, Castledermot, Graney and Baltinglass, jurors' extent reports from 1540 indicate that the houses in each of these districts were standing and functioning (however viably) prior to their destruction in the course of the Kildare rebellion or in the Gaelic raids which followed.

According to those reports, Baltinglass Abbey and St John's Hospital in Castledermot were not far from extinction at the time of their suppression. None the less, it is important to bear in mind that it was in the interests of the jurors to emphasise and perhaps exaggerate the decadent state of the monasteries. Secondly, the decrepit state of monastic sites and estates in 1540 cannot be explained solely in terms of the worldliness and disinterest of their religious personnel. For example, in 1537 the buildings in the precincts of Baltinglass Abbey were comprised of a castle, a hall, a dormitory with two cellars beneath it, a chamber with a vault below it as well as a kitchen and a barn.[26] Yet by 1540, most of the buildings were found to be in a ruinous state. This proves that their rapid deterioration resulted from disturbances and neglect in the aftermath of the Kildare rebellion rather than from the monks of Baltinglass

pp 292-4; Gwynn and Hadcock, *Medieval religious houses: Ireland*, p. 193. **23** *Extents Ir. mon. possessions*, p. 173. **24** The lord deputy and council of Ireland to Cromwell, 21 May 1539 (*S.P. Hen. VIII*, iii, pt 3, p. 130; *L. & P. Hen. VIII*, xiv, no. 1005). **25** *Extents Ir. mon. possessions*, pp 157-63. **26** County Kildare exchequer inquisitions, Hen. VIII, no. 16 (N.A.I.).

allowing their house to slide into decay over a long period.[27] It is also significant that it was in 1536, a year after the suppression of the Geraldine rebellion
which hit Castledermot so hard, that St John's Hospital was said to serve no
purpose.

The monastic life still continued to attract young men and women in
Kildare right down to the 1530s, with Connall Priory and the Franciscan
houses at New Abbey near Kilcullen and Clane all recruiting members. As in
most parts of Ireland, it was the Franciscan friars in county Kildare who
showed dedicated adherence to the monastic life in their survival as a community at New Abbey after its suppression. The Franciscan community also
remained intact in Clane until 1550. In addition, although the Franciscan friary
in Kildare town was destroyed in 1547, it was re-established in 1621.[28]

II

In terms of diocesan organization in county Kildare in the late fifteenth and
early sixteenth centuries, the deaneries of the archdiocese of Dublin which
encompassed the whole of county Dublin, most of county Wicklow, and parts
of modern Carlow also extended their jurisdiction into Kildare. In the northeastern section of the county, the parishes of St Catherine's, Leixlip, Confey,
Leixlip, Castledillon, Kildrought (Celbridge), Stacumny, Donaghcumper, Donaghmore, Killadoon, Straffan, Taghadoe and Laraghbryan (Maynooth) fell
within the compass of the deanery of Leixlip. Further south, the parishes of
Rathmore, Tipper, Coghlanstown (formerly Ballycutland), Yago, Gilltown,
Brannockstown as well as parishes such as Tipperkevin and Ballymore which
were located on the borders between Kildare, Dublin and Wicklow comprised
the west wing of the deanery of Ballymore. In the centre and extreme south of
the county, the deanery of Omurthy encompassed the parishes of Kilcullen,
Kineagh, Davidstown, Fontstown, Tippeenan and Rathsallagh, Killelan, Usk,
Narraghmore, Timolin, Moone, Grangerosnalvan, Belan, Tankardstown, Castledermot, Graney, Ballycoolan, Ballaghmoon and Monemehannok (Dunmanoge), Kilkea, Dullardstown, Nicholastown, Ardree, St Michael's in Athy,
Churchtown (Fassaghreban) and Kilberry, all of which fell entirely or in part
within the shifting boundary of county Kildare.[29] In comparison even with
Armagh, Dublin archdiocese was by far the wealthiest see in Ireland, with the
majority of the metropolitan see lands lying within the maghery of the Pale.

---

27 *Extents Ir. mon. possessions*, pp 125-33.　28 See *Fiants Ire., Hen.VIII*; Gwynn and Hadcock,
Medieval religious houses: Ireland, pp 245, 252.　29 Murray, 'The Tudor diocese of Dublin', p. 402.

Moreover, it also had a sophisticated administrative organization in place: the upshot of these combined factors is that Dublin was characterised by 'tranquillity and a deep-rooted English socio-cultural organization in which conditions approximated reasonably closely to those obtaining in lowland England'.[30]

The archdiocese was unusual in having two cathedrals and two chapters, that of Christ Church and that of St Patrick's, and the above areas of Kildare came under the jurisdiction of St Patrick's. Its cathedral chapter consisted of a dean who was elective by the archbishop of Dublin and a precentor, a chancellor, a treasurer, two archdeacons, the one for Dublin and the other for Glendalough, and twenty-seven prebendaries excluding the archbishop's honorary prebendal stall.[31] Four of these prebends were based entirely in county Kildare at Yago, Tipper, Maynooth and Monmahennoke (Dunmanoge) and a fifth, the prebend of Tipperkevin, lay partly within the county boundary. Since the 1430s, St Patrick's had also had a college of petty canons.[32] The chapter commanded immense wealth and presided over the largest cathedral in the country.[33] According to the *Valor beneficiorum ecclesiasticorum in Hiberniae* of 1538, the four prebends of Yago, Tipper, Maynooth and Dunmanoge were valued at £10 16s. 8d., £16 10s. 0d., £23 2s. 3d. and £11 25s. 11d. respectively. The section of the prebend of Tipperkevin which lay in Kildare was valued at £5 6s. 8d.[34] Yago, situated in northeast Kildare, ranked fourth among the prebends of St Patrick's. In 1230 the earl of Pembroke was invested with the right of presentation to the prebend and thereafter that right was assumed by Pembroke's descendents, the earls of Kildare. In 1545, Henry Darcy was appointed prebendary of Yago.[35] The prebend of Tipper ranked first among those in the cathedral, its incumbent occupying the eleventh stall in the cathedral choir.[36] The prebendaries of Tipper were generally English, with Robert Skerett, William Walsh, John Eustace, Christopher Howth and Bartholomew Fitzsimon holding the office between the years 1494 and 1535, exhibiting general conformity to the rule observed in the appointment of English candidates to key positions in the archdiocesan chapters.[37]

---

30 Ibid., pp 32-3. **31** Ibid., p. 30. **32** Ibid., pp 39, 44. **33** Ibid., p. 39. **34** *Valor beneficiorum ecclesiasticorum in Hiberniae* (reprint, 2nd ed., Dublin, 1780), p. 9; Henry Cotton, *Fasti ecclesiae Hibernicae* (6 vols, Dublin, 1848-78), ii, p. 5 (hereafter Cotton, *Fasti*). **35** *Cal. pat. rolls, Ire., Hen. VIII-Eliz.*, p. 105; Walter Fitzgerald, 'The parish of Yago, and the townland of Gaganstown', in *Kildare Arch. Soc. Jn.*, vii (1912-14), pp 336-7. **36** W.M. Mason, *The history and antiquities of the collegiate and cathedral church of St Patrick near Dublin, from its foundation in 1190 to the year 1819* (Dublin, 1820), p. 59 (hereafter Mason, *Cathedral of St Patrick's*). **37** See *Fiants Ire., Edw. VI*, nos 41-6, 51-60, 76-7, 98 for examples of former English canons of St Patrick's Cathedral.

Archbishop Alen ranked the prebend of Maynooth fourth in the diaconal order in St Patrick's. This prebend had been erected in 1284 by the archbishop of Dublin at the request of Maurice Fitzgerald, lord of Offaly, to whom the church at Maynooth belonged. Thereafter, the perpetual right of presentation to the prebend was invested in Fitzgerald and his successors. The prebends of Maynooth and of Yago were unusual in that they were the only two of the cathedral's twenty-seven canonries (apart from the deanery) which were not in the gift of the archbishop of Dublin.[38] The prebendary of Maynooth was obliged to appoint a vicar in deacon's orders who would officiate in the choir and who was to be paid at the same rate as others of his station.[39] As in the case of Tipper, the incumbents of Maynooth prebend immediately prior to the Reformation were English: Edward Dillon, a close ally of the ninth earl of Kildare, John Bayly and Richard Johnston each served as prebendaries in the late 1520s and in the 1530s. As we will see in the discussion of the foundation of the Geraldine college at Maynooth in 1518, the parish church was traditionally referred to as Maynooth while Laraghbryan enjoyed the status of appendant chapel. The establishment of this college, however, brought about a change in the status of both; Laraghbryan became parochial, and Maynooth church was elevated to prebendal status.[40]

In the cases of the prebend of Tipperkevin situated southeast of Naas and that of Dunmanoge, which lay in the extreme south of county Kildare, little information survives to indicate the origins of their incumbents in the 1520s and 1530s. However, when St Patrick's Cathedral chapter was dissolved in 1547 the incumbents of both benefices appear to have been of English origin: William Cocys was a prebendary of Tipperkevin and Thomas Festam was the incumbent at Dunmanoge.[41] According to Murray, the clergy of St Patrick's Cathedral in particular had

> a clearly defined sense of their own English identity, their loyalty to the crown and its lordship over Ireland, and a sense of superiority to the Gaelic Irish whose church, they argued, fulfilled no proper function and whose clergy they derided as 'unlearned, simpler and unmeet persons'.[42]

The dean and chapter of St Patrick's Cathedral regarded themselves as representing the 'English Irish ecclesiastical order in its purest form'.[43] It

---

38 Murray, 'The Tudor diocese of Dublin', p. 94. 39 Mason, *Cathedral of St Patrick's*, p. 60. 40 Ibid. 41 *Fiants Ire., Edw. VI*, nos 42, 76. 42 Murray, 'The Tudor diocese of Dublin', p. 54. 43 Ibid., p. 83.

comes as no surprise therefore to find that within the area of Kildare under the jurisdiction of the archdiocese of Dublin, both secular and regular clergy appear to have been English in the pre-Reformation and early Reformation eras (down to 1547). Even at the lower levels of parish clergy, several incumbents of rectories and vicarages were of English origin. For example, Richard Weston was prior of St Wolstan's Priory in Celbridge at the time of its suppression, and Richard Niocall was the parish vicar *c*.1537.[44] In the northeast, John Wall was curate of Castledillon in 1540. In Rathmore, Walter Trott was vicar throughout the 1540s and in the south of the county, and John Wogan held the vicarage of Castledermot *c*.1535. Further west, in Athy, Alexander Baron served as rector of the parochial church in Athy.[45] The origins of these clerics also partly reflect the composition and orientation of the upper strata of the laity to whom they ministered in the eastern and southeastern sections of the county. In the district of Rathmore, names such as Lang, Trott, Bayly and Weston appear, though in all of these eastern districts there was still a mix between English and Gaelic elements in the local population.[46] In Athy, a similar situation obtained with names such as Fitzgerald, St Michael, Moultell, Pelles and Wolfe appearing among the list of local jurors.[47] Further south, in Castledermot, the ethnic composition of local worthies was more decidedly (though still not exclusively) Gaelic. In the vicinity of Castledermot, for instance, the names of the local notables included Eustace, Kelly, Browne, Alen, O'Doran, Surgion, MacMurrogh, McJames, O'Garran, O'Connor and Oerman. In all of these areas, however, the majority of the local population were Gaelic, as the crown surveys of lands, the extents of monastic possessions and the Kildare rental collectively indicate.

The diocese of Kildare spanned the northern, central and western sections of the county. In the north, it stretched east to encompass Kilcock, Cara, Kill, Bodenstown, Clane, Naas, Walterstown, Harristown, Oughterard and Lyons. Further south lay the parishes of Ballysax and Nurney. The diocese stretched westwards as far as Geashill in the O'Connor country of east Offaly and Tinnahinch (Oregan) in O'More territory in east Leix. The Valor describes six rectories and seven vicarages as being 'all Irish'. While some of these lay, as one might expect, in the western extremes of the diocese at Geashill, Ballynakill and Oregan, others such as Rathernan were situated in the central plain of county Kildare, an indication of the expanse of the Gaelic presence in the county. This situation was acknowledged by the ninth earl of Kildare in 1523 when he stated that the substance of the see of Kildare 'lieth in the Irishry, and

---

44 Archdall, *Mon. Hib.*, ii, pp 292-4; *Calendar of inquisitions*, pp 49-50, 63, 97, 103. **45** *Extents Ir. mon. possessions*, pp 22, 47, 91, 94, 155, 161; *Calendar of inquisitions*, p. 44; *Crown surveys*, p. 166. **46** *Crown surveys*, p. 144. **47** Ibid., p. 152.

will not be lightly had but by temporal power'.[48] The earl, however, had reason to exaggerate the extent to which the diocese of Kildare was under Gaelic influence. At that time, Kildare was seeking to have his candidate, Edward Dillon, appointed to the bishopric and his statement appears to imply that the incumbent of the see could only be effective if he had the backing of secular rule, that is, Geraldine rule. The extents of the monastic possessions in county Kildare recorded in 1540 list several rectories which were affiliated to Kildare houses and which lay in Gaelic-occupied territories to the west and south of the county. Numerous satellite rectories of Connall Priory including Kylsen and Tullaghevyn, situated in Offaly, were found in the possession of the O'Connors in 1540.[49] The extents of the monastic possessions of all four counties of Kildare, Dublin, Meath and Louth provide similar instances of outlying rectories and vicarages being subsumed into Gaelic territories.[50]

III

In the medieval period the bishops of Kildare were appointed either by papal nomination, by royal appointment or through election by the diocesan chapter. From the early fifteenth century onwards the papacy and the crown had a more active involvement in the nomination and appointment of candidates to bishoprics. By the 1430s, the papacy had gained primacy in episcopal appointments because royal government was too weak to control the administration of temporalities or to prevent papal provisions in the lordship.[51] However, the appointment of Geoffrey Hereford OP, an English Dominican, to the see of Kildare on 23 August 1447 marked a significant break with tradition in two important respects. Firstly, Hereford's advancement was instigated by Henry IV, and secondly, he was the first of a number of incumbents to be imposed from outside the diocese of Kildare. Although his appointment was therefore unusual in the context of the history of the episcopacy in late medieval Kildare, it was an unremarkable development by 'national' standards, as the appointment of English-born bishops to Irish sees was a very common occurrence in the later middle ages.

---

48 The earl of Kildare to Wolsey, 8 Feb. 1523 (*S.P. Hen. VIII*, ii, pp 98-9; *L. & P. Hen. VIII*, iii, no. 2824); 'Obligationes pro annatis diocesis Darensis, 1413-1521', ed. Ambrose Coleman in *Archivium Hibernicum*, ii (1913), pp 39-72 (hereafter 'Obligationes' ed. Coleman). **49** *Extents Ir. mon. possessions*, pp 94-5. **50** Ibid. **51** Comerford, *Collections*, i, p. 18; W.H. Grattan Flood, 'The episcopal succession of Kildare, 1206-1577', in *Irish Ecclesiastical Record*, 5th ser., xxi (1923), p. 157 (hereafter Grattan Flood, 'Episcopal succession of Kildare').

Hereford was consecrated on Easter Sunday 1449 but almost immediately was confronted by formidable difficulties. He stayed for only three years; the native Irish, he told Pope Nicholas V, drove him from his church and forced him to return to England in 1452. The pope accepted Hereford's explanation and promptly granted him another benefice.[52] Hereford's episcopacy is especially valuable to this study since it indicates that before Protestantism was even conceived, an English-born bishop, ministering to his faithful in line with orthodox Catholic regulations, was treated with overt hostility by the Gaelic population of Kildare. Although merely one case, Hereford's experience provides a useful reference point from which we can gain some appreciation of the strength of resistance which Protestant prelates such as Alexander Craik and Robert Daly encountered in their efforts to spread Protestantism in the diocese in the later sixteenth century. It was this same hostility shown to Hereford which over a century later caused the English-born Puritanical Bishop Daly to be 'three times turned in a manner almost naked out of his house'. In the course of these attacks, Daly's property was plundered by rebels and it is believed that the last raid led to his death in winter 1582.[53]

Hereford's successor, Richard Lang, was a controversial figure whose career exemplifies the practice and perils of 'Rome running', which was common in the Ireland in the late medieval period and which is regarded as a significant contributor to the decline of the church in the lordship. Lang was allegedly elected by the chapter of Kildare in 1468 and Edward IV duly recognised him as bishop and granted him restitution of temporalities. In July of that same year Lang attended a parliament at Drogheda in his capacity as bishop of Kildare. However, following the death in 1471 of Archbishop John Bole of Armagh (1457-71), Lang's interests turned to the primacy, encouraged by the king's grant of the temporalities of Armagh to his custody.[54] In November 1474 the dean and chapter of Armagh made representations to the papacy on Lang's behalf to secure his promotion to the archbishopric. Lang had apparently administered the archdiocese during the intervening three years and he was recommended in excessively complimentary terms as being

> noble, both by birth and merit, well instructed in apostolic and ecclesiastical discipline, in faith truly catholic; prudent, wise, docile and

---

52 Grattan Flood, 'Episcopal succession of Kildare', p. 158. 53 *The whole works of Sir James Ware concerning Ireland*, ed. Walter Harris (2 vols, Dublin, 1764), i, p. 391 (hereafter *The works of Ware*); William Sherlock, *Some account of St Brigid and of the see of Kildare with its bishops, and of the cathedral, now restored* (Dublin, 1896), p. 30 (hereafter Sherlock, *Some account of St Brigid*). 54 Comerford, *Collections*, i, pp 18-19; Grattan Flood, 'Episcopal succession of Kildare', p. 159.

patient, temperate, chaste, sober, humble, affable, compassionate, and learned; well read in the law of God; wary in expounding the scriptures; and deeply versed in the tenets of the church.[55]

Unwittingly, the dean and chapter's attempt to ingratiate Lang with the pope worked to the detriment of his suit since, in the eyes of the curia, his advocates were 'simple enough to write commendatory letters to the pope, wherein they gave Richard so high a character for his virtue, learning, chastity, and temperance, that he was with one voice, cried down at the court of Rome'.[56] But that was not all. By advocating his suit, the dean and chapter drew Lang's entire standing as bishop of Kildare into the limelight, and it emerged that Lang had no proof of his provision to the see of Kildare. This led the pope to question his canonical position. Lang's toying with 'Rome-running' ultimately had serious negative repercussions, and the primacy was instead conferred on Octavian de Palatio (1478-1513).

The pre-eminence of the papacy in episcopal appointments to Kildare was also evident when in July 1474 the pope ejected a certain 'John' who 'had himself elected' and instead provided David O'Connell, archdeacon of Kildare, to the see. At the time of his appointment, the bishop-elect was in Rome where he resigned his office as archdeacon early in December. However, O'Connell died before his apostolic letters had been completed.[57] His successor, James Wale OFM, a minorite and doctor of divinity, was English-born and was consecrated on 5 April 1475. He occupied the see for a period of five years but resigned on 7 July 1480 owing to the 'very disturbed state of the country'. He then returned to England where he ministered in London, and died in April 1494.[58] His successor in Kildare was William Barrett, who resigned soon after his appointment.

The accession of Edmund Lane in 1480, following Barrett's resignation, coincided with an upturn in the state of the church both in Kildare diocese and at county level.[59] Lane was bishop for over forty years (1480-1522/3). The longevity of his episcopacy, combined with his reputation as a 'zealous and generous prelate', brought stability and improvements to the church organization. Lane, a native of Kildare, involved himself in both the governmental and ecclesiastical affairs of the Pale in the late fifteenth century. Like his contemporary, Bishop Payne of Meath, he complied with the eighth earl of Kildare's

---

55 Quoted in Sherlock, *Some account of St Brigid*, p. 26. 56 Rowley Lascelles, *Liber munerum publicorum Hiberniae* (2 vols, London, 1852), pt v, p. 41 (hereafter *Liber mun. pub. Hib.*). 57 Comerford, *Collections*, i, p. 19. 58 Ibid.; Grattan Flood, 'Episcopal succession of Kildare', p. 160. 59 Comerford dates his accession 1482; see Comerford, *Collections*, i, p. 19.

instruction to attend the coronation ceremony of Lambert Simnel in 1487. When the pope took retaliatory action on behalf of Henry VII, the adherents of the eighth earl, including Bishop Lane, were threatened with excommunication.[60] Along with the other spiritual and temporal lords involved, Lane was subsequently pardoned and followed the eighth earl in doing homage and fealty before Sir Richard Edgecombe at St Thomas's Court in Dublin in 1488.[61] He also assisted at a provincial synod in Christ Church in 1494 under the presidency of Archbishop Walter Fitzsimons of Dublin, though this was by no means exceptional since even bishops from Gaelic dioceses travelled regularly to attend these provincial councils.[62]

But it was at diocesan level that Lane proved his real dynamism. He introduced practical improvements in the diocese, his principal achievements being his restoration of the cathedral church of St Brigid in Kildare town and his foundation of a college at Kildare in which the dean and chapter could reside in a collegial manner. Indeed, as was generally the case with prelates at this time, Lane was a generous benefactor of the cathedral throughout his life, and his remains were interred there.[63] Given that his episcopacy spanned over forty years of the immediate pre-Reformation period, the state of the church in county Kildare as a whole during his term of office and beyond will hereafter be investigated with a view to examining its structures, its personnel and the role of the county's laity in church life.

I V

Lane administered the diocese with the assistance of a 'four-square' cathedral organization based on the English model and comprised of a dean, a precentor, a chancellor and a treasurer. Some ambiguity surrounds the number of canons. Kildare is said to have had a total of eight canons, although the printed valor only lists those who represented Lullymore, Rathangan, Ballyshannon, Dunmarkill and Donadea.[64] The deanery of Kildare was elective and the

60 *The works of Ware*, i, p. 89; Aubrey Gwynn, *The medieval province of Armagh, 1470-1545* (Dundalk, 1946), p. 27. 61 *The works of Ware*, i, pp 388-9; Comerford, *Collections*, i, p. 19; Mary Hayden, 'Lambert Simnel in Ireland', in *Studies*, iv (1915), p. 627; John O'Hanlon and Edward O'Leary, *History of the Queen's County* (2 vols, Dublin, 1907-14), i, p. 107; Grattan Flood, 'Episcopal succession of Kildare', p. 160. 62 *The works of Ware*, i, p. 389; Comerford, *Collections*, i, pp 19-20; Lynch, 'Religion in late medieval Ireland', p. 6. 63 Comerford, *Collections*, i, pp 19-20. See also Jefferies, 'Diocesan synods and convocations in Armagh', p. 127. 64 See 'Obligationes' ed. Coleman. The prebend of Harristown is referred to in *Cal. pat. rolls, Ire., Hen. VIII-Eliz.*, p. 118. Harristown is termed a prebend in the mid-1540s. See Geoffrey

canons held no titles. According to the succession lists of Lascelles and Cotton, neither the archdeacon nor these prebendaries were members of the chapter; however, the prebendaries did have stalls in St Brigid's Cathedral in Kildare town and they had a vote in the election of a dean. The chapter also owned land in the county.[65] From the thirteenth to the mid-fifteenth centuries the diocesan chapter was granted royal licence to elect candidates to the see of Kildare. Not surprisingly, therefore, certainly right down to the early fourteenth century, the vast majority of the bishops appointed were former members of the chapter. The cathedral revenues were enjoyed in common by the dignitaries, including the archdeacon and canons.[66]

Unfortunately, the dearth of source material relating to the incumbents of the posts of the deanery and chapter of Kildare in the late fifteenth and early sixteenth centuries militates against any attempt to draw decisive conclusions regarding the origins of the diocese's chief administrators. What few records there are, however, appear to suggest that the positions of dean and archdeacon tended to be open to both Gaelic and English candidates. In 1500 the papacy ordained that Maurice Oqueronaten was to have the deanery of the diocese of Kildare.[67] Edward Dillon, the ninth earl of Kildare's chaplain, was dean in 1521 and Cornelius Conyll was archdeacon of Kildare in 1498, a post which he still held in 1510 when he made an endowment to the prior and convent of Christ Church Cathedral in Dublin.[68] David Wellesley, a member of a long-established county family, was archdeacon at the time of his death in 1535, his kinsmen, Walter and Robert, being bishop of Kildare and prior of Connall respectively. In 1540 another Englishman, Maurice Staunton, was archdeacon. The post of diocesan treasurer also appears to have been open to Gaelic incumbents since in 1547 Philip Egerton was appointed to the treasurership of Kildare diocese, vacant as a result of the treason and deprivation of the previous incumbent, an Irishman named William Doyne.[69]

Hand, 'The medieval chapter of St Mary's Cathedral, Limerick', in J.A. Watt, J.B. Morrall, F.X. Martin (eds), *Medieval studies presented to Aubrey Gwynn* (Dublin, 1961), p. 78. See Murray, 'The Tudor diocese of Dublin', p. 40. **65** *Liber mun. pub. Hib.*, pt v, p. 92; Cotton, *Fasti*, ii, p. 236; 'Obligationes' ed. Coleman, p. 67. **66** K.W. Nicholls, 'Medieval Irish cathedral chapters' in *Archivium Hibernicum*, xxxi (1973), p. 104. **67** *Calendar of entries in the papal registers relating to Great Britain and Ireland, papal letters, xvii, pt 1 (Alexander VI- 1492-1503), Lateran registers, pt 2 (1495-1603)*, ed. Anne Fuller (Dublin, 1994), no. 1213. **68** The earl of Kildare to Wolsey, 8 Feb. 1523 (*S.P. Hen. VIII*, ii, p. 99; *L. & P. Hen. VIII*, iii, no. 2824); Cotton, *Fasti*, ii, p. 237; 'Obligationes' ed. Coleman, p. 68; Comerford, *Collections*, i, pp 20-1; Grattan Flood, 'Episcopal succession of Kildare', p. 161; J.T. Gilbert, *A history of the city of Dublin* (reprint, abridged ed., 3 vols, Dublin, 1903) i, p. 108 (hereafter Gilbert, *A history of the city of Dublin*); Valkenburg, 'Walter Wellesley', pp 530-1. **69** *Cal. pat. rolls, Ire., Hen. VIII-Eliz.*, p. 146; *Fiants Ire., Hen. VIII*, no. 112.

Lower down the ranks, the diocesan canons were a mix of English and Gaelic in origin. In the early 1500s John Davy and Walter Wellesley, later bishop of the diocese, were both canons. In the western districts of the diocese such as Geashill in Offaly, the canons were of Gaelic origin; in 1523, for example, John O'Maenaigh was parson of Geashill and a canon at Kildare Cathedral. The clerics appointed to the vicarage, the rectory and the prebend of Geashill also appear to have been Gaelic down to 1541: Gaelic diocesan clergy therefore enjoying a degree of formal representation at canonical level. At parish level, the majority of the diocesan clergy seem to have been Gaelic. However, as one moves closer to the Dublin parishes in the east of county Kildare, the transition from the Gaelic to mixed Gaelic and English composition of the local population is partly reflected in the origins of the clergy. This was also true of the diocese of Meath.[70] Names prevalent in western, northern and central Kildare such as O'Malaghelen, O'Morey, O'Doyne, O'Molagane, Dempsey, O'Moryne, O'More, O'Beghen, O'Hanlon, Maguire, O'Downlen, O'Dogherty, Becon and O'Daly gradually become interpersed with names such as Wallington, Rawson, White, Lang, Browne, Tansey, Eustace and Gray in the eastern districts of Rathcoffey, Kildrought, Naas, Bodenstown, Kill, Ballymore and Lyons in the years down to *c.*1540.[71]

However, these distinctions were by no means clear cut or constant. In 1523, for example, an Englishman, Oliver Eustace, was rector of Rathangan and in the mid-1530s William FitzRedmond was appointed vicar of Rathangan, which lay in the western marches of county Kildare. On the other hand, in 1548 the vicar of Kildrought, whose benefice lay within the Pale maghery, was an Irishman, then *in absentia*.[72] As in the case of Armagh archdiocese, several of the parish clergy appear to have been drawn from families within the immediate localities.[73] Philip O'Malaghelen, a native of Ballyshannon, was presented by the bishop of Kildare to the rectory of St James's in Ballyshannon in December 1536.[74] Richard Flatisbury, a vicar of Kildrought (Celbridge), was a member of a local gentry family. Walter and Thomas Trott, clerics in Rathmore, had at least one other relative, Richard, who was resident in the district.[75] Likewise, Edmund Eustace's benefice in Ballymore lay within the bounds of his extended family's estates, and Alexander de Saint Michael who held the rectory of St Thomas in Athy was a member of a long-established local family. There is, however, evidence to suggest that clerics from

70 Brady, 'The medieval diocese of Meath', p. 39.   **71** See for example 'Obligationes' ed. Coleman; *Calendar of inquisitions*, pp 75, 102-3; *Crown surveys*, pp 10, 19, 20, 149, 156, 160. **72** *Cal. pat. rolls, Ire., Hen. VIII-Eliz.*, p. 26; *Calendar of inquisitions*, p. 120.   **73** Jefferies, *Priests and prelates in Armagh*, p. 44.   **74** *Calendar of inquisitions*, p. 51.   **75** *Crown surveys*, pp 99, 144, 207-8, 219.

outside the county were promoted to the more senior positions in Kildare diocese. In 1541, Lewis Tudor (alias Tidder) was promoted to the vicarage of
Dromiskin in Armagh *inter Anglicos* by Lord Deputy St Leger, but he resigned
that benefice the following year in favour of a prebend in Kildare.[76]

v

Throughout the sixteenth century, the diocese of Kildare was particularly
marred by financial paralysis. It ranked sixth after Dublin, Meath, Armagh,
Ferns and Waterford and Lismore on the basis of the annual income of the
bishopric as recorded in the various valuations in the period 1537-40.[77] The
ninth earl of Kildare informed Cardinal Wolsey in 1523 that the 'bishopric [of
Kildare] do not exceed the yearly value of one hundred marks sterling'.[78] The
duke of Norfolk, also in correspondence with Wolsey, added further credence
to the earl's estimate, stating that in 1528 the bishopric 'was not worth more
than 100 marks a year'.[79] In comparison with the episcopal estates of other
Irish sees, those of the bishop of Kildare were very modest indeed. None the
less, Michael Devitt has suggested that in the medieval period the bishop
would have had ample choice of suitable residences, and he identifies castles
at Kildare town, Bishopscourt-by-the-Liffey, Bishopscourt near Oughterard
and Cloncurry as likely locations. Devitt also claims that none of the bishop's
episcopal lands extended beyond the county boundary.[80]

 While no account of the episcopal lands exists for the immediate pre-
Reformation period, an inquisition recorded in 1549 following the death of
Bishop William Miaghe of Kildare (1541-8), provides a valuable inventory of
the see lands. Miaghe was seized in fee of an estate of in excess of 900 acres
in Bishopscourt-by-the-Liffey and Beiston, alias Ballyvy, Le Narrey, Corbally,
Kildare town, Bishopscourt in Oughterard, Ballylogwas, Karne and Rath-
gelney. The property also extended into Killaurence, Athgarvan, Clongorey,
Killovras and Relickstown and included the manor of Cloncurry and land in
Keppagh Enargid, Ballyndrenane and Lullymore. All buildings, lands and
rents pertaining to those holdings were also owned by the bishop.[81] Miaghe

76 *Cal. pat. rolls, Ire, Hen. VIII-Eliz.*, p. 117; *Crown surveys*, pp 152, 207-8, 222, 291, 340;
Jefferies, *Priests and prelates in Armagh*, p. 154. **77** Murray, 'The Tudor diocese of Dublin', p.
31; see also Ellis, 'Economic problems', p. 250. **78** The earl of Kildare to Wolsey, 8 Feb. 1523
(*S.P. Hen. VIII*, ii, pp 98-9). **79** The duke of Norfolk to Wolsey, 17 May 1528 (*L. & P. Hen. VIII*,
iv, pt 2, no. 4277). **80** Michael Devitt, 'The see lands of Kildare', in *Kildare Arch. Soc. Jn.*, ix
(1918-21), p. 365 (hereafter Devitt, 'See lands'). **81** County Kildare exchequer inquisitions,
Edw. VI, no. 2 (N.A.I.); Devitt, 'See lands', pp 361-62; Gerald Ponsonby, 'Bishopscourt and its

was not seized of 'some lands' belonging to the bishopric, from which it may be inferred that some alienation of the see's land had occurred during his tenure of office or that of his predecessors.

Even this record presents a somewhat exaggerated representation of the assets in the possession of the bishop of Kildare. In 1527, Thomas Dillon, bishop of Kildare, had granted all of his messuages, lands, tenements, rents and other payments pertaining to his episcopal holdings in Bishopscourt to Piers, earl of Ormond and his wife, Margaret, for the duration of the grantor's life.[82] In 1548 this same property at Bishopscourt, along with its lands and tenements and all its rents, reversions, remainders and profits of courts and customs, had been leased for a term of eighty-one years to Sir John Alen under such generous terms as to approach alienation of the property. Indeed the diocese had become so poor by the mid-sixteenth century that successive incumbents were forced, out of financial necessity, to further alienate episcopal lands in order to subsidise their meagre income, an expedient which in the long term accelerated the deterioration in the finances of the diocese.

These problems were further compounded by the uncertain exactions imposed by members of Kildare's aristocracy and gentry on the county's regular and diocesan religious. Like the Butlers, members of the extended Fitzgerald family, and not just the earls of Kildare alone, imposed coign and livery on churchmen within their districts. The ninth earl of Kildare cessed horsemen and carts on the bishop of Kildare as he also did mainly on the laity of counties Carlow and Kildare.[83] In 1531, Sir John Fitzgerald and his son, along with Sir James and Sir Edmund Butler and Sir Richard Poer and their kinsmen, were said to have imposed exactions to the point where 'the churchmen cannot support themselves, serve the king, keep their places and monasteries in repair not exercise their due and accustomed alms and hospitalities'.[84] Three years later, Philip Morice was accused by David Sutton of having imposed coign and livery on all tenants within the district of Allen in north Kildare 'as though they were his own ... as well as upon my lord bishop's lands there as others'.[85] In her letter patent constituting Alexander Craik, bishop of Kildare in 1560, Elizabeth I conveniently attributed the poverty of the diocese to the 'continual and intolerable oppressions of the Irish rebels'. They had, she claimed, caused the diocese to become 'so small and poor as to be insufficient for keeping of hospitality and maintaining other charges which

owners', in *Kildare Arch. Soc. Jn.*, viii (1915-17), pp 3-29. **82** *Ormond deeds*, iv, pp 114-15. **83** *Crown surveys*, pp 351-2. **84** Walter Harris, 'Collectanea de rebus Hibernicus', ed. Charles McNeill in *Analecta Hibernica*, vi (1934), p. 352. **85** Hore and Graves (eds), *Southern and eastern counties*, p. 165.

the ... bishop is obliged to support'.[86] Not surprisingly, Craik bitterly complained about the poverty of his see, begged to be discharged of his post and in the meantime further impoverished the diocese by alienating very substantial portions of the episcopal lands in an expedient to ease his 'continual and daily torment'.[87] However, local lords were not alone in imposing exactions on the bishop of Kildare, since the latter was also expected to maintain eight archers for the service of the Dublin administration.[88]

The poverty of the diocese had been recognised by both the crown and the papacy since the early 1520s, when both made concessions to newly-appointed incumbents to alleviate their predicament at the outset. The incumbents in the 1520s and 1530s, and also Bishop Craik, were allowed to continue to hold their priories along with the bishopric of Kildare *in commendam*. In addition, the taxation imposed on the diocese was reduced by the pope upon Dillon's appointment in 1526, and Henry VIII paid for the bishop's bulls out of the royal treasury. The latter appears to have been an exceptional case since one of Henry's officials in the Dublin government predicted that it would cause resentment among his subjects in Ireland and hence it provides a clear indication of the poverty of the diocese at this time.[89] The state of the diocesan finances appears to have deteriorated after 1529, since the Valor of 1538 records the annual income of the bishopric as just over £69 (as opposed to 100 marks sterling in 1529).[90]

The valuation of ecclesiastical properties in England suggests that the minimum income on which a rector could comfortably subsist, allowing for ordinary expenses, was £13 sterling annually.[91] Given that thirty-eight of the fifty-three benefices listed in the Valor of the diocese of Kildare (which is not comprehensive) yielded an annual income of less than £5, one gains an appreciation of the poverty in which the clergy of the diocese subsisted in the early decades of the sixteenth century. Studies of the advance of the Reformation in England and Wales have emphasised that a fundamental prerequisite to the successful adoption of the Reformation at local level was a financially well-endowed diocese, particularly in the march areas of Wales, Northern England and Ireland. These have highlighted even more effectively the relative poverty of benefices in Ireland, since the English Valor indicated that three-quarters of all parochial livings in England were worth less than £15 sterling, that a half

---

86 *Cal. pat. rolls, Ire., Hen. VIII-Eliz.*, p. 435.   87 *Liber mun. pub. Hib.*, pt v, p. 41; W.M. Brady, *The Irish Reformation or the alleged conversion of the Irish bishops* (London, 1867), pp 96-8 (hereafter Brady, *The Irish Reformation*).   88 Jefferies, *Priests and prelates of Armagh*, p. 130. 89 *Cal. pat. rolls, Hen. VIII-Eliz.*, p. 435; *Liber mun. pub. Hib.*, pt v, p. 41; Comerford, *Collections*, i, p. 23.   90 Murray, 'The Tudor diocese of Dublin', p. 31; Ellis, 'Economic problems', p. 248.   91 Ellis, 'Economic problems', p. 248.

of these livings were not worth £10, and many less than £7.[92] It is hardly surprising that the Reformation had little impact in Kildare throughout the whole of the sixteenth century.

Partly owing to the poverty of many of its benefices, clerical abuses had inevitably crept into the diocesan church organization as a whole in Kildare by the late fifteenth and early sixteenth centuries, and many of these persisted down to the end of the Henry VIII's reign and beyond. Since there are no ecclesiastical court records extant for the diocese of Kildare, we are obliged to rely on anecdotal information in order to gain a glimpse of the nature of some of these abuses. Parish clergy subsisted on the standard sources of clerical income, namely tithes, altarages, oblations and glebe lands.[93] However, the value of these payments varied greatly. In 1540, the tithes of the rectory of Whitechurch near Straffan amounted to £12. The glebe land was valued at 7*s*. 8*d*., though there is no record of the rector's receipt of any altarages. The rector of Morristownbiller received tithes payments to the tune of £8 13*s*. 4*d*. and an additional 13*s*. 4*d*. in altarage payments.[94] By contrast, the tithes of the rectory of Carnalway only amounted to 13*s*. 4*d*. and its altarages were valued at 26*s*. 8*d*.[95] In an effort to supplement their paltry earnings, some Kildare clerics resorted to pluralism. In certain cases this seems likely to have been unavoidable. For example, in 1538 thirteen Irish clerics whom Bishop Wellesley had appointed to benefices in his diocese were recorded as absent. Eleven of these were valued at less than the £13 minimum income calculated by Ellis.[96] That said, however, financial deprivation alone cannot account for the absence of clerics such as John O'Hanlon, the vicar of Donagh, or Donald O'Doyn, vicar of Castlecarbre, whose benefices were valued at £20 and £15 annually in 1538; they may have been resident elsewhere in the diocese and hence were returned as absent from these benefices.[97] A similar pattern is also evident in the archdioceses of Armagh and Dublin and in the diocese of Meath.[98]

92 Ibid., pp 257-9. See also Peter Heath, *The English parish clergy on the eve of the Reformation* (London, 1969) (hereafter Heath, *The English parish clergy*); Rosemary O'Day and Felicity Heal (eds), *Of Princes and paupers in the English church, 1500-1800* (Leicester, 1981); Christopher Haigh (ed.), *The English Reformation revised* (Cambridge, 1987); Glanmor Williams, *Recovery, reorientation and Reformation: Wales, c.1415-1642* (Oxford, 1987); Robert Whiting, *The blind devotion of the people* (Cambridge, 1989); Eamon Duffy, *The stripping of the altars: traditional religion in England, 1400-1580* (New Haven, 1992) (hereafter Duffy, *The stripping of the altars*); Christopher Haigh, *English Reformations: religion, politics and society under the Tudors* (Oxford, 1993); Peter Marshall, *The Catholic priesthood and the English Reformation* (Oxford, 1994). **93** See Murray, 'Sources of clerical income'. For a discussion of sources of income for clergy in England see Heath, *The English parish clergy*, pp 147-63. **94** *Extents Ir. mon. possessions*, pp 156, 160. **95** Ibid., p. 160. **96** *Calendar of inquisitions*, p. 63. **97** Ibid., p. 103. **98** Ibid., pp 86-7, 102-3 for selected examples. See also Jefferies, *Priests and prelates in Armagh*, pp 50-1.

It is likely that certain individual clerics abused the acknowledged poverty of the church in county Kildare in order to advance their own interests. Steven Crennan was one such individual, named as vicar of Oughterard and Castlewarden in 1540 when he was also rector of Rathangan.[99] He was said to have been absent from his vicarage in Oughterard in 1544, 1546 and again in 1548. His absence from his post in Rathangan was also recorded in 1542 and 1546.[100] As well as being a pluralist, Crennan independently supplemented his income by renting land in Maynooth and Laraghbryan from the ninth earl of Kildare, in addition to holding property which Kildare had demised to him.[101] Other clerics had more modest means of augmenting their income, such as serving as witnesses or third parties in land transactions between members of the laity; this was also the custom in Dublin, Meath and Ormond.[102]

The majority of the diocesan clergy in county Kildare appear to have been of Gaelic Irish origin and there seems to have been a serious lack of English clergy in the county in the pre-Reformation and Henrician Reformation period. This is evident in the number of Gaelic incumbents in the *inter Anglicos* areas of the county and even within the Pale maghery. Walter Wellesley, bishop of Kildare from 1529 to 1539, was an influential member of the Dublin administration and by reputation, 'of singular mind to the English order'. Yet, like his counterparts in Meath and Dublin, he was obliged to appoint Gaelic clerics to minister in both *inter Anglicos* and *inter Hibernicos* parishes in his see.[103] Wellesley also slackened his standards to admit two Gaelic men, Naves O'Daly and Hugh O'Doyn to Connall Priory as canons even though at that time the monastery prided itself on being an impenetrable bastion of English culture.[104]

Both Henry VIII and Edward VI tacitly recognised the inevitability of appointing Gaelic clerics to minister in outlying parishes. This is evident from their selection of Gaelic candidates to fill vacant positions such as chaplain to the vicar of Kilmahuke or to benefices such as the rectory of Seskill or the vicarage of Harristown in Kildare diocese in the 1540s.[105] Significantly, in both cases the more senior post of rector went to members of the extended Fitzgerald family, and other benefices were also entrusted to Englishmen

---

99 *Crown surveys*, p. 160; *Extents Ir. mon. possessions*, p. 41. **100** *Calendar of inquisitions*, pp 97, 110, 120. **101** *Crown surveys*, pp 133, 142, 160, 223. **102** Ibid., pp 245-7, 248-9, 252-2, 258-60; *Ormond deeds*, iii (1413-1509), pp 267-8, 321, iv (1509-1547), pp 52, 99, 127, 142, 157, 170, 173-5, 180, 202, 225, 234, 260, 272, 299, 301; *Calendar of inquisitions*, pp 16-17, 19, 26, 28, 45-6, 49, 59, 101. **103** *Calendar of inquisitions*, pp 24, 39, 53, 44, 51, 63, 69, 75; Valkenburg, 'Walter Wellesley'. **104** *Calendar of inquisitions*, p. 44. **105** *Fiants Ire., Hen. VIII*, nos 65, 185, 354.

named Darcy, Egerton, and White.[106] These measures prove that even after the introduction of the Reformation, both Wellesley and the crown were obliged to rely on Gaelic priests to minister in marginal areas, in spite of their dislike for the Irishry and regardless of their being in breach of the legal bar against appointing Gaelic men to benefices within the Pale.[107] That predicament in turn forced Wellesley and indeed successive archbishops of Armagh to tolerate poor standards of education and morality among those clerics available to them.[108] The strength in numbers of Gaelic clerics in Kildare diocese on the eve of the Reformation and their continued appointment to benefices in the diocese did little to help the spread of Protestantism in the reign of Henry VIII or of his successors. That they were needed is evident in Bishop Craik's exasperated pleas to be removed from a see 'where neither he can preach unto the people, nor [can] the people understand him'.[109]

Moreover, partly due to the high rate of clerical absenteeism in county Kildare and the undoubtedly poor standard of clerical education, there was a serious failure on behalf of the parish clergy to keep schools and to teach English in the early years of the Henrician Reformation. This is true of areas both within and beyond the Pale maghery. In 1543, for example, ten parish clergy in Kildare as compared with eight in Armagh were found by the barons of the exchequer to be in breach of statute twenty-eight of Henry VIII which decreed that schools should be kept for the teaching of English. Interestingly, a number of these parishes, including Oughterard, Castledillon and Kildrought (Celbridge), lay well within the bounds of the maghery.[110] Even in 1549-50, individual clerics including the vicars of Clane, Kilcock, Maynooth, Oughterard and Rathmore and the rector of Leixlip, all of whose benefices lay in the maghery, were non resident and did not keep schools.[111] The situation in Kildare thus contrasts sharply with that obtaining in county Dublin where the early application of the act of parliament of 1537 which ordered the establishment of schools for teaching English is said to have been extremely successful.[112] Clearly, the combination of these impediments made the task of propagating the Reformation in county Kildare a formidable one.

The moral abuses which blighted the church in Kildare in the pre-Reformation period apparently prevailed throughout the sixteenth century though again, in the absence of ecclesiastical court records, the evidence is

106 Ibid., nos 109, 112, 121, 228; *Cal. pat. rolls, Ire., Hen. VIII-Eliz.*, pp 73, 118, 145, 146. 107 *Calendar of inquisitions*, pp 44, 63. 108 Lynch, 'Religion in late medieval Ireland', p. 10. 109 Quotation in Brady, *The Irish Reformation*, p. 98. See Brady, 'The medieval diocese of Meath', p. 39 for similar remarks concerning the language barrier in Meath. 110 *Calendar of inquisitions*, p. 103; Jefferies, *Priests and prelates in Armagh*, pp 144-5. 111 *Calendar of inquisitions*, pp 121, 126. 112 Murray, 'The Tudor diocese of Dublin', p. 104.

necessarily anecdotal. Clerical marriage was apparently not looked upon as unusual: Hugh Dempsey, the last prior of Monasterevin Abbey (who received his pension in 1549) was married and his daughter, Gillis, married Robert Fitzgerald from the Carrickmore branch. They in turn had a son, Shane, who married the vicar of Kilmeague's daughter.[113] There are records of several clerics engaged in illicit sexual relations with members of the laity and with other religious. In 1482, the abbot of Monasterevin, Matthew O'Bithechan, was accused of various offences including having offspring with a nun of the Order of St Brigid in Kildare town.[114] Maurice FitzRichard of Allen, who was of an age to receive gifts of horses from the earl of Kildare in the 1510s, had a child by a woman from the O'More clan. This son, Richard, became a Crutched Friar and master of the preceptory at Kilteel. One of his subordinates in the preceptory was a Gaelic man named Dermot O'Herrell who was married to Margery Ní Beghan. Richard regularly had sexual relations with Margery and 'used her in effect as common as her own husband did'. Margery gave birth to a son, William, who was thought to be Richard's child and for whom Richard allegedly made some provision.[115] Richard had a second son, Shane, by another woman, 'a harlot whom he kept'.

Instances of illicit relationships and clerical marriage within the Fitzgerald family in Allen recur throughout the second half of the sixteenth century. For example Pierce FitzRichard, the vicar of Kilmeague in the 1570s, kept Catherine O'Rourke, the daughter of a previous vicar, as a concubine. His elder brother, Edmund (pardoned in 1574) married Sawve (Sadhbh), Catherine's sister, and his half-brother, Richard McShane of Pollardstown, pardoned in 1582, married another of Catherine's sisters.[116] James McShane of Barnacrow (pardoned in 1582) was married to Elinor, daughter of William McThomas McRedmond, the vicar of Rathangan.[117] These instances of clerical concubinage and clerical marriage illustrate the immense importance which the Geraldines attached to the preservation and advancement of their landed interests, and indicate their unscrupulous regard for both practices as legitimate means to secure those ends. This is also evident in the case of a member of the extended Fitzgerald family, Philip FitzMaurice, who was a friar at Clane in the early sixteenth century. When the need arose for Philip to assume the role of administrator of his family estate, he was forcibly removed from the friary by members of his own family who 'plucked off his habit and put him in other apparel, and caused him to take the government of Allen and

113 Nicholls, 'The Geraldines of Allen', p. 199. 114 Gwynn and Hadcock, *Medieval religious houses: Ireland*, p. 142. 115 Nicholls, 'The Geraldines of Allen', in *The Irish Genealogist*, iv (1968-73), p. 95. 116 Ibid., pp 96, 99. 117 Ibid., p. 200.

the rest of the lands'.[118] Although it is difficult to gauge the prevalence of such practices given the lack of evidence, it is unlikely that the Geraldines of Allen were exceptional in this regard.

VI

This leads us to an examination of the role of county Kildare's laity, and specifically that of the earls of Kildare, in church affairs at local level. Families such as the Fitzgeralds, the Wellesleys, the Eustaces, the Kerdiffs, the Trotts, the O'Doynes, the Dempseys, the Langs, the Saint Michaels de Rheban, the Wogans, the Berminghams and many more provided the church with clerics throughout the period of this study, and several individual members of these families were generous patrons of local churches and monasteries.[119] However, just as the earls of Kildare dominated the political, judicial and economic life of the county, so too they commanded a position of unrivalled authority over local ecclesiastical affairs. The earls wielded very considerable influence over the business of Kildare's monasteries, actively intervening in the appointment procedures and the general running of priories such as Connall and St Wolstan's near Kildrought.[120] They also had close ties with New Abbey in Kilcullen, the burial place for a number of deceased family members. Their close associations with the White Friars of Kildare town is evidenced by Silken Thomas's entrusting his family plate to their charge around the time of the rebellion in the mid-1530s. The earls claimed advowson rights in the archdiocese of Dublin, in the dioceses of Kildare, Limerick, Cork, Meath, and in modern Queen's County.

In that section of county Kildare which fell within the jurisdiction of the archdiocese of Dublin, the ninth earl held the right of nomination of the master and sub-master of his college at Maynooth along with the advowson rights to the parsonage and vicarage of Narraghmore in south Kildare. He had the right of presentation to the prebends of Yagostown and Maynooth and also to the rectory of Maynooth and the vicarage of Laraghbryan. In Kildare diocese, he held the advowson right to the parsonage and vicarage of Geashill and to those of Donadea and Rathangan. He had the right of presentation to the vicarage of

118 Ibid., p. 96.   **119** For a brief discussion of lay involvement in religious affairs see Samantha Meigs, *The Reformations in Ireland: tradition and confessionalism, 1400-1690* (Dublin, 1997), p. 42 (hereafter Meigs, *The Reformations in Ireland*).   **120** For details of the controversy surrounding appointments at St Wolstan's Priory see *Calendar of Archbishop Alen's register, c.1172-1534*, ed. Charles McNeill (Dublin, 1950), pp 280-81 (hereafter *Cal. Alen's register*).

Lye (Monasterevin), to the parsonage of Thomastown and to the rectory of Ballybracken in Kildare. Every second presentation of the vicarage of Decimore and the benefice of Dunmurray in Kildare diocese was also in the earl's gift.[121] Prelates and abbots, along with priors and deans and his chaplain, Edward Dillon, are listed among recipients of gifts of horses which the ninth earl presented to persons of standing whose continued support he sought to foster.[122]

As feudal overlords the earls of Kildare, like the earls of Desmond and Ormond, made uncertain exactions both on the laity and on the secular and regular religious whose parishes and monasteries lay within their ambits, allegedly spending 'much of their time ... taking meat and drink at their pleasure'. These hostings could be quite grandiose, depending on the wealth of the monastery, Connall Priory being particularly munificent in this regard.[123] Like the earls of Ormond, the ninth earl leased land from monastic houses by individual agreements. He was also in receipt of full or partial payments of tithes pertaining to property in Kildare which was owned by Thomas Court Priory in Dublin, by St Mary's Abbey in Dublin, by Cartmel Priory in England and by Timolin Nunnery. He received similar payments from Connall Priory, from Graney Nunnery, from the Hospital of St John the Baptist outside Newgate in Dublin and from Kilmainham Priory.[124] Kildare negotiated a lease of the tithes of Kildare for a period of five years which he held from the dean and chapter of Kildare diocese, and set some of the tithes in his possession to individuals such as Gerald Sutton of Richardstown and Owen Beady, a galloglas.[125] Along with other clergy, gentry and Gaelic captains who recognized the ninth earl as overlord, Kildare clerics paid fees to the earl. David Wellesley, archdeacon of Kildare, paid 13s. 4d. annually. The prior of St Thomas's of Athy and the vicar of Oregan each paid two rudders yearly. A priest in Kilrush paid his fee in kind, presenting the earl with ten gallons of honey at Shrove. The parson of Geashill who was appointed by the earl was obliged to present his patron with '6 melsh kyne'.[126]

Like their peers, the earls of Ormond, the Kildares had close ties with members of the clergy in both Kildare and Dublin. Two of the eighth earl's brothers were religious, namely Sir James of Leixlip who was a Knight of Rhodes or of St John of Jerusalem, and Sir John who was a Knight of St

121 *Crown surveys*, pp 188, 277-8. 122 Ibid., pp 332-3. 123 'Articles and instructions to our sovereign lord the king for his land of Ireland', 1534 (*S.P. Hen. VIII*, ii, p. 182; *L. & P. Hen. VIII*, vii, no. 264). 124 *Extents Ir. mon. possessions*, pp 46, 66; *Crown surveys*, pp 233-43. See also *Ormond deeds*, iii (1413-1509); iv (1509-1547). 125 *Crown surveys*, pp 250-1, 253. 126 Ibid., pp 235, 257-60.

John.[127] The earls employed abbots and priors from county Kildare on an *ad hoc* basis to engage in negotiations on their behalf with Gaelic clans in border areas. One such instance occurred in 1520, during the ninth earl of Kildare's detention at court, when the abbot of Monasterevin Abbey was despatched by the earl to convey intelligence back to his Gaelic allies, the O'Carrolls.[128] The Kildares also employed Gaelic-speaking priests in their service. 'A gentleman of worship, and one that retained to that old earl of Kildare', named Boice, was at Maynooth at the time of its capture by the king's forces. Speaking in Irish, Boice scorned Paris, the constable of Maynooth Castle, for betraying the Fitzgeralds.[129] Furthermore, the earls surrounded themselves with a coterie of clerical political advisers as well as several pastors. Among these was Thomas Leverous, a native of Kildare, and a member of a family said to have been bound by old ties of clientship to the Kildares.

From the outset of the Geraldine rebellion in 1534 these clerics served as advisers to Silken Thomas. However, with the exceptions of Leverous and Edward Dillon, dean of Kildare diocese, they were not natives of Kildare. (They included Charles Reynolds, the archdeacon of Kells and principal of Meath; Cormac Roth, the archdeacon and official principal of Armagh; James O'Currin, bishop of Killaloe; Simon Walsh, vicar of Rathbegan, and the English theologian, Dr John Travers, chancellor of St Patrick's Cathedral in Dublin).[130] Leverous and one of the ninth earl's chaplains, Prior Robert Walsh, in particular were to the fore in salvaging the dynasty from chaos in the aftermath of the Geraldine rebellion. Together they secured the safe conduct of Gerald, later the eleventh earl of Kildare, away from Maynooth, and Leverous served as the boy's guardian during his exile in France, Flanders and Italy.[131]

---

127 Lodge, *Peerage Ire.* (Dublin, 1789 revised ed.), i, p. 87; Fitzgerald, *The earls of Kildare*, pp 78-9, 204. **128** Surrey to Wolsey, 6 Sept. 1520 (*S.P. Hen. VIII*, ii, p. 44). **129** Duke of Leinster, 'Maynooth Castle', in *Kildare Arch. Soc. Jn.*, i (1891-95), p. 228. **130** John Alen to Cromwell, 1534 (*S.P. Hen. VIII*, ii, pp 219-24); Lord deputy and council to Hen. VIII, 26 Mar. 1535 (*S.P. Hen .VIII*, ii, pp 236-8; *L. & P. Hen. VIII*, viii, no. 448); Walter Fitzgerald, 'Queries', in *Kildare Arch. Soc. Jn.*, i (1891-95), p. 407; Robin Dudley Edwards, 'Venerable John Travers and the rebellion of Silken Thomas', in *Studies*, xxiii, no. 92 (Dec. 1934), pp 687-99; Ellis, *Tudor Ireland*, p. 194; Laurence McCorristine, *The revolt of Silken Thomas: a challenge to Henry VIII* (Dublin, 1987), p. 73. **131** John Alen to Cromwell, 1534 (*S.P. Hen. VIII*, ii, p. 221); The lord deputy and council to Hen. VIII (*S.P. Hen. VIII*, ii, p. 236); 'Articles against Grey', 1540 (*S.P. Hen. VIII*, iii, p. 39); 'Certain articles put to the king's highness most honourable council by the earl of Ormond and Ossory', 1538 (*S.P. Hen. VIII*, iii, p. 80); 'The confession of Connor More O'Connor', 17 Apr. 1539 (*S.P. Hen. VIII*, iii, pp 140-1); Thomas Agard to Cromwell, 1536 (*L. & P. Hen. VIII*, xi, no. 1); Robert Cowley to Cromwell, 5 Aug. 1538 (*S.P. Hen. VIII*, iii, p. 63; *L. & P. Hen. VIII*, xiii, no. 40); O'Donnell to the deputy and council, 15 Aug. 1538 (*S.P. Hen. VIII*, iii, p. 97; *L. & P. Hen. VIII*, xiii, no. 216); Council of Ireland to Cromwell, 12 Dec. 1538 (*S.P. Hen. VIII*, p. 108; *L. & P. Hen. VIII*, xiii, no. 1032); *Liber mun. pub. Hib.*, pt v, p. 41; Comerford, *Collections*, i, pp

The earls were therefore typical of aristocratic and gentry families of their day in employing several clerics as pastors, tutors, attorneys, advisers and mediators, the last two roles being of magnified importance because of the dynasty's political prominence in the lordship. In their capacities as patrons of benefices, as employers and as overlords in the county, the influence of the earls of Kildare thus percolated down to the very grassroots of county Kildare's diocesan and monastic ecclesiastical organization.

Bernd Moeller identifies an intense desire on the part of the laity in pre-Reformation Germany to grasp the forms of religious life and the possibilities for devout exercise which the church offered with rejuvenated independent zeal. Part of this phenomenon was a heightened sense of responsibility which the laity felt for the church.[132] The same was also true of the laity in Ireland.[133] In Pale society as a whole in the pre-Reformation period, even gentry families of very modest means bestowed some patronage on their local chapel, church, monastery or on one of the two metropolitan cathedrals. Members of the laity donated money, chalices and other small church furnishings. It was also common practice for Kildare-based families to bestow patronage on particular churches by repairing or decorating them. For instance, during the 1490s, the eighth earl of Kildare embellished the church of Bective Abbey and had it paved with encaustic tiles. Lower ranking gentry families in Kildare also engaged in this form of patronage, as is illustrated by the case of the Kerdiffs of Kerdiffstown in east Kildare who left a rare remnant of early-sixteenth century piety in the form of a church window which they funded. The window was originally comprised of two ogee-headed lights with a framework surrounding it and bearing Latin inscriptions in Lombardic and Gothic characters. The names of the benefactors, Richard Kerdiff and that of his wife, were inscribed, as was the invocation to pray for those who had erected the window. This example is in some sense even more significant than those projects sponsored by the earls of Kildare, as it is likely to have been representative of the more common and ordinary forms of popular church patronage. It readily fits alongside examples of similarly modest patronage conferred by individual donors such as Thomas Smoth, who paid for four windows in St Mary's Chapel in Christ Church Cathedral to be newly glazed, or Thomas Walshe, who presented a gilt bowl worth four marks to the cathedral.[134]

24-5; Augustine Valkenburg, 'A study in diplomacy: Gerald, eleventh earl of Kildare, 1525-85', in *Kildare Arch. Soc. Jn.*, xiv, no. 3 (1968), pp 296-7. **132** Bernd Moeller, 'Piety in Germany around 1500', in Steven Ozment, *The Reformation in medieval perspective* (Chicago, 1971), p. 60. **133** Lynch, 'Religion in late medieval Ireland', pp 12-13. **134** Gilbert, *A history of the city of Dublin*, i, p. 108; Walter Fitzgerald, 'The Kerdiffs of Kerdiffstown, County Kildare', in *Kildare Arch. Soc. Jn.*, vii (1912-14), pp 182-6.

The Eustace family of Kildare were among the most munificent patrons of the church in the pre-Reformation era. Within the bounds of the extensive Eustace estates in southeastern Kildare there were several small chapels, including St Mary's at Calverstown, which was of Eustace foundation, and the chapel of the Blessed Virgin Mary, built at Castlemain by Sir Thomas Eustace, Portlester's brother, *c.*1455. While many of the advowson rights to the benefices within their districts were in the charge of Christ Church Cathedral chapter, the Eustaces held the right of presentation to St Sylvester's chapel in Brannockstown near Naas. They were also patrons of the Augustinian Friary of the mote in Naas.[135] More than any member of the extended Eustace family, or indeed any of his peers in the Pale, Sir Roland Fitzeustace, baron of Portlester, proved himself to be a generous benefactor of the church to the point of being almost comparable with his son-in-law, the eighth earl of Kildare. One of his earliest projects had been the construction of Portlester Chapel at the east end of St Audoen's Church in High Street, Dublin in 1455. At that time, St Audoen's was the wealthiest parish in the archdiocese. Like so many private chapels founded at this time, Portlester's chapel was dedicated to the Blessed Virgin Mary. He established a chantry, also under the invocation of Mary, in his new chapel, in gratitude for his survival from shipwreck.[136] At a more local level, he was patron to St Malcolin's in Hollywood, south of Ballymore Eustace.

In conjunction with the eighth earl of Kildare, Portlester, his daughter and others, were involved in founding a chantry at Athboy. Portlester also cooperated with Kildare in the effort to re-establish the guild of English merchants trading in Ireland in 1480. His crowning achievement came in 1486 with his construction of the monastery of New Abbey at Kilcullen in his own heartland. Although the abbey was incomplete when Portlester died, both he and his daughter, Alison, countess of Kildare (d.1495), were interred in its chapel. It was eventually completed by Portlester's nephew, Thomas the future viscount of Baltinglass, and was comprised of a chapel, a dining hall, dormitories, a kitchen and two additional rooms.

The Eustaces, like the Berminghams, the Wellesleys, the Plunkets of Malahide and Dunsoghly, and the St Lawrences of Howth erected elaborate

---

135 E.F. Tickell, 'The Eustace family and their lands in County Kildare', in *Kildare Arch. Soc. Jn.*, xiii, no. 7 (1958), p. 308, xiii, no. 8 (1960), pp 372, 374, 395, 400 (hereafter Tickell, 'Eustace family'). **136** Archdall, *Mon. Hib.*, ii, pp 289-90; John O'Hart, *Irish pedigrees* (4th ed., 2 vols, Dublin, 1887-8), ii, p. 185 (hereafter O'Hart, *Irish pedigrees*); Gilbert, *A history of the city of Dublin*, i, pp 277-8; Walter Fitzgerald, 'The fourteenth-century Eustace effigy', in *Kildare Arch. Soc. Jn.*, ix (1918-21), p. 460; Tickell, 'Eustace family', in *Kildare Arch. Soc. Jn.*, xiii, no. 6 (1955), pp 278-80; John Kingston, 'The Catholic families of the Pale', in *Reportorium Novum*, ii, nos 1-2 (1957-60), p. 247 (hereafter Kingston, 'Catholic families of the Pale').

monumental tombs which displayed the characteristic styles of contemporary continental, Renaissance design and which represented the most highly valued elements of their late medieval popular piety. Portlester's family had two effigies of him and his wife erected, one in his private chapel in St Audoen's in Dublin and the other in the grounds of his monastery at New Abbey in Kilcullen. The style of his tomb at New Abbey marked a continuity with the monuments erected for his predecessors in that it bore representations of saints, in his case St Catherine, St Bridget or St Margaret, St Michael the Archangel and also the Blessed Virgin Mary and the Infant Jesus. It was ornamented with standard carved symbols of the Lord's passion and crucifixion. But an idiosyncratic feature of this tomb is its depiction of a Franciscan monk clad in his knotted girdle with his hands in a blessing position. This of course represented Portlester's close affinity with the Franciscan order for whom he had established the monastery at New Abbey.

However, even Portlester could not compete with the eighth and ninth earls of Kildare in their ecclesiastical patronage.[137] The Kildares had ties with both Christ Church Cathedral and St Patrick's Cathedral where they regularly attended Mass and, on special occasions, solemn high Mass.[138] Often their attendance at Mass was part of an entire evening of celebration of a special event; the feast of St Patrick appears to have been among these events which the people of the Pale celebrated. On 17 March 1489 the eighth earl of Kildare, along with several other nobility, was present at a Mass in St Patrick's Cathedral at which John Walton, the retired archbishop of Dublin, preached to the admiration of his audience. After Mass, Kildare, Walton and their peers were hosted in a splendid manner at the palace of St Sepulchre's by the archbishop of Dublin, Walter Fitzsimons.[139] The eighth earl's main personal association was with Christ Church Cathedral, of which he was a generous benefactor, on one occasion making a presentation of a set of vestments of gold fabric.[140] In this regard the earl typified the lay and clerical patronage conferred on churches by contemporaries such as the baron of Portlester, Cornelius Conyll, archdeacon of Kildare (c.1510), the Plunkets of Dunsany and Killeen and Richard Fitzwilliam of Baggotrath, county Dublin.[141]

---

137 For a discussion of the Kildares' involvement in contemporary church affairs, see Mary Ann Lyons, 'Sidelights on the Kildare ascendancy: a survey of Geraldine involvement in the church, c.1470-c.1520', in *Archivium Hibernicum*, xlviii (1994), pp 73-87.   **138** Fitzgerald, *The earls of Kildare*, pp 46-7.   **139** Mason, *Cathedral of St Patrick's*, pp 139-40.   **140** Bryan, *The great earl*, p. 260.   **141** *Calendar of inquisitions*, p. 23; Gilbert, *A history of the city of Dublin*, i, p. 108; *The registers of Christ Church Cathedral, Dublin*, ed. Raymond Refaussé with Colm Lennon (Dublin, 1998), p. 125.

The eighth earl drew up tentative plans for the foundation of a chantry college at Maynooth in his will, and also established a far more modest chantry endowment in Christ Church Cathedral. He assigned the town of Coporan for the maintenance of a canon who would celebrate his funeral rites. This cleric would also pray for his soul and the soul of Thomas Plunket, former chief justice of the common pleas (also a great benefactor of Christ Church) and the souls of all the faithful. Kildare made provision for a yearly commemoration with an office comprised of nine lessons to be held in his honour after his death.[142] A year before he died, he built St Mary's Chapel, popularly known as 'my lord of Kildare's chapel', in the choir at the east end of Christ Church.[143] Of course this form of expression of popular piety was not unique to English-occupied areas of the lordship; even in such an isolated location as Achmore in the barony of Magheraboy in northwest Fermanagh, Gilbert and Margaret O'Flanagan of Tuath Ratha had a chapel erected in honour of God and Mary in the fifteenth century.[144] Following his death at Kildare in September 1513, Gearóid Mór's body was interred in his private chapel at Christ Church Cathedral.[145] In this regard Kildare again conformed to the general custom, since Sir Christopher Plunket had requested in his will that he would be buried before the statue of Mary at his church in Killeen in Meath.[146] The eighth earl of Kildare was also typical of many of his contemporaries, such as Manus O'Donnell's father, in going on pilgrimages, some of which lasted as long as a week.[147]

The Fitzgeralds were unique in that their wealth and court contacts allowed them to compile an extensive library at their residence at Maynooth, a substantial portion of which was made up of devotional literature. They also succumbed to a *penchant* for spiritual books, which had become increasingly popular with pious lay-folk in towns and rural areas throughout Ireland since the fifteenth century.[148] The ninth earl's collection, for example, contained a

---

142 *The registers of Christ Church Cathedral*, Dublin, p. 69.   143 Gilbert, *A history of the city of Dublin*, i, pp 107-08; Bryan, *The great earl*, p. 260.   144 *Annála ríoghachta Éireann: annals of the kingdom of Ireland by the Four Masters, from the earliest period to the year 1616*, ed. John O'Donovan (7 vols, Dublin, 1851), ii, p. 1247 (hereafter *A.F.M.*).   145 *Annála Uladh; annals of Ulster: a chronicle of Irish affairs 431 to 1541*, eds W.M. Hennessy and Bartholomew MacCarthy (4 vols, Dublin, 1887-1901), iii, p. 507 (hereafter *A.U.*); *Annála Connacht: the annals of Connacht, AD 1224-1544*, ed. A.M. Freeman (reprint, Dublin, 1970), p. 623.   146 Gilbert, *A history of the city of Dublin*, i, pp 277-8; Colm Lennon, 'The Reformation in the Pale' (unpublished paper).   147 *A.F.M.*, v, pp 1308-9; *A.U.*, iii, pp 494-7; Brendan Bradshaw, 'Manus "The Magnificent": O'Donnell as Renaissance prince', in Cosgrove and McCartney (eds), *Studies in Irish history*, p. 17; Art Cosgrove, *Late medieval Ireland, 1370-1541* (Dublin, 1981), p. 65; Ellis, *Tudor Ireland*, p. 71; Yolande de Pontfarcy, 'Pre-Reformation pilgrimages to St Patrick's Purgatory', in *Ulster Local Studies*, xv, no. 2 (winter 1993), pp 7-21. See also Meigs, *The Reformations in Ireland*, pp 37-40.   148 Lynch, 'Religion in late medieval Ireland', pp 12-13.

Psalter of Cashel, the prophecies of St Berehan, editions of lives of various saints, the Bible, the New Testament, as well as the Works of St Anthony, St Gregory, St Jerome and St Augustine. An examination of the composition of this collection provides telling evidence of their interest in acquiring if not indeed studying standard works of piety which were popular among the gentry and aristocracy at this time. The library also suggests that the ninth earl of Kildare was more than a mere antiquarian collecting old devotional works for posterity. Rather, his possession of works such as *The king of England's answer to Luther* and *Sir Thomas More's book against the opinions that hold against pilgrimages* bear testimony to his being aware of the controversy which Martin Luther was causing in the very early stages of the Protestant Reformation, and the hostile reaction which it was provoking in England.[149] Murray suggests that Kildare's involvement with the cathedral chapter of St Patrick's would also have sensitized him to the developing reactions of the canons to the ecclesiastical changes which were being introduced by the crown in England in the early 1530s.[150]

As with all wealthy families, the Fitzgeralds had several religious tokens and memorabilia, including a chalice which presumably belonged to the ninth earl's chaplain and the college chapel, among their plate collection at Maynooth. The sumptuousness of their religious icons, which included heavily decorated Spanish pieces studded with jasper stones, garnished with silver and gilt detail and bearing the salutation of Mary, testified to the piety of the Kildares on the eve of the Reformation.[151] Another salient feature of their piety was their endowment of chantries and religious guilds on both an individual and corporate basis; the eighth earl in particular was involved in the establishment of several such bodies from the early 1480s onwards. In 1480 he was instrumental in reviving the fraternity or guild of English merchants trading in Ireland under the invocation of the Blessed Virgin Mary. One or more chaplains of this fraternity was to celebrate daily divine service for the king, Edward IV, for the earl of Kildare and for all of the other sponsors of the fraternity and their relatives, both living and deceased.[152] Five years later he and a number of others gained parliamentary approval for a licence to establish a chantry in the church of St Nicholas in Dundalk.[153] In 1491 Kildare, his wife, Alison, his father-in-law the baron of Portlester, and four others received another licence to found a chantry under the invocation of St Anne at St Jake's parochial church in Athboy.[154]

149 *Crown surveys*, pp 355-6; Fitzgerald, *The earls of Kildare*, pp 268-9. 150 Murray, 'The Tudor diocese of Dublin', p. 114. 151 *Crown surveys*, pp 304-5, 316. 152 Bryan, *The great earl*, pp 48-9. 153 'Parliaments and great councils, 1483-99: *addenda et corrigenda*' presented by S.G. Ellis, in *Analecta Hibernica*, xxix (1980), p. 102 (hereafter 'Parliaments and great councils, 1483-99: *addenda et corrigenda*'). 154 'Parliaments and great councils, 1483-99: *addenda*

There is no indication of the number of chantries which existed in Ireland in the pre-Reformation period. However, a conservative estimate of the number of chantries in England prior to the 1530s suggests a figure of 2,374, which provides an insight into the immense popularity of such endowments among the laity. The earls of Kildare thus exhibited their particular regard for chantry endowments, a favourite mode of expression of popular piety in aristocratic and gentry circles in the greater Pale areas and in Irish towns.[155] Their chantries resembled those of the Eustaces in the parish church in Skreen, county Meath, the St Lawrence family chantry at St Mary's Abbey, Howth, that of the Verdons at Ardee, and the trinity of chantries established at St David's Church, Naas whose priests formed a corporate body with rich endowments described by an inquisition in 1606.[156]

Inevitably, the immense wealth and political prominence of the Kildares enabled them to undertake larger projects and to provide more lavish patronage. The foundation of the College of the Blessed Virgin Mary at Maynooth in 1518 by the ninth earl was one of the grandest projects in church patronage undertaken by any member of the laity at this time. Indeed, it was only rivalled by the college founded by Sir Christopher Fleming and his wife in Slane in 1512 which housed four priests, four clerics and four choristers.[157] The establishment of the Geraldine college serves as a striking testimony to the vitality of lay piety in pre-Reformation Ireland, mirroring the dynamic role of the laity in church patronage in contemporary England and Western Europe.[158] Significantly, several of the fraternities and chantry endowments established by the earls of Kildare were founded on a permanent basis, a testimony to their exceptional wealth. In this regard they were very unusual since in Wales and

---

et corrigenda', pp 107-8; 'The bills and statutes of the Irish parliaments of Henry VIII and Henry VIII' ed. D.B. Quinn, in *Analecta Hibernica*, no. 10 (1941), pp 86-7. **155** A.G. Dickens, *The English Reformation* (14th ed., Glasgow, 1988), p. 286 (hereafter Dickens, *The English Reformation*); L.P. Murray, 'The ancient chantries of County Louth', in *Louth Arch. Soc. Jn.*, ix, no. 3 (1939), pp 181-208 (hereafter Murray, 'The ancient chantries of County Louth'); Colm Lennon, 'The chantries in the Irish Reformation: the case of St Anne's Guild, Dublin, 1550-1630', in R.V. Comerford, Mary Cullen, J.R. Hill and Colm Lennon (eds), *Religion, conflict and coexistence in Ireland: essays presented to Monsignor Patrick J. Corish* (Dublin, 1990), pp 6-25; Mary Clark and Raymond Refaussé (eds), *Directory of historic Dublin guilds* (Dublin, 1993) (hereafter Clark and Refaussé (eds), *Directory of historic Dublin guilds*). **156** Archdall, *Mon. Hib.*, ii, pp 288-9; Gwynn and Hadcock, *Medieval religious houses: Ireland*, p. 361; Lennon, 'The Reformation in the Pale'. **157** John Bradley, 'The chantry college, Ardee', in *Louth Arch. Soc. Jn.*, xxii, 1 (1989), p. 18. For a detailed recent discussion of the establishment of the Geraldine college at Maynooth see Mary Ann Lyons, 'The foundation of the Geraldine college of the Blessed Virgin Mary, Maynooth, 1518', in *Kildare Arch. Soc. Jn.*, xviii (1994-5), pp 134-50. **158** Ronald Hutton, 'The local impact of the Tudor Reformations', in Christopher Haigh (ed.), *The English Reformation revised* (Cambridge, 1987), p. 115.

England, the common practice was to make provision for temporary chantries, usually for a period of between four and eight years.[159]

The ninth earl's father had made provisions for the foundation of a college of clerics at Maynooth prior to his death in 1513. However, the project only came to fruition five years later. Official procedures were initiated on 7 October 1515 when the ninth earl received licence from Henry VIII to erect a college at Maynooth, along with other independent grants of privileges to the towns of Kildare and Athy. In 1518, Gerald petitioned William Rokeby, archbishop of Dublin, for licence to establish and endow a college at Maynooth for which purpose, he explained, his father had allocated certain parcels of land in county Meath. In his will, the eighth earl had assigned the manor of Rathbegan and lands in Kiltale and Carbreston in Meath, to Thomas Rochfort, dean of St Patrick's Cathedral, Nicholas Kerdiff, chancellor, and Robert Sutton, archdeacon, for the use of his son, Gerald, and his successors. The grant was made so that

> if in future times a college should be founded in the church of the Blessed Virgin of Maynooth, according to form of law, the said feoffees, should grant the manor and lands … to the master of the college and his successors if they should be incorporated, and be by law capable of receiving lands.

At the time, Rathbegan contained 271 acres, and the holdings at Kiltale and Carbreston were comprised of 140 and eighty acres respectively.[160] Further to the ninth earl's petition Rokeby confirmed the foundation of the college of clerks at Maynooth and on 10 September 1519 the college of minor canons and choristers was incorporated by letters patent. On 6 October 1521 licence for the establishment was confirmed by Rokeby. Six days later the privileges and ordinances with which the college was to be invested were ratified by letters patent and these provide a useful glimpse into the machinations, prerogatives and vested interests at stake in the legal establishment of such an endowment.

The terms of the foundation charter for the college at Maynooth resemble those stipulated in the charters for chantry endowments in England, Scotland

---

159 Glanmor Williams, *The Welsh church from conquest to Reformation* (Cardiff, 1962) (hereafter Williams, *The Welsh church*). See also Duffy, *The stripping of the altars*, p. 370. **160** John Healy, 'The college of the Blessed Virgin Mary of Maynooth, County Kildare', in *Irish Ecclesiastical Record*, 3rd ser., i (1880), p. 539; M.T. MacSweeney, 'The parish of Maynooth, AD 1040-1614', in *Irish Ecclesiastical Record*, 5th ser., lvi (July-Dec. 1940), p. 318 (hereafter MacSweeney, 'The parish of Maynooth').

and Wales at this time. The majority of chantry chapels in England were established to contribute to 'the increase of divine service' and the Maynooth charter makes similar explicit reference to the envisaged role of the college being the promotion of 'a divine reverence and other works of piety'.[161] Chantry endowments, like other forms of conspicuous consumption, were designed to display the testator's wealth and social status. But their religious *raison d'être* was none the less fundamental to their foundation and they served as a constant reminder to the local community of the continuing spiritual needs of the founder. The ninth earl was typical of many of his English contemporaries in his apparent aim to provide for the spiritual well-being not only of himself and other deceased persons prayed for, but also for the living community of the parish of Maynooth. At the time of the establishment of the college, the earl rebuilt the church of St Mary at Maynooth as the college chapel in a very beautiful manner. This church had been attached to the Geraldine castle from the mid-thirteenth century and its re-edification undoubtedly assisted 'the increase of divine service' in Maynooth.

That it was a chantry endowment is certain since the charter states that

> He [Gerald] would set up, found and establish the perpetual celebration of two clerics for our souls [Henry VIII's soul] when we [Henry VIII] shall have departed this life, and for the souls of ... Gerald and his antecedents and for all the faithful departed.[162]

The chantry endowment was made in perpetuity. The college seems to have been conceived out of a widely-held medieval notion that the church's most important role was that of intercessor for the dead. An unashamedly utilitarian view of the Mass existed at popular level in the pre-Reformation period. It was commonly held that the benefits which the living and the dead received varied in direct proportion to the number and munificence of the Masses offered for their souls and to the amount of offerings made at each Mass. The earls of Kildare, by virtue of the number and elaborateness of their chantry endowments, clearly subscribed to that belief.

The ninth earl's dedication of his college to the Blessed Virgin Mary also conforms to a trend obtaining across the whole of Western Europe. Since the affirmation of the doctrine of the Immaculate Conception at the Council at Basel in 1439, the cult of Mary had enjoyed increasing popularity throughout Christendom, as she was widely regarded as the most effective intercessor.

161 *The red book of the earls of Kildare*, ed. Gearóid MacNiocaill (Dublin, 1964), pp 176-8 (hereafter *Red Bk Kildare*); Duffy, *The stripping of the altars*, p. 139.   162 *Red Bk Kildare*, pp 176-8

More chantries, guilds and fraternities in Wales were dedicated to her than to any other saint. In Dublin too, the guild of shoemakers (est. 1465), the guild of weavers (est. 1446), the guild of carpenters, millers, masons and heliers (est. 1508), the guild of butchers (est. 1569) and the guild of saddlers, upholsterers, coach and coach harness makers, bridle cutters and wheelwrights (est. 1558) all designated Mary as their patron.[163]

The corporate nature of the organization of the college at Maynooth also made it typical of contemporary lay endowments. Corporate intercession for the dead, one of the fundamental features of late medieval popular religious practice, was highly regulated and formalized as the stipulations laid down for the appointment of the Maynooth college personnel clearly illustrate. Right from its inception, the college was constituted a corporate entity with its own common seal. This empowered the trustees and the college body and their successors to 'pursue all manner of complaints and actions real, personal, and varied in whatever meeting place [tribunal] of whatever kind or nature and [to] be able to proceed, respond and defend regarding these matters, before judges, both spiritual and temporal in perpetuity'.[164] Many of the lordship's monastic houses, for example the convent of Timolinbeg, Connall Priory, St Thomas Court Priory in Dublin, and those at Granard and Kilbeggan, had similar seals which were used in the ratification of indentures between these institutions and the ninth earl of Kildare. The college seal was used on at least one occasion, in 1530, to ratify an agreement which formalized the payment of tribute by the Gaelic lord, MacRannal, to the ninth earl. The chantry's personnel were invested with the power to sue or to be sued as a corporate entity but on condition that, in exercising that right, they would undertake not to infringe upon the rights of the prebendary of Maynooth, the vicar of Laraghbryan or the dean and chapter of St Patrick's Cathedral.

The long-standing question of whether the college at Maynooth fulfilled any educational role is one to which no conclusive answer is forthcoming. In relation to the functions of chantry priests, it appears from the contemporary English context that they generally helped the parish incumbent in administering parochial duties. They also assisted at parish services, attended in the choir at matins, Mass and evensong, and sang the gospel at the parish Mass when required.[165] The fact that no explicit reference to the provision of education is made in the foundation charter for the college at Maynooth does not necessarily mean that it did not fulfil an educational role. Again in the English

163 Clark and Refaussé (eds), *Directory of historic Dublin guilds*, pp 17–18, 25–7, 30–1. 164 *The 'dignitas decani' of St Patrick's Cathedral, Dublin*, ed. N.B. White (Dublin, 1957), no. 71 (hereafter *Dignitas decani*). 165 Duffy, *The stripping of the altars*, p. 140.

context, even in cases where it is known from the statutes that it was intended that a school would be incorporated as part of a chantry establishment, it is rare to find a reference to a school in the foundation deeds. Moreover, the functions fulfilled by chantry clerics tended to evolve over time according as the demand for various services arose.[166] Therefore while the Geraldine college may not have begun its life as an educational institution, its personnel, like their counterparts in Connall Priory further south in the county, might well have been prevailed upon to provide educational training before its premature demise in the 1530s.

Kildare's prompt receipt of a licence to establish his college was exceptional when compared with the standard procedure for the foundation of a similar endowment in pre-Reformation England. In the fifteenth and sixteenth centuries, the crown opposed the absorption of land into mortmain in order to support chantries; as a result, it became increasingly difficult to obtain licences. Many testators in England who wished to found chantries grew anxious to secure their wills against legal objections and confiscation. Hence their wills display explicit deference to the law, with the inclusion of clauses that their chantries be allowed to function 'from time to time ... as long as the king's laws will suffer it'.[167] Kildare, by contrast, forged ahead with proceedings for his chantry endowment with no apparent regard for such constraints or legal obstacles. This is indicative of his autonomy in bestowing ecclesiastical patronage at local level, and of the more relaxed attitude taken by the crown in monitoring popular religious practices in the lordship. His confidence proved well founded, given the ease and speed with which he secured the licence for his college.

In 1521 Gerald endowed the college more lavishly than had at first been intended, and the chantry was established immediately contiguous with the castle. He formulated a set of rules for the governance of the college, and detailed procedures for the appointment of a provost, vice-provost, five priests, two clerks and three choristers to pray for his soul and those of his antecedents were drawn up.[168] As a consequence of the foundation of the college, a restructuring in parochial organization ensued. In response to the earl's request, the prebend of Laraghbryan, which was vacant at this time, was annexed to the mastership of the newly-instituted college in perpetuity. Thereafter, the prebendary of Laraghbryan (later termed the prebendary of Maynooth) was required to reside at the college. The document which sets out the respective prerogatives of the earl of Kildare and the archbishop of Dublin provides a

166 Dickens, *The English Reformation*, p. 292.   **167** Duffy, *The stripping of the altars*, p. 510.
168 *Red Bk Kildare*, pp 176-7.

valuable insight into the brokering for control which was a fundamental feature of the establishment of such an endowment. It also sheds light on the lines of demarcation which corralled ecclesiastical and lay input and control in such projects.

The archbishop of Dublin, William Rokeby, was, as we will see later, engaged in intermittent attempts to reassert the legal rights and prerogatives of the metropolitan see which had been eroded to the advantage of the laity, in particular the Kildares, in the fifteenth and early sixteenth centuries. His acute concern was to maintain a decisive role in the appointment of the college's ecclesiastical personnel and in aspects of its administration. Rokeby's consent to grant the earl's request for the annexation of the prebend to the mastership of the college had to be ratified by the dean, who at this time had custody of the vacant prebend of Laraghbryan. In addition the prebend's annexation had to be sanctioned by the cathedral chapters of Christ Church and St Patrick's. Furthermore, Rokeby only agreed to Kildare's proposal on condition that the prebendary of Laraghbryan should first be instituted and installed at St Patrick's Cathedral before being admitted as master of the Geraldine college. The archbishop stipulated that after this installation ceremony had been performed, the incoming prebendary was to be appointed to the mastership of the college by the archdeacon. From then onwards, the incumbent was to assume responsibility for the running of the college. Rokeby warned that if the prebendary and master were to be appointed by any alternative means, he would deem it an intrusion and the transgressor would be liable to excommunication.

Constitutions for disciplinary procedures in the college were also drafted. The master was appointed to the most honourable place in the college choir, at its capitular meetings and at table. All members of the college personnel were to obey the master 'in all things lawful and honest and in every thing related to the service of the choir'. Special provision was made for the master's living. A portion of the revenues of the college refectory was reserved for the support of the incumbent and that of a servant who was to attend on him. The master was to receive twenty marks annually from the sub-master and fellows to enable him to maintain the honour and expense of his station as prebendary of St Patrick's Cathedral. The payment was to be made before the feast of the Assumption of the Blessed Virgin Mary and, in the event of its non-payment, the dean and chapter of St Patrick's reserved the right to sequester the revenues accruing to that benefice until such time as the money was forthcoming. The master had two votes in the nomination, election, appointment and dismissal of college personnel. During his absence, the sub-master and fellows were to appoint a substitute to discharge all of his duties as prebendary of Laraghbryan in return for which service the officiating cleric was to receive the altarages. In no circumstances was the master of the college allowed to default in fulfilling his duties or in attending divine service in St Patrick's Cathedral in his capacity as cathedral prebendary. He was at all times obliged to pay canonical obedience to the dean of St Patrick's as his predecessors had done prior to the foundation of this college and the concomitant merge of the posts of prebendary and college master. A further regulation often laid down in relation to parochial clergy in England stipulated that all college personnel were prohibited from going to market. (Maynooth village had a market which had been in existence since 1286). They were ordered not to buy corn on any occasion, however urgent, even on feasts of charity. In cases of extreme need, the regulations allowed that

> lest the said collegiate associates be forced by necessity to go to a public market to buy corn, we lay down that the residue of the fruits and produce, and of all other endowments and gains from the prebend [of Maynooth ... that] are not otherwise being used for the college, which the submaster and the other associates of the said college held, are to be paid by the said prebend twice a year.[169]

These regulations were confirmed when the seal of the earl and that of the newly-erected college corporation were affixed to the documents on 12 October 1521 and they were subsequently entered in the registry of St Patrick's Cathedral. The rules and default provisions for the staffing and governance of the Geraldine college set out by Kildare and Rokeby indicate the deliberate establishment of a clear delineation between secular and ecclesiastical administration. The archbishop, acting on behalf of the dean and chapter of St Patrick's, from the very outset established a firm grip on the prebend of Laraghbryan and on the running of the college, determined, though not in an aggressive way, to restrain Gerald from gaining a monopoly of control over the running of the college, and to prevent it from becoming an *enclave* within the jurisdiction of the earl's liberty in county Kildare. Hence, the right of appointment to the more junior positions of sub master and boys of the college was invested in the earl and his successors, while the appointment of priests and control of the spiritualities were prerogatives reserved to the archbishop. However, given that it was Kildare's personal chantry endowment it was only to be expected that a compromise would be reached between both parties in the selection of its ecclesiastical personnel. Indeed the official confirmation of

---

169 *Dignitas decani*, no. 72.

the establishment of the college in 1518 acknowledged Kildare's 'right' to influence the college's clerical appointments as patron of the chantry endowment stating that 'decisions regarding divine offices shall pertain to us with the approval of the founder. The nomination and appointment of all offices whatsoever shall pertain forever, with the consent of the founder, to the master and the majority within the collegiate'.[170]

The appointment of Edward Dillon to the prebend of Laraghbryan is proof that such mutual accommodation was put into practice. Edward was the son of Sir Bartholomew Dillon, chief baron of the exchequer. Throughout the 1510s he had been in the service of the ninth earl as his chaplain, and his signature appears in the Kildare rental on occasions in the period 1514-19 when he acted as witness to indentures between the earl and landowners. In 1521, in addition to being chaplain to Kildare, master of the Geraldine college and prebendary of Maynooth, Edward was incumbent of the deanery of Kildare diocese. During his occupancy of these positions he became embroiled in a conflict of interest between the ninth earl and King Henry VIII which will be examined at a later point in this study. Such accommodation of the founder's preferences was commonplace in Ireland at this time: a substantial proportion of the chantry chaplains of Ardee, for example, were members of leading families of the town.[171]

At the earl's further request, and having obtained the vicar of Laraghbryan's consent, Archbishop Rokeby by another indenture of 1521 stipulated that in order to enhance existing provisions for the maintenance of the college, the profits of the vicarage should be amalgamated with college funds. Those profits would thereafter be spent in accordance with the wishes of the master and the majority of the college fellows. In return for surrendering the profits of his benefice, the vicar of Laraghbryan was to be paid £6 3s. 4d. annually by the college master and fellows – a substantial income by contemporary standards. Further evidence of Rokeby's proprietorial role in the project can be seen in his insertion of a clause to protect the rights of the vicar should the master and fellows fail to meet their obligations in paying him. In this event, the dean and chapter of St Patrick's Cathedral could exercise their prerogative to sequester the fruits of the vicarage until such time as the vicar received his income.

By this same indenture, the vicar was also appointed to the post of sub master of the college, where he was to reside, and he was to have cure of souls in the parish of Laraghbryan. His duties as sub master were precisely defined vis-à-vis his position in the college choir, at chapter meetings and at table, with

---

170 Ibid., no. 71. 171 See Murray, 'The ancient chantries of County Louth'.

the hierarchical organization of the college's personnel being explicitly enshrined in this indenture. The vicar was invested with the authority of the master during the latter's absence, during which times five marks were to be deducted from the profits of his vicarage of Laraghbryan in lieu of the cost of his table in the college house. Rokeby's indenture also ordained that a 'good and learned curate' was to be appointed at the expense of the Geraldine college. Again the archbishop ensured that the cathedral chapter of St Patrick's would maintain a firm grip on this cleric, who was required to celebrate divine service and to pay 'due respect to the archbishop, the dean, or the officials of the [arch]diocese'.[172]

This marked the final round in the procedures for the foundation and running of the college, which appears to have functioned down to the mid-1530s. By 1538 it is said to have 'ceased to exist' and was formally suppressed along with the monastic houses of Kildare as part of the wide-scale campaign of the suppression of the monasteries in 1539-41. Inevitably, the college buildings were destroyed in the course of the rebellion in 1534-5 though not irretrievably so since, in 1537, a refurbishment of these buildings was evidently envisaged. Lord Leonard Grey pillaged the abbey at Killeigh in O'Connor's country and removed glass from its windows which he then had installed in the windows of the college church at Maynooth Castle.[173] This planned restoration of the college buildings was part of a scheme to repair the Geraldine fortress at Maynooth. In the event, the renovations were at best only partially completed. In October 1540 jurors compiling the extents of the county's religious establishments reported that there were no longer any buildings on the site of the former Geraldine college, except an old house which at that time was the residence of the rector of the parish church of Maynooth.[174] Down to the time of its closure, the college retained possession of its property in Carbreston in county Meath and its eighty acres were occupied by four tenants each holding one messuage and twenty acres in 1540. Its property in Kiltale, also in Meath, had been marginally expanded. In 1540 these combined holdings were leased to Edward Beck.

Further parcels of property belonging to the college and comprising six messuages and 219 acres lay in Porterstown, Little Wareston and Killester. All of this land was leased to John Plunket who was, at the time of the juror's report, a sitting free tenant of certain lands in Porterstown and Little Wareston. During its short existence, the college had acquired further significant holdings, notably the rectory of Killenagh in county Wexford and land in Bally-

172 *Dignitas decani*, no. 73.   **173** Lord Leonard Grey to Cromwell, 31 Dec. 1537 (*S.P. Hen. VIII*, ii, p. 529).   **174** *Extents Ir. mon. possessions*, pp 174-6.

began, Ballybarrack and Timolinbeg in south Kildare. The first of these was leased to John Plunket; the second formed a parcel of the manor of Maynooth which was leased to Lord Deputy Leonard Grey, and Timolinbeg was leased to Edmund Eustace whose extended family estates spanned the greater part of southeast Kildare.[175] The collegiate house itself remained intact down to 1563. In February 1559, the lands belonging to the dissolved college were granted by Queen Elizabeth to Gerald, the eleventh earl of Kildare.[176]

The short lifespan of the Geraldine college at Maynooth was by no means exceptional by contemporary standards. Glanmor Williams points to the fact that many guilds and confraternities were comparatively short-lived since a variety of contingencies could bring their existence to an abrupt end. The most common were the varying popularity of a saint or a clerical incumbent; the removal of a vigorous personality, be it a patron or a cleric; personal disagreements; economic adversity; or poor management.[177] The establishment of the college at Maynooth is especially valuable for the insights which it provides into the nature and the mechanics of Geraldine ecclesiastical patronage in the early sixteenth century. Its foundation testifies to the fact that this leading aristocratic dynasty, like other prominent aristocratic and gentry families of the Pale, adhered to the beliefs and pious practices which were in common currency among the laity of late medieval Western Europe. Moreover it exhibits both earls' initiative and generosity in devising and lavishly sponsoring this chantry independent of any impetus from the ecclesiastical authorities of their day. Certainly, it would be going too far to suggest that Rokeby's carefully contrived outline of the dean and chapter's prerogatives with respect to the running of the college is evidence of medieval churchmen's 'deep-rooted distrust of lay intervention in ecclesiastical affairs'.[178] However, it is clear that while Rokeby was willing to honour Kildare's wishes in making clerical appointments, he did expect the earl to refrain from any interference in those areas of the administration of the college which were explicitly and exclusively reserved as the responsibility of the dean and chapter of St Patrick's.

VII

Both the foundation of this college at Maynooth and the episcopacy of Edmund Lane in Kildare coincided with a period when the Fitzgerald ascendancy was at its zenith. However, from 1519 onwards, the ninth earl of

175 Ibid. 176 MacSweeney, 'The parish of Maynooth', p. 319. 177 Williams, *The Welsh church*, p. 291. 178 Watt, *Church in medieval Ireland*, pp 202-3.

Kildare's career began to be punctuated by intermittent but intensifying attempts on the part of a coterie of Palesmen, the earl of Ormond and Cardinal Wolsey to curb the political dominance of his faction in the lordship. A series of simultaneous and intermittent but significant restrictions upon the earl's authority were also manifest in the ecclesiastical sphere in the 1520s and 30s. Firstly, the see of Kildare was invested to two men, neither of whom were Kildare's nominees and both of whom were declared opponents of the earl. Secondly, successive archbishops of Dublin set about reasserting their archiepiscopal prerogative at Kildare's expense. Both combined to gradually erode Kildare's power in manipulating the ecclesiastical personnel of the Pale and questioned his usurped possession of archiepiscopal lands, and as such served as an extension of the attempt to circumscribe Kildare's political autonomy within an increasingly centralized government framework.

In the early 1520s, the episcopal succession of the diocese of Kildare became embroiled in the factional politics of the period. Kildare's authority in church affairs was most overtly challenged by the crown when he was denied the right to exercise his privilege of nominating Lane's successor, a privilege which he claimed to have been granted by Henry VIII during his sojourn at court in 1515. In February 1523 the earl wrote to Cardinal Wolsey notifying him that the see had become vacant owing to the death of Edmund Lane and he duly exercised his privilege by nominating his candidate, Edward Dillon, as Lane's successor. He described Dillon as a man 'of virtuous living and of English name and condition'.[179] Kildare clearly anticipated no obstacle to his exercising his advowson right, having already requested that Henry VIII present Dillon with his letters of denomination. However, Gerald failed to have his chosen candidate appointed. That in itself was hardly exceptional; his father had at one point failed to have his preferred candidate appointed as prior of St Wolstan's Priory in Celbridge, and he also failed to secure the appointment of Richard Lang to the primacy of Armagh. Neither was such intervention on the part of the earls in clerical appointments unusual.

What made this case different, however, was the fact that Gerald was seeking to exercise a unique prerogative invested in him by the king rather than merely pursuing the more usual presumed or opportunist course of action in trying to determine the outcome of the contest for the see. Recent scholarly studies of Anglo-papal relations have shown that in the era of the early Tudors, royal nomination to bishoprics were usually binding in English areas, that the king frequently had to accommodate local interests in nominating candidates, and that the crown's influence over the appointments procedure was steadily

179 The earl of Kildare to Wolsey, 8 Feb. 1523 (*S.P. Hen. VIII*, ii, pp 98-9).

increasing.[180] The deference with which Kildare was treated by Rokeby and to a lesser extent, Henry VIII, in the foundation of the college at Maynooth and in the appointment of his preferred candidate as its master provides a clear indication of such accommodation of the earl's interest.

In the case of the episcopal appointment, however, Henry discarded Kildare's claims of an advowson right to the see and blatantly refused to allow his decision to be influenced by Kildare's input. Instead Henry recommended Thomas Dillon to the pope as the candidate to be appointed. The fact that the appointment was made during Kildare's detention in England in 1526 accentuated his chagrin. In his history of the diocese, Michael Comerford has suggested that the candidate appointed may in fact have been Kildare's nominee, with the 'Edward' in the earl's letter to Cardinal Wolsey being a scribal error for 'Thomas'.[181] However, it is highly unlikely that Kildare would make such an error in his nomination. Also, in his letter of recommendation to Wosley, Kildare referred to Edward Dillon as the dean of Kildare. The dean of the diocese at the time was indeed Edward Dillon, also the master of Kildare's college at Maynooth and a man said to have been 'of Kildare's bringing up'. The appointee to the see was Thomas Dillon, an Augustinian prior of St Peter's in Trim, county Meath.[182] A native of Meath, he had studied in Oxford and unlike Lane, Lang or many of his more recent predecessors as bishops of Kildare, he was imposed from outside the conduit of the diocesan chapter and the county. The papal bull providing him to the see stipulated that he was to be allowed to retain his priory of St Peter's *in commendam* ('*cum retentione monastereii St Petri, et aliorum beneficiorum prout in cedula*').[183] The extreme poverty of the diocese of Kildare is further illustrated in the bull's provision for a substantial reduction from 205 to seventy-five florins in the taxation of the see and in Henry's payment for Dillon's successor's bulls out of the royal treasury. As already mentioned, this financial deprivation subsequently served as a severe disincentive to Protestant bishops such as Craik and Daly.

Thomas Dillon's papal appointment was eventually confirmed on 11 March 1527; he vacated the see the following year and died in 1529.[184] The earl of Kildare does not appear to have challenged the king on this issue, which undoubtedly caused him considerable affront at a time when he was coming under increasing pressure from Ormond and from steadily more vociferous critics in the Dublin council. Nor does he seem to have attempted to reassert his claimed right to nominate an alternative candidate to the see after Thomas's installation. Perhaps Kildare approved of Thomas's appointment

180 Ellis, *Reform and revival*, p. 201.   **181** Comerford, *Collections*, i, p. 21.   **182** Grattan Flood, 'Episcopal succession of Kildare', p. 161.   **183** Comerford, *Collections*, i, p. 21.   **184** Ibid.

and therefore posed no opposition. However, a more plausible explanation is that the earl probably realized that he was pushing his luck in endeavouring to have Edward appointed to the see. His candidate already held several prestigious and well-endowed benefices, and his appointment to the see would have effectively reduced the bishop of Kildare to the status of his chaplain. Given that Edward was already the earl's private chaplain, the master of his college, a prebendary of St Patrick's Cathedral and the dean of Kildare diocese, it is hardly surprising that Henry VIII used this opportunity to circumvent Kildare's efforts to further extend his virtual monopoly of control over both secular and ecclesiastical affairs within his liberty.

However, controversy concerning the appointment of Thomas Dillon's successor emerged from another quarter. Robert Cowley, later master of the rolls and a formidable adversary of the earl of Kildare, voiced his objection to Dr Peter Stoll, a Dominican friar, as the new incumbent and to the partisan manner in which he had been appointed. In 1528 he complained to Cardinal Wolsey that Anthony Knevet, sometimes a member of the English privy council, had lobbied the king and had secured the bishopric of Kildare for Stoll whom Cowley described as 'a simple Irish priest, a vagabond, without learning, manners, or good quality, not worthy to be a holy water clerk'. He also remarked that the king's payment for Stoll's papal bulls would not be favourably looked upon by those who had served the king well in the lordship.[185] Stoll was promoted to the see by Clement VII in March 1529. These suits were addressed to the royal court rather than to Rome, indicating a common perception among contemporaries that the king played the decisive role in determining episcopal appointments. In the event, Stoll held the bishopric for just over three months and was replaced on 1 July 1529 by Walter Wellesley.[186]

Wellesley's career provides an insight into the competition for benefices and bishoprics in the lordship in the pre-Reformation period and the manipulative speculation for career advancement which went with it. Wellesley owed his appointment to the bishopric of Kildare largely to the persistent suits made on his behalf by his patron, the duke of Norfolk, to Wolsey. However, his was not an automatic ascent to the office. Since the early 1520s and with the support of Norfolk, Wellesley, a native of Kildare, had unsuccessfully attempted to secure various ecclesiastical posts. Significantly, he resorted to mercenary means to secure a benefice at a stage in his career when he had not yet pursued

---

185 Robert Cowley to Wolsey, 1528 (*S.P. Hen. VIII*, ii, p. 141; *L. & P. Hen. VIII*, iii, no. 2824; *Cal. Carew MSS, 1515-74*, p. 36).   **186** 'Obligationes' ed. Coleman, p. 72; Comerford, *Collections*, i, p. 21.

his university education. In 1497, he had sought his appointment to the rectory of the parish church of St Patrick's in Trim by contesting the resident incumbent's title to the benefice; in the event, Wellesley failed to prove the legitimacy of his claim.[187] During the first decade of the sixteenth century, Walter, like Thomas Dillon, was educated at Oxford which was the most popular university among those wishing to study either canon or civil law. There he almost certainly studied at St Mary the Virgin's, the college usually attended by canons regular of the Order of St Augustine. He was conferred with a degree in canon law which at the time was regarded as the best means of advancement for ambitious clerics.[188]

The precise date of his return to Ireland is unknown but he appears to have been resident in the country in 1506 when in the month of January he acted as a witness to a notarial judgement by Thomas Hurley, bishop of Emly. Wellesley's ambition and his Oxford education led to his appointment at some stage before 1520 to the position of prior of Connall, Kildare's wealthiest monastery. By that time he had established ties with the earl of Surrey, who arrived in Ireland in May 1520 to assume the office of lord lieutenant and who was to become his patron from that point onwards. In August 1520 Surrey presented Wolsey with a very sobering picture of the state of the diocese of Cork, whose bishopric had recently become vacant. He advised that the position be entrusted to an Englishman and expressly opposed the appointment of a native or any other cleric who would not reside in the diocese. He warned Wolsey of the challenges which the appointee would face in assuming this bishopric and therefore urged that the new prelate would be a cleric who was able and willing 'to speak and ruffle when need shall be'.[189]

Surrey's first choice of candidate was the bishop of Leighlin, Thomas Halsey, an English absentee then living in Rome. His recommendation was accepted, but Halsey died at Westminster while en route to Ireland. On 6 September, following consultations with the Irish council, Surrey nominated as a second candidate, Walter Wellesley, lauding his qualifications as 'a famous cleric, noted the best in the land, a man of gravity and virtuous conversation and having a singular mind to English order'.[190] Rather embarrassingly for Surrey, Wellesley refused the post on the grounds that he was 'not apt' for the bishopric of Cork since he would be 'but a stranger' there whereas in Connall Priory, he felt well placed among his friends and kinsmen. In the

187 See *De Annatis Hiberniae*, eds M.A. Costello and Ambrose Coleman (Dundalk, 1909), i, p. 103.　188 See Valkenburg, 'Walter Wellesley'; Lynch, 'Religion in late medieval Ireland', p.4. 189 Surrey to Wolsey, 1520 (*S.P. Hen .VIII*, ii, p. 42; *L. & P. Hen. VIII*, iii, pt 1, no. 962).　190 Surrey to Wolsey, 6 Sept. 1520 (*S.P. Hen .VIII*, ii, p. 42; *L. & P. Hen. VIII*, iii, no. 971).

final analysis, however, the main reason for his decision was the refusal of his request to be permitted to continue to hold the post of prior of Connall. In doing so, Wellesley exhibited his very calculated foresight. His forfeiture of the post of prior would have meant the loss of a very substantial annual income and a very highly esteemed position as head of one of the Pale's wealthiest and most vital monastic houses. Perhaps even more importantly, it would have made his attendance at parliament wholly impracticable and thus would have deprived him of the opportunity to foster the valuable political connections which were so essential to his career advancement.

The following year, his supporters in the Irish council wrote to Henry VIII, this time nominating Wellesley for the vacant bishopric of Limerick on the grounds of his 'good qualities'.[191] However, in spite of Henry having 'laboured earnestly' on Wellesley's behalf, the Kildare cleric was not appointed to the see.[192] Given his grounds for refusing the offer of the bishopric of Cork, it is improbable that Wellesley was actively seeking appointment to Limerick. Rather, it is far more likely that with the backing of Surrey and his supporters in the Irish council he was throwing his hat in the ring in these contests for vacant sees in order to gain the attention of Henry VIII and Wolsey, strengthening his chances in the event of a more suitable see becoming available. Interestingly, neither Wellesley nor Surrey appears to have had any input into the controversial appointment of Bishop Lane's successor, Thomas Dillon. This possibly stemmed from a general reluctance to overtly challenge the earl of Kildare's prerogative. However, following Bishop Thomas Dillon's resignation in 1528, Wellesley was presented with an opportunity to secure a bishopric on his own terms. In May of that year Surrey, who had by then been elevated to duke of Norfolk, wrote to Cardinal Wolsey requesting that he procure the king's letter to Pope Clement VII for Wellesley to be appointed bishop of Kildare. Dillon's immediate successor, Peter Stoll, was ousted from the bishopric when Henry VIII fully backed Wellesley's candidature, and on 1 July the appointment received papal sanction.[193] His delayed promotion proved fortuitous as in addition to being invested with the bishopric he was permitted to retain his post as prior of Connall *in commendam* in consideration of the poverty of his see.

By this stage, Wellesley had carved out a niche for himself as an influential member of the Irish council, having occasionally served as master of the rolls and as a privy councillor. In his joint capacities as prior of Connall and bishop of Kildare, Wellesley needed to exercise caution in his dealings with the earl of Kildare, especially since he had been appointed to the see during

191 Comerford, *Collections*, i, pp 21-2. **192** *The works of Ware*, i, p. 510. **193** Comerford, *Collections*, i, pp 21-2.

Kildare's detention at court. However, by virtue of his close association with Norfolk and with senior members of the Irish council, he was in a position to operate independently of the earl's control for the most part. Although listed as a recipient of a royal pardon following the Geraldine revolt, Wellesley was certainly no supporter of the house of Kildare.[194] This deep-seated animosity appears to have stemmed at least in part from the fact that his kinsman, Sir Thomas Plunket of Rathmore, had been killed in a skirmish with the eighth earl's forces in the late fifteenth century. By 1528, Wellesley had emerged as an outright opponent of the earl, and his signature appeared among those of the members of the Irish council who complained regarding Kildare's alleged maladministration.

In his capacity as a member of the Dublin government, Wellesley remained a thorn in the side of the earl throughout the early 1530s, all the while supported by the duke of Norfolk in his independent stance. But while he may have been overtly antagonistic towards Kildare in the council chamber, the earl taught Wellesley a memorable lesson in subordination to his authority within his liberty of Kildare. During one of Wellesley's visits to England, Norfolk had obtained for him a liberty for Connall Priory. In the course of a feast in the great hall at Connall at which 300 guests were in attendance, the ninth earl found out about this liberty and immediately 'went into a great rage, and drew out a long Irish knife, so that ... [Wellesley] ... could with difficulty escape from him'. Wellesley, clearly petrified and chastised by the assault, afterwards sheepishly confessed to Norfolk that as long as he lived he dared not to speak about the liberty which had 'almost caused my death'.[195] Other monastic houses such as Thomas Court Abbey in Dublin enjoyed similar liberty status at this time. But the fact that Kildare's principal monastery was claiming exclusion from the earl's liberty of the county constituted a serious challenge to his authority in his immediate heartland; hence his extreme anger at Wellesley's connivance and insubordination.

The factional politics of the Irish council and the Henrician court in the 1520s and early 1530s thus had reverberations in the episcopal appointments to the see of Kildare and forced the ninth earl to contend with an increasingly truculent incumbent. Whereas before the earls of Kildare could rely on the support, albeit enforced, of the bishops of Kildare, who generally lacked political clout, Wellelsey broke that mould. A driven careerist, he proved a formidable opponent of Kildare both as an ecclesiastic and as a member of the Irish

---

194 *Cal. pat. rolls, Ire., Hen. VIII-Eliz.*, p. 22.   195 Walter Wellesley, bishop of Kildare, to the duke of Norfolk, 15 May 1539 (*Cal. Carew MSS, 1515-74*, p. 151; *L. & P. Hen. VIII*, xiv, no. 970).

council. And while Kildare could effectively constrain his freedom of action in his capacity as prior of Connall and as bishop of Kildare, there was little that he could do to quieten Wellesley in government circles given his ties with influential courtiers. While the eighth earl had been able to supplant opposition from prelates including Octavian, primate of Armagh and Bishop Payne of Meath in the 1470s as a result of his having a virtual monopoly of control over the Irish council, Gearóid Óg seemed to find it difficult though not impossible to curtail the mounting opposition which was directed against him by a handful of hostile ecclesiastics in the Pale.

VIII

By far the greatest threat to Kildare's control over local ecclesiastical affairs had its genesis in the archiepiscopacy of William Rokeby, and reached a fraught climax during John Alen's term of office (1529-34) when the archbishop was 'cruelly and shamefully murdered' by Kildare's forces at Artane on 27 July 1534.[196] Archbishop Alen's calculated and systematic assertion of the rights and prerogatives of the metropolitan see in the early 1530s directly infringed on Kildare's landed interest. His two predecessors had already set about reasserting the rights of the archiepiscopacy which had lapsed to the advantage of the earls of Kildare, amongst others, during the fifteenth century. This was part of a more general drive on the part of primates such as Archbishop Mey of Armagh to regain church lands which had been lost to Gaelic or English neighbours. During his episcopacy William Rokeby, a Yorkshire man who had been bishop of Meath prior to his elevation to the archbishopric, proved an obstruction to the vested interests of the earls of Kildare when he set about reasserting the prerogatives of his office. In contrast with Mey, who had adopted a conciliatory course of action, negotiating an agreement with the O'Neills regarding their payment of dues from church lands which they had taken over, Rokeby adopted a more confrontational stance.[197]

In 1514, he initiated proceedings to reclaim archiepiscopal lands which had been confiscated by Gerald, the eighth earl of Kildare, in 1484. Rokeby made his case to Henry VIII for the restoration of these lands, claiming that the eighth earl had illegally assumed possession of more than twenty-four parcels

---

196 John Rawson to Hen. VIII, 7 Aug. 1534 (*S.P. Hen. VIII*, ii, p. 201); James Murray, 'Archbishop Alen, Tudor reform and the Kildare rebellion', in *Proceedings of the Royal Irish Academy*, lxxxix, sect. C (1989), p. 1 (hereafter Murray, 'Archbishop Alen'). **197** Lynch, 'Religion in late medieval Ireland', p. 10.

of lands and towns in the lordship of Ballymore and Castlekevin in the Fertir district and in the barony of Collacht, retaining possession of these towns until the time of his death in 1513. Rokeby would have us believe that when he was close to dying, the old earl was stricken in conscience for withholding these towns which were the property of the metropolitan see. As a result, the archbishop claimed that the earl declared his will in the presence of his son, the future ninth earl and other witnesses, that the archbishop ought to have possession of these holdings. On 18 October 1514 the case was referred to Patrick Bermingham, chief Justice of the king's bench, Richard Delahide, chief justice of common pleas, and Sir Bartholomew Dillon, chief baron of the exchequer and father of the ninth earl's chaplain, Edward. They examined all available grants made by the king to Rokeby's predecessors as well as rentals and muniments concerning the towns in question. They ruled that there was no evidence to exclude Rokeby from assuming title to these towns and so he was granted possession of them.[198]

As might be expected, the ninth earl of Kildare contested that ruling and when the dispute re-emerged in Rokeby's successor's term of office, it was finally ended with the restoration of the property to the possession of the metropolitan see in 1521. The death of the bishop of Kildare, Edmund Lane, in 1522/3 afforded Rokeby's successor, Hugh Inge, the opportunity to further advance this drive to reassert traditional rights accruing to the office of archbishop. As part of that project, in November 1523 Robert Sutton, the dean of St Patrick's Cathedral, collected precedents from the cathedral's archives with the purpose of vindicating a right claimed by Archbishop Inge to exercise archiepiscopal jurisdiction over the diocese of Kildare and to secure custody of its spiritualities while the see remained vacant. This intended infringement on the prerogatives of the dean and chapter of Kildare diocese was, however, successfully contested by the former and it cost Archbishop Inge dearly, since he was forced to acknowledge himself bound to pay the sum of £40 to the dean, archdeacon and chapter of Kildare. At this early stage the deleterious effects of this revival of archiepiscopal prerogatives had little real impact on the influence of the ninth earl in the ecclesiastical affairs of the Pale. That, however, was to change with the appointment of John Alen in 1529.

Alen had been implicated in the political machinations orchestrated by Cardinal Wolsey in the period 1529-30 with a view to mitigating the dominance of the earl of Kildare in the government of the lordship. Alen's appoint-

---

198 *Cal. Alen's register*, p. 262; Walter Fitzgerald, 'Ballymore Eustace and its neighbouring antiquities', in *Kildare Arch. Soc. Jn.*, iii (1899-1902), p. 348; M.V. Ronan, 'Anglo-Norman Dublin and diocese', in *Irish Ecclesiastical Record*, 5th ser., xlv (1935), p. 158.

ment as archbishop therefore caused him to become an embodiment of the fusion of the two previously separate processes of erosion of Kildare's political dominance on the one hand, and his control over ecclesiastical matters on the other. Wolsey intended that Alen would act as his agent on the Irish 'secret council' as he experimented with this alternative to Kildare's rule of the lordship. Alen's hostility towards the earl stemmed from his belief that Kildare was involved in causing the depredation to the metropolitan see's patrimony in the southern districts of the archdiocese, namely modern south county Dublin, southeast Kildare and north Wicklow. He held the earl and his predecessors culpable for turning a blind eye to this destruction of archiepiscopal land by the O'Tooles, the O'Byrnes and other Gaelic clans, and he also accused the Kildares of sanctioning such attacks in order to facilitate their own aggrandizement.

Alen's opposition to Kildare first manifested itself in the political arena. Only a month after his arrival in Dublin to assume his office as archbishop, he conducted an investigation which unearthed evidence that Kildare was inciting his retainers to stage disturbances in the lordship during the earl's detention in order to prove his indispensability and to persuade the king to reappoint him to the deputyship.[199] Kildare got his own back on Alen by refusing to authorize certain allowances on his account relating to expenditure of royal subventions in 1529-30.[200] Murray suggests that Kildare exacted his revenge on Alen in an overt manner following Cardinal Wolsey's fall in 1531, possibly playing a role in the factional intrigue at court which resulted in Alen's being served a burdensome *praemunire* fine in spring 1531.[201] Kildare further countered Alen's attempts to undermine his authority in political and ecclesiastical affairs when upon being re-appointed lord deputy in 1532, he secured the archbishop's removal from the chancellorship and replaced him with his rival, George Cromer, archbishop of Armagh. In 1532, the ninth earl was still capable of flexing his political muscle in order to manipulate ecclesiastics as his father had done, so as to strengthen the Geraldine faction and to isolate his opponents within the council. For the time being, Kildare appeared to have isolated the threat posed to his position by Alen. However, the archbishop's alliance with Cardinal Wolsey's replacement as royal secretary, Thomas Cromwell, augured badly for the earl of Kildare.

In spite of being marginalized in the Irish council by Kildare, Alen set to work to build a systematic and determined case for clawing back metropolitan

---

199 Ellis, *Tudor Ireland*, p. 119; Murray, 'Archbishop Alen', p. 14. **200** 'Account of John [Alen], archbishop of Dublin ... of the king's money', 1531 (*L. & P. Hen. VIII*, v, no. 398); 'Ireland', 7 Feb. 1533 (*L. & P. Hen. VIII*, vi, no. 1588); Ellis, *Tudor Ireland*, p. 120; Murray, 'Archbishop Alen', p. 14. **201** Murray, 'Archbishop Alen', p. 14.

lands which the Kildares and others had illegally acquired over several generations. A highly accomplished legalist whose competence was superior to that
of his predecessor, Alen claimed that on the basis of documents dating back to
the episcopacy of John Walton (1472-84), John Inge was in fact legally entitled to temporarily sequester the spiritualities of the vacant see of Kildare, a
legality of which Inge was evidently unaware.[202] Alen's challenge of the ninth
earl's occupation of metropolitan lands in this southern district of the archdiocese hinged on a statute passed in 1483 which legalized the then earl of
Kildare's claim to the lands of absentee landowners in counties Kildare,
Carlow and west Wicklow. Although the act purported to protect the church's
landed interest in these areas, in reality the metropolitan see lost out in this
arrangement. In a move to retrospectively rectify this situation, Archbishop
Alen had a statute passed in the 1531 parliament which rendered null and void
the terms of the act of 1483. He also claimed full dominion through the right
of escheat over several townlands in the district. Among these were Dunboyke
and Tulfarris which, according to Alen, the earls of Kildare had claimed in
right of the Lords Butler. This property also incorporated three carucates of
land in the parish of Kilberry in Kildare of which Russellstown in county
Wicklow formed a part. Alen explicitly accused Kildare of occupying these
lands which were rightfully the property of the archbishop in 1533, without
any legal claim and without paying any chief rent. Murray suggests that Alen
probably challenged Kildare's illegal occupation through the courts as he was
unlikely to waive a legal title to property without a contest. However, in the
event, Kildare emerged as victor since Tulfarris and Russellstown were seized
following the Fitzgeralds' attainder in 1536.

　　While the political fallout from the demise of the Kildares was momentous,
and its impact at county level profound, it is clear that their removal left a real
vacuum in the ecclesiastical sphere also. The most immediately identifiable
impact was the forfeiture of the ninth earl's advowson rights to upwards of
twenty-eight benefices which he held in his gift at the time of his death, half
of which were located in the county and diocese of Kildare. From a broader
perspective, the revolt facilitated an easier passage of the ecclesiastical legis-
lation in the Reformation parliament of 1536. Fear of punishment and confiscation of their estates in the wake of the suppression of the Kildare revolt
cowed many of the Pale gentry into submission. Moreover, many of the most
obstinate clerical opponents of the reform measures, most notably Dr John
Travers, had by that stage been removed from office or executed owing to
their support for the Geraldine rebellion. An entry in the patent rolls for the

202 *Cal. Alen's register*, p. 271.

year 1535 provides an apposite epilogue to the demise of the earl of Kildare's authority in the ecclesiastical affairs of county Kildare. In April of that year, John Bayly was appointed to the prebend of Maynooth, the latter at that time being vacant by the death of Edward Dillon, and in the presentation of the crown 'for certain reasons'.[203]

At county level, the removal of the Kildares and the suppression of the county's liberty provided the Dublin government with the opportunity to extend effective royal control throughout the whole of the shire. The Reformation had an impact on the diocesan church in the county in several respects. The episcopal succession of the see of Kildare was complicated by rivalry between papal and royal appointees. Bishop Walter Wellesley died in 1539 and the pope nominated Donald O'Beachan, a minorite from Kildare town, as his successor in July 1540. However, O'Beachan died within days of his appointment and Thady Reynolds, rector of the church of Olmar in the diocese of Meath, was advanced to the see by Pope Paul III. Henry VIII opposed this appointment and had Reynolds's election annulled, replacing him with his candidate, William Miaghe, in 1540. Miaghe was bishop until his death in December 1548.[204] The financial state of the see deteriorated throughout the remainder of the Tudor period. Clerical absenteeism and pluralism continued. In spite of efforts to encourage all clergy in the *inter Anglicos* areas of the county to hold schools and to teach English to their parishioners, a significant proportion of those clerics fulfilled neither of these duties throughout the reign of Henry VIII and beyond.[205] Furthermore, as is evident from the discussion of the impact of the Reformation on the county's lesser nobility and county gentry, the careers, beliefs and practices of subsequent generations of both strata point to the survival of Catholicism throughout the sixteenth century in county Kildare.

The suppression of St Patrick's Cathedral chapter in 1547 resulted in the incumbents of the prebends of Maynooth, Yago, Tipper, Dunmanoge and Tipperkevin being pensioned off in the early Edwardian period, some more handsomely than others. While the prebendaries of Maynooth and Tipper received pensions worth £30 and £25 respectively, those retired from the prebends of Dunmanoge and Yago were granted £10 and £8 respectively. The two incumbents of the prebend of Tipperkevin, William Cocys and Richard Wakefield, each received pensions of £4 and £6 13s. 4d.[206] The crown

203 *Cal. pat. rolls, Ire., Hen. VIII- Eliz.*, p. 15; Steven Ellis, 'The Kildare rebellion and the early Henrician Reformation', in *Historical Journal*, xix (1976), p. 817. **204** Comerford, *Collections*, i, pp 22-3. **205** See *Calendar of inquisitions.* **206** *Fiants Ire., Hen. VIII*, nos 41, 42, 51, 60, 76, 77, 98.

assumed the advowson rights to the vast majority of the county's benefices, including those affiliated to monastic houses within and outside of Kildare. The right of presentation to only a handful of benefices was reserved to lay men: Sir John Alen was granted the advowsons to Donacomper, Stacumney, Killadoon and Donaghmore churches and chapels in 1538. Following the suppression of St Patrick's Cathedral chapter in 1547 John Sutton of Tipper and Nicholas Eustace of Craddockstown were granted the right of presentation to Tipper rectory. That same year Robert St Leger was conferred with the advowson to Tipperkevin church, and Maurice Eustace of Castlemartin was to have the right to nominate a cleric to Brannockstown church. Sir Thomas Eustace, Viscount Baltinglass, enjoyed the right of presentation to Kilberry rectory and Sir Thomas Luttrell was entrusted with a similar right in the case of the churches of Dunmanogue and Aderge in 1547.[207] As this study has shown, Henry VIII, Edward VI, and Bishops Walter Wellesley and William Miaghe were compelled to appoint Gaelic clerics to minister in the county and the large number of Gaelic clerics, especially in Kildare diocese, did little to help the propagation of Protestantism. The records for crown presentations in the Henrician and early Edwardian periods are scant; nonetheless, references to sitting clerics being deprived of office are rare, William Doyn's deprivation of the treasurership of St Brigid's Cathedral, Kildare, in 1547 and his replacement with Philip Egerton, being one instance.[208] While each of these developments may be viewed as manifestations of the impact of the Reformation in county Kildare, it was the dissolution of the monasteries which had the most profound impact on Kildare society. It is to this campaign that we now turn our attention.

---

207 *Cal. pat. rolls, Ire., Hen. VIII-Eliz.*, p. 40; *Fiants Ire., Edw. VI*, nos 51, 89, 90, 97. For the allocation of advowsons in the case of rectories affiliated to monastic houses see chapter three. **208** *Cal. pat. rolls, Ire., Hen. VIII-Eliz.*, p. 146; *Fiants Ire., Hen. VIII*, no. 112.

3

The Dissolution and Distribution of Monastic Properties in County Kildare

The removal of the earls of Kildare from the political arena which the dynasty had dominated for over two generations had a predictably dramatic impact on both English and Gaelic elements in the lordship. In the immediate aftermath of the suppression of the revolt, there followed a spate of sporadic attacks on the Pale launched by Gaelic septs, principally O'Connors. These raids and the formation of the Geraldine league, which ostensibly aimed to have Gerald Fitzgerald restored to the inheritance and political prominence of his predecessors, clearly indicate a reluctance on the part of the Gaelic septs involved to accept the displacement of the Kildares as an irrevocable reality.

As might be expected, the population of county Kildare suffered most in the turmoil of the 1530s. Apart from their political ascendancy in the lordship, the influence of the Kildares pervaded county society down to grassroots level; they were an integral part of the very fabric of county society as its leading landed magnates, as chief military captains, as patrons and feudal overlords of the county's regular and secular clergy, as heads of a very large, widely-dispersed and influential extended family and as overseers of judicial process within the liberty of Kildare. The execution of Thomas, the tenth earl, and five senior members of the extended Fitzgerald family, the confiscation of their principal seat of Maynooth and the attainting of leading members of the collateral branches had a profound impact on the gentry and on the majority of the county's population. The associated suppression of the shire's liberty resulted in Kildare again being open to the direct influence of the Dublin administration, although that authority still had to be more forcibly asserted in the county's western and southern marches.

But the most immediate impact of the rebellion and the reduction of the Kildares was the destruction of substantial areas of the county resulting from the rebellion itself and from subsequent raids mounted by neighbouring Gaelic chiefs, mainly Kavanagh, O'More, O'Toole and O'Connor. The inhabitants of Kildare were not unaccustomed to such attacks: in 1521, when several Gaelic septs had gathered in O'Connor country, the earl of Surrey, then lord lieutenant of the lordship, was convinced that an imminent 'continual war' would result in 'the Englishry, and most especially the county of Kildare' suffering 'some hurts'.[1] Government officials emphasized that it was not the Gaelic raids alone which caused destruction and oppression in the county. In 1521 the under-treasurer, Sir John Stiles, complained of the ineptitude of Kildare's brother, James, as captain of the county, alleging that he 'defended not the country, but rather did great oppression thereunto, with coign and livery' which he is said to have imposed for his own purposes.[2] A year later, Stiles painted a bleak and ominous picture of the inhabitants and the landscape of county Kildare. He described how

> the king's subjects of the county of Kildare be in great fear and danger to be destroyed, in case that … Conell [O'More] go to war; for the said county of Kildare is almost destroyed already by the gentlemen of the same county, and their servants, with coign and livery. And all the country is almost waste.[3]

The persistent quarrelling between the earls of Kildare and Ormond (created earl of Ossory in 1528) which intensified during the 1520s increased the ferocity of attacks inflicted in the population of Kildare and led to a deterioration in the county's already partially wasted state. The viciousness of these raids is indicated by Ossory's descent on the small town of Levitstown in the extreme south of Kildare in the early 1520s. The earl's troops robbed the townspeople of £200 worth of goods. They then burned and spoiled the town and 'cruelly murdered and burned seventeen men and women, diverse of them being with child, and one of them that fled out of the fire to the church, was slain on the high altar'.[4] In the early 1530s, even before the outbreak of the Geraldine revolt, Sir James Fitzgerald, alarmed at the devastated state of the county, urged the king that unless he took remedial steps to ensure

> the redress and relief of your poor subjects of the counties of Kildare and Carlow, they shall be utterly destroyed, and the land left waste, for they be oppressed so extremely, and [more so] than ever was seen, that they must depart and leave the ground waste, and so is a great part of it already.[5]

According to contemporary accounts, the rebellion of 1534-5 brought this deterioration in the state of the country and its population to crisis point.

---

1 Surrey to Hen. VIII, 29 July 1521 (*S.P. Hen. VIII*, ii, p. 76). 2 John Stiles to Wolsey, 19 Oct. 1521 (*S.P. Hen. VIII*, ii, p. 86). 3 John Stiles to Wolsey, 25 Apr. 1522 (*S.P. Hen. VIII*, ii, pp 97-8). 4 'Articles to be shown on the behalf of the earl of Kildare', 1525 (*S.P. Hen. VIII*, ii, p. 122). 5 Sir James Fitzgerald to Hen. VIII, 31 Aug. 1533 (*S.P. Hen. VIII*, ii, p. 180).

Gerald Aylmer, chief justice of the king's bench, and Sir John Alen, master of the rolls, both of whom were also residents of Kildare, described to Thomas Cromwell, Henry VIII's chief secretary, how they 'marvelled at the state of the Pale which was 'so far altered from the condition, that we left it'. Kildare, they said, was particularly badly affected, with six of its eight baronies 'in effect, all burned, few or no people inhabiting there, but leaving their corns in the ground to the traitors'.[6] Late in 1535, both officials optimistically related how the greater Pale area had been subdued with the execution of several malefactors, particularly in county Kildare. The upshot of this purge was that local farmers resumed their peaceable occupation of the land and were no longer afraid 'to complain upon them by whom they be hurt'.[7] In spite of the retrieval of the county from much of the lawlessness which prevailed during the rebellion, over the next two years English soldiers and government officials regularly remarked the ruinous state of Kildare.[8] It is important, however, to regard these accounts with some degree of scepticism as the extent of the alleged devastation appears to have been heavily exaggerated. Admittedly jurors' extents compiled in 1540-1 contain many references to the devastated state of the earl of Kildare's confiscated manors and that of some of the county's monastic houses in the march areas of the county. However, in central and eastern Kildare, the property of both the earl and several monastic houses appear to have been relatively unscathed as a result of the disturbances and hence the evidence does not conform to the impression of wholesale destruction conveyed by Alen, Aylmer and several others.[9]

In mitigation of these officials, and leaving aside their motives for exaggerating the destruction of the countryside, their accounts may not have been entirely inaccurate. This stems from a question of the terminology which they used as it is possible that in referring to waste land they were describing property which had been given over entirely to pastoral farming.[10] Underlying these reports was a concern that the county would not be allowed to lie indefinitely in this wasted state since, as such, it was worthless to the exchequer. Sir John Alen in particular wrote to both Henry VIII and Thomas Cromwell urging them to rent the confiscated lands of the attainted Fitzgeralds as soon as possible. Lord Deputy Leonard Grey amplified Alen's concern, explaining to Henry VIII that the inhabitants of Dublin, Meath, Kildare and Louth 'hath been so spoiled, oppressed, and robbed, as they be not of ability to give Your

6 Sir Gerald Aylmer and Sir John Alen to Cromwell, 21 Aug. 1535 (*S.P. Hen. VIII*, ii, p. 263). 7 Sir Gerald Aylmer and Sir John Alen to Cromwell, 31 Dec. 1535 (*S.P. Hen. VIII*, ii. p. 295). 8 Francis Herbert to Cromwell, 21 Mar. 1536 (*S.P. Hen. VIII*, ii, p. 308). 9 My thanks Dr Vincent Carey for drawing my attention to this point. 10 Jefferies, *Priests and prelates in Armagh*, p. 29.

Grace any notable thing [that is, revenue]'.[11] Following the execution of Lord Offaly and his uncles at Tyburn, Kildare was still said to be lying in a devastated and therefore unprofitable condition. As a consequence of the executions the county's inhabitants were said to have been 'in such fear … as they dare not trust to abide in the country, but wander about'. The result, according to Lord Deputy Grey, was that they left their estates unattended, 'fearing more the loss of their lives, than the decay of their goods and lands', though the extent of this response is almost certainly exaggerated. He went on to urge that pardons be issued to these landowners in the belief that having been pardoned, they would return to farming their land by May 1537.[12]

With the removal of senior branches of the Fitzgerald dynasty from Kildare, and given the much cowed state of the population of the four shires and of Kildare specifically, the Dublin administration was eager from 1536 onwards to assert and extend its effective control in the Pale's march districts. In October 1536 Sir John Alen presented Henry VIII with a set of proposals for the reform of Ireland. Alen posited that the Gaelic elements of Leinster, especially the MacMurroughs, the O'Byrnes, and the O'Tooles, might be 'conquered, reformed, or subdued' to the king's rule by using 'goodly garrisons already built' in 'diverse propice places' which ought to be supplemented with a few more strategically located outposts. Alen further recommended that the king should rent his march lands to freeholders, since soldiers or farmers-at-will, would, he believed, be unable to adequately preserve and defend them. Alen's sense of expectancy was also articulated by Francis Herbert, a young soldier who had come to Ireland with Grey's army and who secured a place in the Irish council. After the attainders and confiscations authorized at the first parliamentary session in 1536, Herbert exclaimed that the king had never as much in Ireland, that the millennium had come when all loyal servants of the crown would be rewarded.[13]

As early as the summer of 1534, there were tentative signs of the onset of this climate of opportunism which prevailed in the immediate aftermath of the Geraldine revolt. During the throes of the rebellion, hostility to monasteries in the Pale marches had been voiced in government circles, and their propensity for political subversion was advanced as justification for their suppression. Sir Patrick Finglas, chief baron of the exchequer, tabled a set of proposals for the reform of the lordship in which he accused the monastic personnel of border areas of giving 'more aid and supportation to those Irishmen than to the king's subjects, part against their will'.[14] Finglas's salutary warning was echoed in 1536 by Sir William Brabazon, vice-treasurer, who advocated a scheme for widespread suppression on the grounds that 'they nourish rebels'.[15] The campaign for the suppression of the monasteries in both England and Ireland aimed at replacing the religious by laymen holding the lands by patent from the crown. Three factors dictated the distribution of the dissolved monastic possessions, namely, politics, patronage and revenue, and the first two were of the greatest importance.

Thomas Cromwell, in the first phase of the suppression campaign (1536-8), and Anthony St Leger in the second (1539-41), both exploited the property of the dissolved monasteries as capital for political investment, though their patterns of patronage distribution differed. Generally speaking Cromwell used the lands which came into the crown's possession as a result of the act of attainder, the act of absentees and the first act for the limited suppression of the monasteries in order to firmly establish a coterie of his supporters in the Pale. In the case of Kildare, Sir John Alen, Sir Gerald Aylmer, Richard Aylmer and Sir Thomas Eustace benefited from that patronage and formed part of this faction. In contrast, St Leger concentrated on conciliating the existing political establishment in Ireland and extended his patronage to those members of the politically influential group in the Pale who supported his policy. By granting monastic property to hand-picked gentlemen of the Pale whom he elevated to peerages in the early 1540s, St Leger aimed at fostering in them a vested interest at the seat of government while facilitating contact between their localities and the central administration. In coordinating the distribution of dissolved monastic possessions in Kildare and Wexford, St Leger aimed at 'taking order in Leinster' by infiltrating the border areas with loyal and strong landowners who would exercise a restraining influence on lawlessness.[16]

St Leger was faced with the challenge of formulating a policy in which the threat of coercion could be used to elicit a positive response from the various Gaelic elements to a conciliatory approach. The foundations for subjugating Leinster were laid by agreements with the O'Tooles and the O'Byrnes in Wicklow in 1541 and 1542 respectively and with the Kavanaghs in Wexford in 1543. Each of these clans was required to permit peaceable possession to tenants of any crown properties, including castles and monastic properties. The distribution of the majority of Kildare's monastic possessions thus coincided with and served as a vital element in this process of conciliatory politi-

14 See Bradshaw, *Dissolution of religious orders*, p. 42. 15 Letters from the deputy and council, 1536 (*L. & P. Hen. VIII*, x, no. 1032). 16 Bradshaw, *Dissolution of religious houses*, p. 193.

cal appeasement of the province's Gaelic septs. By examining the distribution of Kildare's dissolved monastic properties in the wider context of a drive in the early 1540s to consolidate and extend effective royal control within and beyond the four English shires, one can appreciate the political dimension to the suppression campaign in the rather unique case of Kildare. The distribution of dissolved monastic lands in county Kildare also formed part of a larger process of redistribution of land in the Pale in the aftermath of the Kildare revolt. Where relevant, this redistribution of the estates of the earl of Kildare and his supporters will be referred to in this section and in the next, though the primary focus of this study is specifically on the impact of the distribution of dissolved monastic property on gentry society. In addition, while Dublin-, Leix-, and Kilkenny-based monastic houses held land in Kildare, this study concentrates on the fate of Kildare's houses and their properties.[17]

I

The county had eight independent monastic houses located in rural areas, and four houses affiliated to monasteries outside of Kildare.[18] The five towns of Naas, Athy, Castledermot, Clane and Kildare were also centres of monastic settlement. Two of the county's houses, the nunnery at Graney and St Wolstan's Priory, were the first houses in the lordship to be dissolved by individual commissions. Baltinglass Abbey was nominated for suppression in a commission in 1536 and the nunnery of Timolin was closed by act of parliament in 1537. With the exceptions of Connall Priory and Monasterevin Abbey, the remaining monastic houses in Kildare were suppressed in the widespread campaign conducted between summer 1539 and April 1541. As we shall see, the dissolved properties served as substantial rewards conferred on military personnel, government officials or members of the local gentry, particularly those who had distinguished themselves in their service in quashing the

---

17 For a less detailed discussion of the impact of the dissolution campaign in Kildare see Mary Ann Lyons, 'Revolt and reaction: the Geraldine rebellion and monastic confiscation in County Kildare, 1535-1540', in *Kildare Arch. Soc. Jn.*, xviii (1992-3), pp 39-60.   18 County Kildare exchequer inquisitions, Hen. VIII, no. 27 (N.A.I.); *Extents Ir. mon. possessions*, p. 177; O'Murethi, 'Ballysax and the Nangle family' in *Kildare Arch. Soc. Jn.*, vi (1909-11), pp 96-7; *Fiants Ire., Edw. VI*, no. 1131; *Cal. pat. rolls, Ire.,Hen. VIII-Eliz.*, p. 385. A large old church or a monastery of Conventual Franciscans stood at Moone and a religious house or chapel existed at Clonagh. Given that the exact status and purpose of both is indeterminable, they have been omitted from the present discussion. See Archdall, *Mon. Hib.*, ii, pp 256, 284; Gwynn and Hadcock, *Medieval religious houses: Ireland*, pp 364, 367.

Geraldine rebellion. More importantly the dissolved monastic houses, many of which were located in vital urban centres or in the county's marches, provided the Dublin administration with strategic outposts which in several cases became the 'goodly garrisons already built' located in 'diverse propice places' referred to by John Alen in his scheme for the extension of effective government throughout and beyond the marches of the Pale.

The Arroasian convent at Graney, Kildare's third most valuable independent house, was the object of the first commission for the suppression of monastic houses issued for Ireland and it provides a good illustration of the fusion between the suppression campaign and both Cromwell's and St Leger's political agendas. Graney was situated on the Kildare-Carlow border, a mile and a half south of Castledermot and is variously referred to as being located in county Kildare and county Carlow in contemporary sources. Owing to its peripheral situation, its personnel had reluctantly been obliged to interact with the neighbouring Gaelic septs. King Henry IV officially recognized the extreme isolation of the nunnery and its services to the crown in adverse conditions in a patent which he granted in 1409; he acknowledged that by virtue of their being 'so surrounded by Irish enemies, and English rebels ... neither the prioress Margery nor her tenants could there dwell without holding communication with them'. On the grounds that the house served as 'a great comfort and support to his large [number of] subjects of the ... county', Henry IV granted the prioress and her tenants permission to have communication with these Gaelic elements. The Irish were to be permitted to donate or sell their goods such as bread, wine or ale to the nunnery and to the inhabitants of the surrounding district.[19] Its location on the very borders of this Gaelic country made Graney nunnery the Dublin government's most valuable strategic acquisition in the county in the 1530s. This is highlighted in the status of the contestants and of the eventual owner of the dissolved property, Sir Anthony St Leger, who spearheaded the political programme for the strengthening of the county's border defences through the secularization of Kildare's monastic properties.

In 1534 Finglas had singled out the nunnery as one of the border monasteries which allegedly assisted rebels. A year later, a commission for the suppression of Graney was issued to Lord Leonard Grey, marshal of the king's army. It suggested that the nuns be transferred to reside in other religious houses and it explicitly referred to the king as founder of the house, thereby affirming an uncontestable title to the property in the event of its dissolution. The motive for this early dissolution was to reward Lord Grey for his service

---

19 Archdall, *Mon. Hib.*, ii, pp 259-60.

as marshal during the Geraldine rebellion. The commission was, however, abortive, and the suppression was temporarily postponed, partly because it was overtaken by political events and partly as a result of the nuns' payment of a fine. Proceedings for Grey's receipt of the dissolved nunnery and its lands resumed in early October 1536, by which time he had been appointed lord deputy. Henry VIII issued instructions that letters patent be prepared which would provide for the elevation of Grey to the dignity of Viscount Graney. A further attempt at the closure of the nunnery was made in May 1537 when Graney was listed in another suppression bill.[20] Although Graney was then formally dissolved, no revenues were collected by the administration. The eventual dissolution of the nunnery proved considerably more difficult than envisaged in the 1535 commission for its suppression. That commission had intended that the last abbess, Aegidia Wale, would be transferred to another nunnery. However, the abbess proved a formidable obstacle to Grey's plans as well as a shrewd stewardess of her monastic property. She managed to hold out to qualify for the pension conferred on all of the superiors who surrendered in 1537. Moreover, she used the intervening period to cut her losses even further by leasing out the convent's lands in return for substantial entry fines.[21] The nunnery was eventually suppressed on 7 February 1539 and Aegidia Wale was seized of the manor and its lands on 20 July and received a pension worth £4.[22]

The fact that the nunnery was earmarked in this first suppression commission, coinciding with the Kildare rebellion and predating the more widespread dissolution campaign, clearly signals the overtly strategic intention of this policy in the minds of policy-makers in the Dublin administration from a very early date. This is borne out in the lists of houses selected for dissolution in the second commission of 1536 and in the act of suppression passed in 1537. In the first of these, Baltinglass Abbey, bordering on the O'Toole country, and Dunbrody and Tintern Abbeys in Wexford, both of which were adjacent to Kavanagh's territory, were targeted for dissolution. Another three houses, the monastery in Ferns, also near Kavanagh country, the nunnery of Timolin in southeast Kildare bordering on O'Toole territory and the priory of Ballyboggan in Meath close to O'Connor's lordship, were listed in the act of 1537.[23] As Bradshaw has observed, in all of these cases overtly defensive mil-

---

20 Bradshaw, *Dissolution of religious orders*, p. 73. 21 Ibid., p. 67. 22 Archdall, *Mon. Hib.*, ii, p. 260; Comerford, *Collections*, iii, p. 154; Walter Fitzgerald, 'The priory or nunnery of Graney, County Kildare', in *Kildare Arch. Soc. Jn.*, vii (1912-14), p. 377 (hereafter Fitzgerald, 'Nunnery of Graney'); Gwynn and Hadcock, *Medieval religious houses: Ireland*, p. 318. 23 Bradshaw, *Dissolution of religious orders*, pp 75-6.

itary considerations determined the choice of crown leasees to occupy them following their suppression.[24] The preferential grant of Graney Nunnery to Lord Deputy Leonard Grey in 1539, along with his being invested with the monastery of Ballyboggan in county Meath, was obviously conceived in the belief that his proven military ability would enable him to hold both properties as outpost for the king.[25] Further recognition of the particular strategic value of the convent at Graney came following Grey's execution in June 1541 when his successor as lord deputy, Sir Anthony St Leger, received a grant of the property within the year.[26]

St Leger's installation at Graney provided a crucial link in the tripartite chain which he himself devised for the strengthening of Kildare's defence system. While he secured the most southerly quarter of the county, Sir Thomas Eustace, Viscount Baltinglass, and David Sutton oversaw defence in central and northern Kildare. In the short term, St Leger's presence there appeared to yield results: in 1542, the O'Mores bound themselves to concede the possessions of certain monasteries in county Kildare, including Graney, to the tenants of the crown.[27] However, St Leger's occupancy of the property was short-lived and in 1548 he obtained a royal licence to alienate his holdings at Graney as a result of which possession passed to David Sutton of Tully in central Kildare.[28] The house and its property remained in the possession of the Suttons until 1558 when Gerald Sutton of Connall sold it for the sum of £1,600 to the restored eleventh earl of Kildare; it remained in the hands of the Fitzgeralds down to the early seventeenth century.[29] The nunnery at Graney was therefore a valuable acquisition for Grey and later St Leger as individuals by virtue of its very substantial financial worth (£73 13s. 4d.) but even more so for the Dublin administration owing to its strategic value as a traditional English outpost in southern Kildare. As such it was to be used in the Dublin government's drive to expand its sphere of effective influence throughout the Pale and specifically Kildare in the wake of the Geraldine revolt.

Provision for the dissolution of the Augustinian priory of St Wolstan's, located near the village of Kildrought (Celbridge) in northeast Kildare, was made in an individual commission of December 1536 and by an act of parlia-

---

24 Ibid., p. 76. **25** Ibid., pp 76, 233. **26** Hen. VIII to lord deputy and council of Ireland, 1541 (*S.P. Hen. VIII*, p. 335); *Fiants Ire., Hen. VIII*, no. 304; Archdall, *Mon. Hib.*, ii, p. 260; Comerford, *Collections*, iii, p. 154; Fitzgerald, 'Nunnery of Graney', p. 377; Gwynn and Hadcock, *Medieval religious houses: Ireland*, p. 308. St Leger was also invested with the monastery at Ballyboggan which he continued to occupy in 1548 (*Extents Ir. mon. possessions*, p. 321). **27** Bradshaw, *Dissolution of religious orders*, p. 73. **28** *Fiants Ire., Edw. VI*, no. 162. **29** See Walter Fitzgerald, 'Great Connell Abbey, County Kildare', in *Kildare Arch. Soc. Jn.*, ii (1896-9), pp 304-14 (hereafter Fitzgerald, 'Great Connell Abbey').

ment of 1537. Though its dissolution roughly coincided with the first round of suppressions under the commission of May 1536 which brought the closure of Bective, Tintern, Dunbrody, Baltinglass and Duiske Abbeys, the suppression of St Wolstan's priory remained an entirely independent transaction.[30] At Easter 1536, the crown was in receipt of revenues from St Wolstan's and in May, prior to his return from court, John Alen, then master of the rolls, secured a promise from the king of a grant of the priory. News of the intended closure of the monastery quickly spread throughout the Pale and on 26 June, the prior, Richard Weston, and the religious of St Wolstan's wrote to Thomas Cromwell alerting him to their awareness that the priory was to be suppressed and granted to John Alen. Weston presented Henry VIII with a supplication for the preservation of the priory and sought Cromwell's support in advocating his cause.[31] His plea was ignored, the suppression was authorized on 15 September 1536 and on 28 October, he was seized of all the priory's possessions.[32] The estate consisted of over 1,000 acres and in excess of twenty-four cottages. The property was worth approximately £41 though some of the possessions were not valued, being in a wasted state, no doubt as a direct result of the Geraldine rebellion.

The exceptional nature of the suppression of this house is evidenced by the special provisions made for the prior, Richard Weston. By an act of parliament (1537) he was granted the right to reside in the dissolved priory for the duration of his life. He was to be provided with a decent chamber with a chimney, along with a supply of wood and other necessities for his fire. A proper diet, both food and drink, and all of his provisions to the value of £6 annually were to be provided. The act also stipulated that Gerald Aylmer and Thomas Luttrell were to reserve to themselves and their heirs, during the life of Richard Weston, the annual sum of £4 from the dissolved priory lands for the late prior's own use.[33] Little time elapsed between the suppression and the transfer of ownership to Alen as on 1 December, he received a grant of the house and all its properties and rectories to hold forever at a rent of £10.[34] Alen immediately took up residence at St Wolstan's which thereafter became known as Alenscourt. St Wolstan's was of little strategic use; rather, its value stemmed purely from its being a sizeable and well-maintained property, which readily suited Alen's requirements for a county seat. The nunnery at Graney and St

30 Ronan, *The Reformation in Dublin*, p. 138.   31 Prior and convent of St Wolstan's to Cromwell, 26 June 1536 (*L. & P. Hen. VIII*, x, no. 1211).   32 Archdall, *Mon. Hib.*, ii, pp 292-4; Kirkpatrick, 'St Wolstan's', p. 285; Gwynn and Hadcock, *Medieval religious houses: Ireland*, p. 193.   33 Archdall, *Mon. Hib.*, ii, p. 295; Kirkpatrick, 'St Wolstan's', p. 285; Gwynn and Hadcock, *Medieval religious houses: Ireland*, p. 193.   34 *Fiants Ire., Hen. VIII*, no. 57.

Wolstan's Priory were therefore the only monastic houses in the lordship whose suppression was authorized before the crown resorted to a more systematic though limited policy of monastic suppression. Although political factors determined the allocation of both properties, the conferring of patronage on two loyal servants of the crown was the principal motive behind the dissolution of these houses.

Kildare's second most valuable monastery was the Cistercian abbey at Baltinglass. Situated on the shifting border between southeast Kildare and west Wicklow, the abbey is variously referred to as being in Kildare and Wicklow in contemporary accounts.[35] Because of its location in the district of Imail, the heartland of the O'Tooles, nestled between the Slewdagh mountain on the east and Cyhill mountain on the west, the abbey was open to frequent attacks from neighbouring Gaelic septs. As a result of its strategic location, Baltinglass Abbey was nominated for suppression in the second commission for the dissolution of religious houses issued in May 1536.[36] At a parliamentary session held in October 1537 it was enacted that possession of the sites and properties of the abbey be assumed by the crown. John Galbally, the last prior, was granted a pension of £10 backdated to Easter 1537 which he was to hold until such time as he might be promoted to a benefice worth twenty marks.[37] The monastic estate was largely wasted and left unoccupied from the time of its dissolution in May 1537 as a result of the war waged by Terence O'Toole, MacMurrough and their adherents. The 1540 extents jurors described the abbey buildings as in need of repair but necessary for the defence of the inhabitants and their goods.

Baltinglass was therefore a valuable acquisition for the Dublin government. On 30 June 1541, Sir Thomas Eustace, lord of Kilcullen, on the occasion of his elevation to the viscountcy of Baltinglass, was granted the site of the abbey and all of its possessions in county Wicklow, with the remainder to his male heirs. In doing so, the Dublin government was handsomely rewarding Eustace for valuable services rendered in the suppression of the Kildare revolt and in the subsequent effort at pacifying the Gaelic elements in the marches. But it was also, more importantly, ensuring the constant defence of

---

35 Given that Baltinglass Abbey is described as being in Kildare in some contemporary sources and in view of the fact that it subsequently formed part of the Viscount Baltinglass's estate, the dissolution and subsequent history of this monastery has been incorporated into this study. **36** Bradshaw, *Dissolution of religious orders*, p. 76. **37** County Kildare exchequer inquisitions, Hen. VIII, no. 16 (N.A.I.); Walter Fitzgerald, 'Baltinglass Abbey, its possessions and their post-Reformation proprietors', in *Kildare Arch. Soc. Jn.* v (1906-08), p. 393 (hereafter Fitzgerald, 'Baltinglass Abbey'); Comerford, *Collections*, pp 144-5; Gwynn and Hadcock, *Medieval religious houses: Ireland*, p. 128.

the southwestern periphery of the maghery and the march lands beyond. Eustace's co-recipients, the earl of Ormond and Robert Browne, an English soldier, were also clearly chosen with this purpose in mind.[38] The abbey itself appears to have remained in the possession of the Eustaces since James, third viscount, was its owner at the time of his insurrection in 1580 when he 'broke down the abbey and house, and burned the whole town, which together with the lands ... continued utterly waste during the ... rebellion and long after'.[39] Baltinglass Abbey and its land were thereafter successively leased to Captain Francis Stafford, to Captain William Russell and in 1587, Sir Henry Harrington, seneschal, received a grant of the property.[40] The credentials of the recipients of the Baltinglass property prove that it was a prize well worth competing for and one which was reserved for conferral on loyal servants of the crown over two generations. Moreover, they further amplify the administration's heightened sensitivity to the strategic importance of the district of Baltinglass in the defence of the Pale marches, when in the aftermath of the Baltinglass revolt, it was jolted into tightening its defence structures as it had previously been forced to do in the wake of the Geraldine rebellion.

The Arroasian nunnery of Timolin or Timolinbegg was the fourth house in Kildare to be targeted for closure by the act of 1537 which also provided for the dissolution of border houses at Ferns and Ballyboggan. The circumstances surrounding the closure of the nunnery were exceptional, however. In 1530 Archbishop Alen had suppressed the nunnery, ostensibly owing to its derelict state which resulted from its location in the extreme southern marches of the county. The nunnery served as a valuable defence fortress for the local population, a fact which was acknowledged in 1540 by the extent jurors. It was included in the 1537 act in order to confirm the crown's legal title to the property.[41] The possessions of the house, as recorded in several inquisitions in the early 1540s, were substantial, being valued at 106*s*. 8*d*., though their worth had been depreciated owing to their wasted state.[42] Since the property was partly overrun by the O'Mores, no income was forthcoming to the crown down to 1540.[43] In spite of his having received a grant of the nunnery and its possessions by royal indenture in 1538, Edmund Eustace failed to retain ownership of the property, which became fragmented in the 1540s and early 1550s

---

38 Bradshaw, *Dissolution of religious orders*, p. 76.   39 County Dublin exchequer inquisitions, Jas. I, no. 17 (N.A.I.).   40 *Fiants Ire., Eliz.*, nos 3745, 5081.   41 Bradshaw, *Dissolution of religious orders*, p. 73.   42 County Kildare exchequer inquisitions, Hen. VIII, no. 24 (N.A.I.); County Kildare exchequer inquisitions, Edw. VI, no. 3 (N.A.I.); Archdall, *Mon. Hib.*, ii, p. 297; Walter Fitzgerald, 'Timolin', in *Kildare Arch. Soc. Jn.*, ii (1896-9), p. 415 (hereafter Fitzgerald, 'Timolin'); Ronan, *The Reformation in Dublin*, p. 231.   43 Bradshaw, *Dissolution of religious orders*, p. 73.

when it was leased in parcels to loyal government officials. These included Richard Brasier, auditor of Ireland, John Goldsmith, clerk of the council and Walter Peppard of Kildare, one of the gentlemen ushers of the king's chamber.[44] St Leger's policy of installing loyal servants of the crown in the Pale marches was thus evident, with Dublin officials gaining precedence over the influential local family of Eustace.

II

In 1539 the commissioners charged with the widespread suppression of Ireland's monasteries began operations, and all but two of Kildare's houses were dissolved during the following two years. Among those suppressed was the preceptory of Knights Hospitallers at Tully, about a mile south of Kildare town. In peace times it ranked among the six most wealthy monastic houses of the county, being valued at over £31.[45] It was affiliated to the Hospital of St John of Jerusalem in Kilmainham, with its last preceptor, John Walinton, also serving as sub-prior of Kilmainham. Tully had been farmed out by the prior of Kilmainham, John Rawson, c. 1527.[46] In spite of the fact that much of its land lay waste in 1540 and that other parcels of property could not be valued by jurors as they lay adjacent to the marches of O'More country, the preceptory itself was still valued at £13 8s. 8d. The monastery's land, cottages, tithes, customs in Moortown, Friarstown, Brallistown, Duneany, Rathbride, Calverstown, Terwen and Frumpolston, Fontstown, Kilcale near Connall, Kylcorker and Ballycullane, were collectively valued at approximately £21.[47] Further evidence of the wealth of the house is provided by the very substantial pension of £16 granted to Walinton, the last preceptor. Because of its very considerable value, the sound state of its castle and in particular, its strategic location, it was only to be expected that the imminent prospect of this property coming on the speculator's market would arouse the interest of the Dublin administration and of influential members of the county's lesser nobility and gentry. In 1538, the interests of both dovetailed in the granting of the preceptory and its possessions, comprising in excess of 330 acres, to David Sutton whose political career was in the ascendant at this time. In 1545 that grant was further endorsed by Henry VIII.[48] As already noted, in 1548 the Suttons secured possession of the nearby priory of Connall and both acquisitions provided that

44 *Fiants Ire., Edw. VI*, nos 391, 601, 728, 806, 1083. **45** Gwynn and Hadcock, *Medieval religious houses: Ireland*, p. 339. **46** *Registrum de Kilmainham*, ed. Charles McNeill (Dublin, 1932), p. 171. **47** *Extents Ir. mon. possessions*, pp 96-7. **48** Ibid., p. 97; *Cal. pat. rolls, Ire., Hen. VIII-Eliz.*, p. 113.

family with a very substantial estate and a strong base from which to serve in the coordination of the defence of the central plain of Kildare.

The preceptory for Knights Hospitallers at Kilteel, due east of Naas, was also among the county's most substantial monastic properties to be dissolved at this time. Like its counterpart at Tully, the house at Kilteel was affiliated to the Hospital of St John of Jerusalem in Kilmainham. Well before its dissolution, this monastery's strategic worth was recognized by the prior of Kilmainham: 'Because the said preceptory or lordship is situated in the marches, near the Irish enemies, the Tholes, where resistance and defence are necessarily required'. John Rawson leased the preceptory and its possessions to Thomas Alen and his wife, Mary Rawson, in whose hands the property remained after its dissolution.[49] This lease had come about as part of Rawson's preemptive strategy designed to salvage what he could from the impending suppression of his house and all its properties, including Kilteel. By virtue of his own status in the Irish council, and given that Thomas Alen was the lord chancellor's brother, Rawson managed to get a licence under the Great Seal for a transaction in February 1540 which leased the entire property to Alen and his wife to hold forever.[50] This included a rectory and also lands in Kilteel, Cromwelston, Kilwarden, Kilbride, parcels of land near Three Castles in Wicklow, and property in Johnstown, Rathmore, Sherlockstown and Naas.

In 1542, Alen's leases of Kilteel, which were viewed by certain members of the Dublin administration as particularly flagrant, became the subject of a judicial inquiry and one of his leases was reduced to a fifty-one year duration.[51] Alen, however, withstood the challenge, being too well entrenched politically and legally to be ousted. Like his brother, Sir John, he was a loyal servant of the crown; his political career was in the ascendant in the late 1530s, and he owed his establishment as a member of the county gentry in Kildare almost exclusively to his acquisition of dissolved monastic lands such as Kilteel. As in the case of David Sutton at Tully, Alen's continued presence in this important march area went some way towards meeting the Dublin administration's need to assert its authority in the area while rewarding his loyal service in government and facilitating his self-aggrandizement.

A far more modest preceptory of Kilmainham Hospital was that of Killybeggs, which was situated west of Clane in the northeast of the county. It is believed to have been farmed out by the hospitallers in the fourteenth century and in 1540 the jurors found a capital messuage for the farmer's lodgings

---

49 Gwynn and Hadcock, *Medieval religious houses: Ireland*, p. 338.   50 *Extents Ir. mon. possessions*, p. 91.   51 *Cal. pat. rolls, Ire., Hen. VIII-Eliz.*, i, p. 79; Bradshaw, *Dissolution of religious orders*, pp 89-90.

which was said to be worth nothing above repairs, two messuages and 180 acres of demesne lands along with a further 100 acres of common pasture. The tithes and altarages pertaining to the property were valued at £13 6s. 8d. and the manor and rectory were held from Kilmainham at £10 by David and Edward Sutton in 1540, at which time a stipendary priest served the church.[52] Another of these houses affiliated to a parent monastery outside of the county was a cell located at Kilrush in the southeast of Kildare, the property of Cartmel Priory in England. Although the jurors only gave a return for the cell's lands and tithes in 1540, the property also consisted of a castle, as well as several messuages and cottages which were eventually granted to Thomas, earl of Ormond, in 1558.[53]

The Franciscan house at New Abbey near Kilcullen was of relatively recent foundation (est. 1486) and its buildings were therefore in a good state of structural repair at the time of the dissolution campaign. Like its sister house at Multyfarnham, New Abbey was exceptional as a Franciscan monastery in enjoying the patronage of a powerful local nobleman, and in its isolated location, since most mendicant houses tended to be situated in towns and generally had no special connection with a powerful patron.[54] In spite of its modest financial worth, its isolated strategic location caused this house to attract the attention of Archbishop George Browne of Dublin in 1538 as a premises which could be useful to him in his provision of defence of the southeastern front of the maghery. In the aftermath of the Geraldine revolt, the Dublin administration realized that the existing defence structures in the district of Ballymore Eustace were wholly inadequate. The Eustace estates spanned the areas of Coghlanstown and Ballymore Eustace. For five generations, that family had manned the castle at Ballymore which served as an important Pale fort, guarding as it did a vital crossing of the river Liffey and fending off the attacks mounted by Gaelic septs from their bases in the Wicklow mountains. That Ballymore was recognized as a strategic fortress is evident in its being targeted for plunder as part of the property of Sir Maurice Eustace, the constable of the castle, at the time of the Geraldine revolt.

Having witnessed the vulnerability of this flank of the Pale borderland during the revolt, Dublin officials took immediate remedial steps towards overcoming the fragility of royal government control in the southwestern quarter of the Pale. The first of these measures was taken in 1537 when Patrick

---

52 *Extents Ir. mon. possessions*, pp 91-2; Gwynn and Hadcock, *Medieval religious houses: Ireland*, p. 337. 53 *Extents Ir. mon. possessions*, p. 177; *Cal. pat. rolls, Ire., Hen. VIII-Eliz.*, p. 385; Gwynn and Hadcock, *Medieval religious houses: Ireland*, p. 184. 54 Bradshaw, *Dissolution of religious orders*, p. 145.

Barnewall, sergeant-at-law, was invited to accept the constableship of Ballymore. Concern for the provision of adequate defence in this region in particular was also voiced by Robert Cowley, master of the rolls, in this same year. He stressed that

> as Ballymore and Tallaght ... stand most for the defence of the counties of Kildare and Dublin against the O'Tooles and O'Byrnes, therefore it should be ordered that the commissioners shall see that the farmers and tenants there shall be ... able to defend those marches.[55]

Ballymore Castle and manor were in the possession of the archbishop of Dublin, and Browne refused the king's request to allow his castle at Ballymore to be occupied by Barnewall. He did so on the grounds that he suspected Barnewall 'would not attend there' but would instead appoint a gentleman as a substitute who would reside ... and report to him while at the same time oppressing 'the poor tenants ... under pretence of their defence, as the Geraldines and Eustaces used to do in times past'.

Browne went on to explain his personal reservation about surrendering possession of the castle as he often had occasion to 'resort thither and lie there, as my predecessors have done, for the stay [defence] of the country'. Were he to be deprived of access to the castle he would have neither provision nor lodgings in that entire area.[56] Meanwhile the archbishop was actively canvassing to gain possession of New Abbey, though with little success. In May, he petulantly complained to Thomas Cromwell that while he had asked the latter to obtain this 'very poor house of friars ... .which lay very commodious for me by Ballymore, to repair unto in times of need', he was denied this request, with preference having been given to an Irishman which led him to the indignant conclusion that 'I am an unworthy person'.[57] In the same letter to Cromwell, Archbishop Browne requested that he might be granted instead the abbey of Grace Dieu, near Lusk, in exchange for a promise that the constableship of Ballymore would be entrusted to someone other than Barnewall. In this way, New Abbey Priory became entangled in the brokering of dissolved monastic properties which occurred between opposing factions in the Dublin administration in the late 1530s.

At the time of its dissolution, New Abbey was in the possession of Thomas Eustace, lord of Kilcullen and later Viscount Baltinglass, who was, as we shall

---

55 Robert Cowley to Cromwell, 26 June 1537 (*S.P. Hen. VIII*, ii, p. 451; *L. & P. Hen. VIII*, xii, p. 157). 56 Ibid. 57 Archbishop George Browne to Cromwell, 21 May 1538 (*S.P. Hen. VIII*, iii, p. 10).

in the next section of this study, richly rewarded with dissolved monastic properties in recognition of his role in suppressing the Geraldine rebellion. Given his loyalty to the crown during the crisis of the mid-1530s and later, Eustace was the obvious candidate to be invested with New Abbey. His presence there, combined with his ownership of the dissolved property of Baltinglass Abbey further south, served to significantly bolster the government's recently strengthened presence in the broad catchment areas of Ballymore, east and southeast Kildare. Ironically, it is possible that Browne's request for New Abbey was refused on the grounds that while his presence there would only be occasional and brief, Eustace (whose estates spanned the district) would have a more permanent and therefore less penetrable hold in the march lands of the Pale. The suppression of the monasteries did not mean automatic and entire secularization, as the post-dissolution history of New Abbey illustrates. Like the Franciscan communities at Multyfarnham, Trim, Enniscorthy, Ardee, Dundalk and Wexford, all of which were nominally dissolved in 1539-40, the monks at New Abbey survived the Henrician suppression.[58] It was only in the first year of Edward VI's reign that the friars were expelled from the house and even then the attempt proved ineffective since in 1549, Eustace himself died in the care of the monks in New Abbey.[59] At the time of Eustace's death, the abbey was in ruins, except for a few rooms which were apparently used for tending the sick. Thereafter the house passed to Roland, second Viscount Baltinglass. Roland's adherence to Catholicism is apparent in the fact that in 1554, under the Marian regime, the guardian and community of the monastery near Kilcullen requested that their convent and those in Enniscorthy, Trim, Multyfarnham, and Carrickfergus be restored, thus implying a considerable degree of cohesion among these supposedly disbanded religious of New Abbey.[60]

There is evidence to suggest that even prior to the suppression of the house, the monks at New Abbey had planned their re-emergence at a future date when a more favourable climate again prevailed. In anticipation of New Abbey's imminent suppression, the Franciscans had entrusted many of their goods to the safekeeping of their patron, the lord of Kilcullen. In this respect they merely conformed to a general trend, as their brethren in the Carmelite house in Ardee and in Limerick also entrusted most of their valuables to local people until they could return to claim them.[61] The relatively recent foundation of the house, and its having been entrusted to two direct descendants of its founder, the Baron

---

58 Bradshaw, *Dissolution of religious orders*, p. 144. **59** 'Brevis synopsis provinciae Hiberniae FF. Minorum', ed. Brendan Jennings in *Analecta Hibernica*, vi (1934), p. 154; Gwynn and Hadcock, *Medieval religious houses: Ireland*, p. 252. **60** Gwynn and Hadcock, *Medieval religious houses: Ireland*, p. 252. **61** Bradshaw, *Dissolution of religious orders*, pp 140-41.

Portlester, undoubtedly strengthened the resolve of its religious personnel in their reluctance to accept the monastery's dissolution as an irrevocable reality. The dissolution of this house therefore provides an insight into how the contest for possession of monastic properties was beset by interpersonal rivalries, in this case the suit of a minor Kildare aristocrat being afforded precedence over that of an English-born cleric. More importantly, it highlights the overriding importance of defence considerations in dictating the allocation of dissolved properties which in this instance took priority over personal suits for possession of a property that was otherwise of relatively little real value.

The Carmelite friary at Cloncurry, situated northwest of Maynooth, was the least valuable of the county's isolated monastic houses to be dissolved. It was a small monastery which in April 1540, was comprised of a church and belfry, a chapter-house, a dormitory, a hall, two chambers, a kitchen, an orchard, three cottages and ten acres of land in Cloncurry.[62] Yet the extent jurors who visited the site between October and November 1540 reported that they found no buildings there. William Dixon, who had received a grant of the Carmelite friary at Kildare, took the timber from the site at Cloncurry. The total valuation of the extent amounted to a mere 12*s*. 8*d*. As a result, it was only of interest to local individuals, mainly farmers. The property was granted to William Dixon in 1543 and he, along with Edward Dixon, farmed the land for at least the next five years during which time Nicholas Carden was also an occupant of the dissolved property.[63] Later in the sixteenth century the monastery was evidently reconstructed as in 1602, Andrew Forester was seized of its church, a dormitory, a hall and other possessions. In this respect Cloncurry is not entirely unique in county Kildare. The Franciscan house in Kildare town which was destroyed in 1547 was re-constructed in 1621 and the Dominican priory of Athy, which was utterly devastated in a raid by McCare Kavanagh in 1539, was re-established by Ross MacGeoghegan, bishop of Kildare (1629-44).[64] The unremarkable post-dissolution history of Cloncurry Friary throws into greater relief the unique circumstances surrounding the fate of New Abbey near Kilcullen, highlighting the Dublin authorities' very singular interest in the acquisition of strategic outposts.

III

Apart from these individual, isolated monastic settlements, the towns of Naas, Athy, Castledermot, Clane and Kildare all had monastic houses which were

---

62 Archdall, *Mon. Hib.*, ii, p. 257. **63** *Extents Ir. mon. possessions*, p. 172. **64** Comerford, *Collections*, i, p. 257; Gwynn and Hadcock, *Medieval religious houses: Ireland*, pp 222, 252.

suppressed in the widespread dissolution conducted by the commission and whose structural state and post-suppression history was inevitably shaped by their being situated in such strategic locations. Spanning the very borderline of the Pale, the principal town within the maghery in county Kildare was Naas. Given that it was viewed as the last main loyal outpost west of the city of Dublin, the town was subjected to frequent raids by Gaelic septs. Faced with ongoing pressure from hostile Gaelic elements on the maghery in the late fifteenth century, the Dublin government was at constant pains to protect and retain an English presence in the town. On several occasions, when rumours of imminent raids were in circulation, and realising the potentially ominous consequences for Dublin itself should this outpost be lost to rebel Gaelic forces, Dublin officials were quick to mobilize forces in order to establish a protective presence there.

During the 1520s and 1530s, Naas was singled out for reinforcement as a priority strategic point. In 1521, Sir John Stiles reported that within days of Surrey's hearing that O'Carroll, O'Connor and other allies were intending to burn the town of Naas, the lord lieutenant had departed for Naas to ensure its defence. His intervention was required according to Stiles because the inhabitants of the district of Naas 'will not defend themselves; for they be Geraldines, or of diverse opinions'.[65] Predictably, during the Geraldine revolt, the security of the town was high on the agenda of the government. Sir John Alen warned that Lord Offaly 'is in purpose to burn Trim, Navan, Athboy, Naas, Kildare, and other incorporate towns' and he advised that the Englishmen in each of these towns should garrison themselves, ensuring they had lodgings and a sufficient supply of food.[66] In the event, Naas was well fortified: in June and August 1535, Sir John Alen and Gerald Aylmer commended the treasurer for his service in preserving the town. Had he not stayed in Naas along with Thomas Eustace and their small band of men, they believed that the town would have been burned in a manner similar to the rest of the county and the countryside would have been laid waste right to the very gates of Dublin.[67]

This protection afforded the town by the English forces, especially during the mid-1530s, shielded its three monastic houses from the destruction inflicted on houses in remote marches such as the Dominican house of Athy and the Franciscan friary in Kildare town during and in the aftermath of the rebellion. The largest of the monasteries in Naas was the Augustinian Hospital of St John. On 26 July 1540, Thomas Possick, the last prior, surrendered the

65 John Stiles to Wolsey, 30 July 1521 (*S.P. Hen. VIII*, ii, p. 80). 66 John Alen to Cromwell, 26 Dec. 1534 (*S.P. Hen. VIII*, ii, p. 221; *L. & P. Hen. VIII*, vii, no. 1573). 67 Sir Gerald Aylmer and Sir John Alen to Cromwell, 27 June 1535 (*S.P. Hen. VIII*, ii, p. 260; *L. & P. Hen. VIII*, viii, no. 1124).

house and all of its possessions.[68] Two days later, Thomas Alen, its occupant, received a lease for a period of twenty-one years of the site of the former hospital with its lands in Naas, Johnstown, Jigginstown, Walterstown, Castledermot and Eadestown, and the affiliated rectories of St John's in the town of Naas and Whitechurch which lay due north of the town.[69] The wealth of the monastery is evident in the rent paid by Alen for the property (in excess of £35) and in the generous pensions provided for its former religious. Possick received a handsome annual pension of £9 while another member of the community, Laurence Birley, was assigned a pension of 40s., to be funded from the revenues of the rectory of Whitechurch.[70]

The evidence therefore points to St John's Hospital's being a very generous grant to be conferred on one individual, Thomas Alen, whose social status was immensely inflated as a direct result of his receipt of dissolved monastic properties in northeast Kildare.[71] The Dominican priory of St Eustace was the second most valuable house in the town of Naas, being valued at 113s. 6½d. at the time of its dissolution.[72] On 30 March 1540, Richard Walshe, its last prior, was seized of the priory's buildings, all of which were still standing, and which were worth 66s. 8d.[73] Although a more modest concern than St John's Hospital, this monastery none the less provided some rich pickings mainly for members of the county gentry, particularly those who already had a vested interest in the property such as Thomas Eustace, lord of Kilcullen, who, along with Patrick Barnewall, lord of Trimleston, had a quit rent out of the house's property in the town of Naas. Richard Aylmer of Lyons in northeast Kildare bought the church and chancel for £4 and also all of the superfluous buildings. The site and properties of the former Dominican house formed part of a grant made in 1542 to Robert Eustace and others for the use of Thomas Luttrell of Luttrellstown, chief justice of the king's bench.[74]

The least valuable of the town's three monastic houses was the Augustinian friary, commonly called the monastery of the mote. In an extent recorded in November 1540, the jurors found that, like the other two houses in Naas, the friary was in a good state of structural repair with its buildings being valued at £10 sale price. Its holdings, however, were minute: in the town itself, the monks had a tenement with four gardens and six acres of land. Thomas

---

68 Cal. pat. rolls, Ire., Hen. VIII-Eliz., p. 56. 69 Fiants Ire., Hen. VIII, no. 80. According to this lease, Alen was to pay £39 3s. 4d. rent. However, in April of the following year, that lease was again issued, without reference to the rectories, and the rent was £35 18s. 2d. See Fiants Ire., Hen. VIII, no. 120; Gwynn and Hadcock, Medieval religious houses: Ireland, p. 189. 70 Cal. pat. rolls, Ire., Hen. VIII-Eliz., pp 59-60. 71 Extents Ir. mon. possessions, pp 154-7; Gwynn and Hadcock, Medieval religious houses: Ireland, p. 189. 72 Extents Ir. mon. possessions, p. 166. 73 Ibid. 74 Fiants Ire., Hen. VIII, no. 313.

Eustace, lord of Kilcullen, had a quit rent from these lands and the total valuation of the house and its modest properties amounted to 8s. 11d.[75] While in April 1540 Thomas Alen had been granted a twenty-one year lease of the site and possessions of the monastery, John Sutton occupied the property down to 1548.[76] The constant defence of Naas during the Geraldine revolt by the Dublin administration can therefore be seen to have benefited the monasteries of St John's, St Eustace's and the Augustinian friary and by implication, their recipients, given the relatively sound structural state of these houses on their suppression.

The Franciscan priory of friars minor at Clane was also situated on the very border of the Pale maghery and its good state of structural repair contrasts sharply with that of the houses in the marches. The buildings in the precincts of this monastery all appear to have been intact in 1537 as the church, chancel, and part of the dormitory had to be knocked by order of Lord Leonard Grey for the purpose of repairing the king's castle at Maynooth.[77] Clane Priory was by no means unique in this regard; the timber from Bective Abbey was used for repairs to the king's mills at Trim in Meath.[78] Further testimony to the sound state of the monastery at Clane is provided by the extent report that the buildings, with the exception of the dormitory, were considered suitable for the local farmer's use. In the village itself they owned two messuages, though these were dilapidated and unoccupied in 1540. Apart from a garden and a small close of three acres, the friars also held considerable landed assets in the greater Clane area. At Bodenstown, to the south of Clane, they held twelve acres and received payment of tithes from this property. The total value of this priory was 103s. 2d. and the sale of its chattels yielded a very substantial return of £15 6s.[79] On 29 March 1541, the site of the Franciscan priory and its possessions were leased to David Sutton.[80] But the property changed hands several times in the 1540s. Sutton's initial lease was

---

75 *Extents Ir. mon. possessions*, p. 165. Curiously, Archdall lists the possessions of the three chantries of St David's Church in the town as part of the property which the Augustinian friars were said to have held at the time of the suppression of their friary. See Archdall, *Mon. Hib.*, ii, pp 287-9. 76 *Fiants Ire., Hen. VIII*, no. 119; *Extents Ir. mon. possessions*, p. 165. 77 In 1537 Grey brought a pair of organs, as well as glass, wooden hallows, and other necessary commodities from the abbey of Killeigh in O'Connor country to furnish repairs to the castle and former college church and building in Maynooth. He also brought building materials and adornments from Dundalk to embellish the church. See *Extents Ir. mon. possessions*, pp 164-5; Leonard Grey to Cromwell, 31 Dec. 1537 (*S.P. Hen. VIII*, ii, p. 529); Bradshaw, *Dissolution of religious orders*, p. 140. 78 *Extents Ir. mon. possessions*, p. 267. 79 Ibid., p. 165; 'Accounts of sums realised by sale of chattels of some suppressed Irish monasteries', ed. Charles McNeill in *Journal of the Royal Society of Antiquaries of Ireland*, lii (1922), pp 21, 28, 34. 80 *Fiants Ire., Hen. VIII*, no. 174.

soon superseded in June 1542 by a lease of the site and its possessions along with those of the Dominican priory in Naas to Robert Eustace and others, to the use of Sir Thomas Luttrell of Luttrellstown.[81] The following year, Robert Eustace, prebendary of Rathmichael and four others received a lease of the same property.[82] Like their counterparts in New Abbey in Kilcullen, the friars remained resident in Clane until 1550 when the remains of the monastery were entirely destroyed.[83]

IV

Beyond the maghery, however, strategic concerns took precedence in the distribution of the possessions of the dissolved monastic properties in Athy, Castledermot and Kildare just as it did in the case of the individual isolated monastic houses in the march areas which we have already examined. The scene in the southwestern town of Athy in 1540 provides a stark contrast to that obtaining in Naas or in Clane. Because of its frontier location, Athy was, as already noted, well fortified. In 1500 the eighth earl of Kildare had thoroughly repaired the castle at Athy and thirty years later, the ninth earl garrisoned and fortified Woodstock Castle nearby. As a result of its strategic location and its close association with the Kildares, the town and its inhabitants suffered considerable destruction during numerous raids in the course of the rebellion in 1534-5.[84] One can only imagine the extent of the damage inflicted by Ossory's campaign in 1535 in the area of north Carlow, Athy, Castledermot and Kilkea during which his forces continually burned, spoiled and destroyed that district for three full days.[85]

Athy's strategic importance in the 1530s was highlighted in the Dublin government's acute concern that the bridge in the town along with the earl of Kildare's garrison at Woodstock should be recaptured by English forces, both having been occupied by the Irish since the outbreak of rebellion. Their efforts suffered a serious setback, however, when the chief of the O'Mores and his forces outnumbered those of Thomas Alen, who was in charge of the restoration project. O'More razed the bridge and broke all doors, windows and battlements in the manor at Woodstock 'thinking utterly [that] the king would

---

81 Ibid., no. 313. **82** *Cal. pat. rolls, Ire., Hen. VIII-Eliz.*, p. 90. This grant was made to Eustace and his partners in consideration of the sum of £177 3*s.* 4*d.* which Thomas Lutrell paid (*Cal. pat. rolls, Ire., Hen. VIII-Eliz.*, p. 90). **83** Gywnn and Hadcock, *Medieval religious houses: Ireland*, p. 245. **84** Lord Leonard Grey to Thomas Cromwell, 24 June 1536 (*S.P. Hen. VIII*, ii, p. 338; *L. & P. Hen. VIII*, x, no. 1194). **85** Ossory to Walter Cowley, 1535 (*S.P. Hen. VIII*, ii, p. 251).

have built the same no more'. He held the bridge and the fortress as 'his own, not surrendering nothing without the power of his sword'.[86] However, Lord Leonard Grey reacted by sending his footmen, ordnances and a supply of victuals to garrison the bridge of Athy until such time as those provisions were spent, in which event, the troops were to base themselves at nearby Kilkea. The restoration of the bridge and the manor of Woodstock was obviously arduous and expensive. In August 1536, Grey informed Thomas Cromwell that while he campaigned against O'Brien and James FitzJohn of Desmond, he left William Brabazon with a company in Dublin partly for the defence of the city and also to oversee the 'continuing [of] the works of Athy and Woodstock'.[87] The enormous amount of labour and supplies invested in the re-edification of the castle and bridge at Athy and the manor of Woodstock after the suppression of the rebellion indicate the lengths to which the Dublin administration was prepared to go in order to keep this foothold in the southwestern march of the county.[88]

Given that Athy suffered such extensive destruction, the town's monastic houses necessarily fell prey to the attacks of hostile Gaelic elements. The monastery of the Crutched Friars called the Hospital of St Thomas the Martyr, appears to have especially suffered since it lay beyond the town walls.[89] In 1536, the house and its revenues were valued at £20, but Myles Ronan claims that the revenues of the house were in reality much greater than this, amounting to over £33 annually. At the time of its dissolution, the property had depreciated in value to just over £20. Following its dissolution, the monastery and all its possessions were granted to a local man named Anthony Power.[90] The precincts of the Dominican house of friars preachers suffered more extensive damage, being almost entirely devastated by mid-1540. In their extent recorded at Kilkea in November 1540, the jurors reported that all of the buildings of the house itself had been burned during a raid by Donald McCare Kavanagh in the previous June. Those superfluous buildings which had survived were only of use to a farmer, and six of the ten

86 Thomas Alen to Cromwell, 17 July 1536 (*S.P. Hen. VIII*, ii, p. 346; *L. & P. Hen. VIII*, xi, no. 101); O'Murethi, 'The white castle of Athy', p. 53. **87** Lord Leonard Grey to Cromwell, 10 Aug. 1536 (*S.P. Hen. VIII*, ii, p. 353; *L. & P. Hen. VIII*, xi, no. 266). **88** Thomas Alen to Cromwell, 17 July 1536 (*S.P. Hen. VIII*, ii, p. 345; *L. & P. Hen. VIII*, xi, no. 101); Comerford, '"The ford of Ae"', p. 61. **89** The Hospital of St Thomas the Martyr is also variously referred to as the priory of St John, and the priory of St Thomas. See Gwynn and Hadcock, *Medieval religious houses: Ireland*, pp 210-11. According to Bradshaw, it was passed over by the suppression commissioners in 1539-40 (Bradshaw, *Dissolution of religious orders*, p. 123). **90** *Cal. Alen's register*, p. 277; 'Irish monasteries', 1536 (*L. & P. Hen. VIII*, xi, no. 1416); Archdall, *Mon. Hib.*, ii, p. 249; Ronan, *The Reformation in Dublin*, pp 222, 224; Gywnn and Hadcock, *Medieval religious houses: Ireland*, p. 210.

acres belonging to the vicarage of Athy were waste as a result of the raid. The reduced state of the monastery and its property is evident in its valuation of 28*s.* 8*d.* at the time of its dissolution, compared with a figure of 32*s.* recorded in an extent taken in 1539 prior to its destruction.[91] The site of the priory and certain parcels of its property were leased in April 1540 to Martin Pelles of Athy.[92] Four years later, he received a grant of the site and lands of the dissolved priory along with several other possessions; he still occupied this property in 1548.[93]

The Dublin government's donation of this monastic property to Pelles was a purely strategic move. Like other recipients of dissolved monastic estates, he had played an active role in the suppression of the Geraldine revolt. He had served under Lord Deputy Grey in his invasion of O'Connor's territory in 1537 and had particularly distinguished himself at the capture of the Gaelic chief's castle at Phillipstown. In 1538 he was rewarded for his services with the constableship of Athy, which was a post of considerable responsibility.[94] In the early 1540s, in addition to receiving grants of monastic property, he was also invested with parcels of the estate of the ninth earl of Kildare. In April 1540, on the same day as he received a lease of the site of the Dominican priory, Pelles was granted a lease of the manors of Athy and Woodstock, formerly possessions of Gerald, the ninth earl of Kildare. In July 1541, he secured a lease of more parcels of the former estate of the earl of Kildare, located in Oldragh (Shanragh) and Percivalstown (Prusselstown) due southwest of Athy. Three years later, he was invested with a lease of parcels of the estate in the districts of Narraghmore and Moone.[95] Martin Pelles therefore managed to elevate himself from the status of a soldier as a result of being rewarded with both dissolved monastic property and portions of the attainted earl's estate in the greater Athy region. His installation there served as one of several measures adopted by the Dublin administration in their aggressive efforts to strengthen their hold in this county marchland. He also became one of a number of beneficiaries from both events who joined or were raised to the ranks of the established county gentry and thereby fundamentally changed its composition.

As in the case of Athy, the town of Castledermot, located in the southern extreme of county Kildare, was subjected to frequent attacks by neighbouring Gaelic septs, by the forces of the earl of Ormond and indeed by those of the ninth earl of Kildare. We gain an insight into the destruction caused by such

---

91 *Extents Ir. mon. possessions*, pp 172-3. **92** *Fiants Ire., Hen. VIII*, no. 126. **93** Ibid., no. 399; *Extents Ir. mon. possessions*, p. 173; Archdall, *Mon. Hib.*, ii, p. 251. **94** *Cal. pat. rolls, Ire., Hen. VIII-Eliz.*, p. 34. **95** *Fiants Ire.,Hen. VIII*, nos 125, 232, 445.

attacks in the example of a lightening raid by the ninth earl on the town in 1532. He entered the town fair 'crying havoc upon the king's subjects which thither had resorted' and then proceeded to attack and rob them of their goods, and murdered a number of people in the course of the raid.[96] During the Geraldine rebellion, Castledermot was garrisoned by Fitzgerald's Gaelic allies. The earl of Ossory claimed that in September 1534 MacMurrough, O'More, O'Connor, O'Byrne and the majority of the county's gentlemen were retained by the baron of Offaly's military personnel. Ossory alleged that they were then dispatched to camp at Carlow, Castledermot, Athy, Kilkea and the surrounding districts and were equipped with provisions to last them three weeks so that they might resist his attempts to invade Kildare. In reaction, the earl mobilized his forces into counties Carlow and Kildare where he campaigned for three full days as a result of which 'the traitors were ... put from abode in that marches, lacking both housing and victual there'.[97] He proceeded to occupy the town in the king's name. In 1540 he was appointed constable of the fortress at Castledermot as part of the broader policy of establishing a tighter grip on these borderlands which was implemented in the districts of Baltinglass, Ballymore, Athy and Monasterevin.

Castledermot's two monastic houses, St John's Hospital and a Franciscan friary, suffered serious damages to their property and loss of income to the neighbouring O'More clan. Undoubtedly as a result of these raids which intensified during the Geraldine rebellion, St John's Hospital, property of the Crutched Friars, had lapsed in fulfilling its pastoral duties by 1536. In that year, the house was said to have 'serveth of no purpose' and the extents of both houses compiled in 1540 testify to their being in an utterly decrepit state.[98] In April 1540, the last prior of St John's surrendered his houses and its appurtenances, some of which lay in Connacht.[99] On the site the jurors found only the stone walls of the former church, which was roofless in November 1540, and the belfry, which was used as a fortress for the defence of the local population, as in Baltinglass Abbey. Its hall and chamber were both in a very ruinous state, uninhabited and unvalued by the jurors. The cemetery had been waste since 1534. In Grangeford the monastery owned an old castle which was broken down and in Maudlins the prior held eight cottages, all of which were waste, and fourteen acres of land which were not cultivated. The tithes from Timahoe which the friars formerly received were no longer paid, as that area was among the Irishry. The friars' house in Priorstown in Leix also lay in

---

96 Fitzgerald, *The earls of Kildare*, p. 111.   **97** Ossory to Cowley, 1535 (*S.P. Hen .VIII*, ii, p. 251).   **98** 'Irish monasteries', 1536 (*L. & P. Hen. VIII*, xi, no. 1416).   **99** Ronan, *The Reformation in Dublin*, p. 225.

Gaelic hands and had long since been in a wasted state.[100] The total value of the dissolved monastic house and its possessions in 1540 was £7 10s. 2d.[101] On 15 June 1543, a lease of the site of the hospital and its lands in Castledermot, Grangeford, Haystown, Tomenston, Cullinstown, Kilkea and Bray was granted to William Keating, a gentleman who was captain of the kerne in Castledermot.[102] Like Pelles in Athy, Keating benefited from the distribution of the estates of those involved in the Geraldine rebellion. In 1547, he received a grant for life of the manor of Fontsland and its possessions in Fontsland itself, in Little Boley, and in Rathsillagh in Kildare, which had comprised a portion of James Fitzgerald's confiscated estate.[103]

The town's second monastic house, the Franciscan friary, was considerably less valuable than St John's but it appears to have been in a somewhat better state of structural repair, perhaps having been spared the worst excesses of raids by Kildare's forces because it was a Geraldine foundation.[104] The extent jurors found in the precincts a church, a cloister and a dormitory, all fit only for demolition, though the tiles, timber, glass, iron and stones were valuable. There was also a tower, two halls, a kitchen, a garden, an orchard and a cemetery on the site along with a walled bawn, three messuages and ten acres of land, most of which was waste or in Gaelic hands. The friars also owned three cottages and were still in receipt of customs. They owned a water mill and the total valuation of the house and its possession was 54s. As such it ranked well above the Austin friary in Naas (8s. 11d.), the house at Cloncurry (12s. 8d.) or the Dominican house in Athy (32s.).[105]

As in the case of St John's Hospital, this house was suppressed in April 1540. Though it is not known who subsequently received a grant or lease of the dissolved monastic property, the occupant at the time of its dissolution was Robert Butler. He continued to occupy what would appear to be virtually the entire property in 1548.[106] In spite of their strategic location, the two houses in Castledermot, because of the dilapidated state of one and the modest financial value of the other, offered little of any real substance either to the Dublin government or to members of the Pale gentry. Yet St John's was sufficiently substantial to handsomely reward the more modest expectations of the captain of the kerne in the district, and the Dublin administration availed of this oppor-

---

100 *Extents Ir. mon. possessions*, pp 168-9; Ronan, *The Reformation in Dublin*, p. 226; Gwynn and Hadcock, *Medieval religious houses: Ireland*, p. 211. 101 *Extents Ir. mon. possessions*, p. 169. 102 *Fiants Ire., Hen. VIII*, no. 364. 103 *Fiants Ire., Edw. VI*, no. 24; *Extents Ir. mon. possessions*, p. 207. 104 *Liber mun. pub. Hib.*, pt v, p. 244; Archdall, *Mon. Hib.*, ii, p. 253; Fitzgerald, *The earls of Kildare*, p. 19; Ronan, *The Reformation in Dublin*, p. 227; Gwynn and Hadcock, *Medieval religious houses: Ireland*, pp 244-5. 105 *Extents Ir. mon. possessions*, pp 165, 172, 173. 106 Ibid., p. 170.

tunity to secure a stronger foothold in the town as it had also done in the case of Athy.

Lastly, the county town of Kildare was the site of three monastic houses, a Franciscan friary, a Brigittine nunnery and a Carmelite priory. The Franciscan house was one of a number of Kildare monasteries to be reformed by the Observant order in 1520. The friary was surrendered on 30 April 1539 by the guardian who was seized of a church, a belfry, a kitchen, a cemetery, two gardens, two closes containing three acres, four messuages, two cottages and thirty-five arable acres, all of which was valued at 46s. 8d.[107] The jurors who compiled the 1540 extent of the monastery found it in a similar state to the houses in Athy and Castledermot. Lying beyond the maghery boundary, all of the friary's buildings had been burned by O'Connor during a raid on Kildare in May 1540. Only the church and two-thirds of the cloister had survived intact and even these were said to be only fit for demolition.

In spite of the decrepit state of the friary's buildings, as in the case of the Franciscan friary in Castledermot, the stones, tiles, glass and iron were quite highly valued at a market price of 53s. 4d.[108] The friars owned twenty-four acres of land in Kildare town and a further eleven acres in Collerland, and enjoyed receipt of customs and tithes payments from both holdings. Immediately after its dissolution in 1539, Philip FitzMores entered the monastery's lands in Collerland, and was in receipt of all tithes from that land though paid no rent whatsoever. In 1543, the Franciscan friary, along with the lesser Carmelite priory in the town, was granted to David Sutton who was based at Tully further south. Both houses remained in the hands of the Sutton family during the Henrician period as David's executor, Gerald Sutton, was found in possession of them in 1548.[109] The Franciscan friary was destroyed in 1547 but was re-established in 1621 and throughout the sixteenth and early seventeenth centuries, it was the burial place of four successive earls of Kildare.[110]

The second most valuable of the town's houses was one of Ireland's oldest monastic foundations, having been established in the late fifth or early sixth century by St Brigid. In an extent recorded in the town in November 1540, the jurors found in its precincts a small castle, suitable for the farmer's use, and in the town the nuns held eight acres which, at the time, were occupied by a Gaelic tenant. They also owned two cottages and enjoyed receipt of customs

107 *Archdall, Mon. Hib.*, iii, p. 279. **108** *Extents Ir. mon. possessions*, p. 166. **109** *Fiants Ire., Hen. VIII*, no. 345; *Extents Ir. mon. possessions*, p. 167; Archdall, *Mon. Hib.*, ii, p. 279 records the name of the recipient of the property as Daniel rather than David Sutton. **110** Gwynn and Hadcock, *Medieval religious houses: Ireland*, p. 252.

from the town. In Calaghton in Newcastle, county Dublin, the nunnery held forty-four acres farmed by Francis Cosby and Raymond Oge FitzGarret of Rathangan. The total value of the nunnery and its possessions was 43*s*. 6*d*. which put it on a par with the neighbouring Franciscan house (46*s*. 6*d*.).[111] In 1547, Raymond Oge FitzGarret was granted a lease to this parcel of the possessions of the dissolved nunnery, a measure which probably had the effect of simply legalising an existing arrangement. The commissioners appear to have passed over this house in 1539-41 and no record of other grants of the house or its property exists.[112]

The third monastery in Kildare was St Mary's, a Carmelite priory. As in the case of the Franciscan house, the jurors found in November 1540 that with the exception of the church and one messuage which the friars used for their hall, all of this priory's buildings had been burned during O'Connor's raid. The church was only fit to be thrown down and the messuage was considered suitable for the local farmer's use. All that remained within the precinct was a garden and a small close of one acre. In the town itself, the friars owned four acres, two of which lay waste, and a messuage, and they enjoyed receipt of customs payments. Following its dissolution, the Carmelite priory is said to have been granted to William Dixon, a yeoman, who also received a grant of its sister house at Cloncurry though this, as already noted, was occupied by David Sutton's executor, Gerald Sutton, in 1548.[113] The distribution of the dissolved properties in Kildare town was therefore beneficial only to members of the established local gentry and was particularly important in bolstering Sutton's position as superintendent of the central plain's defences from his base in Tully.

V

County Kildare's most richly endowed monastic house was the last to be suppressed under the auspices of the commissioners. The Augustinian priory of Connall was situated beyond the Pale rampart in the central plain of the county. The monastery and its possessions were immensely valuable, its total value in 1540 being recorded as £168 20*s*.[114] Apart from its wealth, Connall was an attractive concern as it enjoyed a reputation for being a loyal English stronghold, which it had struggled to maintain down to the late-1530s. Twice in the

---

111 *Extents Ir. mon. possessions*, pp 163-4.   **112** *Fiants Ire., Hen. VIII*, no. 519; Bradshaw, *Dissolution of religious orders*, p. 123.   **113** Gwynn and Hadcock, *Medieval religious houses: Ireland*, p. 290.   **114** *Extents Ir. mon. possessions*, p. 162.

course of the fifteenth century the priory had been subjected to vicious attacks by neighbouring Gaelic septs. In 1406, the prior was described in Marlborough's chronicles as having 'fought valiantly and vanquished 200 of the Irish that were well armed, slaying some of them and chasing others' even though the prior had only twenty Englishmen to fight on his behalf.[115] The second raid in 1458 appears to have been considerably more destructive as on this occasion, the priory was entirely wasted by the Gaelic forces.[116] In 1476, the priory was styled 'one of the principal keys of the county of Kildare'. The strategic value of the prior of this monastery in working as a negotiator on behalf of the Dublin administration is evident in Walter Wellesley's role as an intermediary in the kidnapping of Vice-deputy Richard Nugent, baron of Delvin by O'Connor Faly in May 1528. Delvin was abducted when, contrary to Archbishop Inge's advice, he refused to pay O'Connor the 'wages', or black-rent, which he and his predecessors had traditionally received. As soon as news of his capture broke, members of the Dublin government sent the prior of Connall, 'a lord of parliament, wise and expert in such causes' to engage in negotiations with O'Connor. Because his house was located beyond the bounds of the maghery, the prior of Connall was regarded as a valuable ally for the Dublin administration in its dealings with troublesome Gaelic lords.

Since the establishment of the commission for the suppression of monastic houses in May 1537, Walter Wellesley, bishop of Kildare and prior of Connall, like the superior of the Augustinian house in Mullingar, could see that the writing was on the wall for the future of Connall Priory. Wellesley, an 'indefatigable court runner', pursed his suit for the preservation of the priory from suppression down to May 1539 when he canvassed both the duke of Norfolk and Thomas Cromwell.[117] He requested that the royal secretary 'aid and strengthen' him in his efforts to maintain possession of the priory which was proving difficult since it lay 'wholly ... in the [territory of the] wild Irish amongst the king's rank rebellers'. Wellesley further emphasised the loyalty of his monks, stating that no brother was elected 'unless he be of a very English nation; in consideration whereof the wild Irish rebellers doth daily ensue all their extremities for the impoverishing of the said monastery'.[118] Lord Deputy Leonard Grey and the Irish council also supported Wellesley's suit and addressed a petition to the king, requesting that the Connall Priory along with five other monasteries be exempted from closure on the grounds of their service to the local community and to the crown.[119]

115 Fitzgerald, 'Great Connall Abbey', p. 308. 116 Ibid.; Archdall, *Mon. Hib.*, ii, p. 263. 117 Walter [Wellesley], bishop of Kildare, to Cromwell, 24 May 1539 (*Cal. Carew MSS, 1515-74*, p. 151; *L. & P. Hen. VIII*, xiv, no. 970). 118 Ibid. 119 Lord deputy and council to Cromwell,

In spite of this impressive representation by the prior and some of the most influential figures in the Dublin administration, the monastery was suppressed on 23 April 1541. Robert Wellesley, Walter's kinsman and the last prior, surrendered the house to the crown with the proviso of a grant of a yearly pension of £13 6s. 8d. issuing out of the rectories of Rathernan and others, and a lease of the vicarage of Bodenstown.[120] The size of his pension and those granted to the monks of the house, a total of £21, also testifies to the unique wealth of the priory.[121] This is particularly evident when the prior's pension is set alongside the sum of £9 yearly granted to the prior of the dissolved Hospital of St John the Baptist in Naas or the £4 annually provided for the abbess of the dissolved nunnery at Graney. Not surprisingly, therefore, the priory and its possessions was a much sought-after prize which was granted to Gerald Sutton of Castletown in Kildrought.[122] During the 1560s it passed to Edward Randolf, who was at that time one of the administration's senior military captains, in reversion to Sir Edward Butler. In 1566 Sir Nicholas White, master of the rolls and later a committed Old English reformer, secured possession of the property, which was in turn acquired by Sir Edmund Butler.[123]

The precise date of the dissolution of the Cistercian abbey at Monasterevin is not recorded. It appears to have occurred well after the suppression commission had wound up as its activities in the early 1540s, as it was only in October 1549 that Hugh Dempsey, the last prior, was granted a pension of £15.[124] Like the house at Graney and Baltinglass Abbey, the monastery at Monasterevin proved a valuable acquisition for the administration's extension of its jurisdiction into the western extremes of Kildare and beyond over the course of the sixteenth century. The abbot of Monasterevin held a seat as a baron in parliament and in the extent recorded upon its dissolution, the abbey's farm was valued at £20 13s. 4d.[125] Like Connall Priory, Graney Nunnery and the Dominican priory in Athy, Monasterevin Abbey was frequently subjected to attacks by Gaelic septs. In 1427, the house was almost completely despoiled of all its goods.[126]

21 May 1539 (*S.P. Hen. VIII*, iii, p. 130; *L.& P. Hen. VIII*, xiv, no. 1005). **120** Robert Wellesley is thought to have been the son of Garret Wellesley of Dangan. *Fiants Ire., Hen. VIII*, no. 147; Gwynn and Hadcock, *Medieval religious houses: Ireland*, p. 177; Bradshaw, *Dissolution of religious orders*, pp 120-1. **121** *Extents Ir. mon. possessions*, p. 163. **122** *Fiants Ire., Edw. VI*, no. 405. **123** *Fiants Ire., Hen. VIII*, no. 1131; Archdall, *Mon. Hib.*, ii, p. 321; *Cal. pat. rolls, Ire., Hen. VIII-Eliz.*, p. 498; Gwynn and Hadcock, *Medieval religious houses: Ireland*, p. 177. **124** *Fiants Ire., Edw. VI*, no. 387; Fitzgerald, 'The proprietors of the manor of Monasterevin', p. 80. **125** Ware, *Antiquities*, p. 79; *Liber mun. pub. Hib.*, pt v, p. 243; Gwynn and Hadcock, *Medieval religious houses: Ireland*, p. 142; *Extents Ir. mon. possessions*, p. 177. **126** Gwynn and Hadcock, *Medieval religious houses: Ireland*, p. 142.

In the early 1520s, the abbot of Monasterevin Abbey served as a strategic ally of the earl of Kildare in orchestrating his show of indispensability through complicity with neighbouring Gaelic septs. At Easter 1520, the abbot named Heke, brought a letter to the Gaelic chief, O'Carroll, which had been entrusted to him by the earl who was then detained at court. In the letter, Kildare allegedly instructed O'Carroll to 'keep the peace to Englishmen, till an English deputy come there, and when an English deputy shall come thither, do your best to make war upon Englishmen there, except such as be towards me, whom you know well yourself'.[127] The abbot was suspected by Surrey of having written the letter which was in Irish but O'Carroll's brother's confession removed this suspicion as the letter bore the earl of Kildare's seal. By virtue of its borderline location, Monastervin Abbey was therefore recognised firstly by the earl of Kildare and later by the Dublin administration as a valuable strategic outpost facing onto O'Carroll and O'Connor countries which could serve their respective interests.

Following its suppression, the abbey, like the priory of Mullingar, became the preserve of successive lord deputies. In addition, the hay, oats, and all other produce yielded by the abbey's lands were reserved for provisioning the deputy's household.[128] Apparently very soon after its suppression, building operations and structural improvements in the precincts of the abbey were commenced by the Dublin administration. The government clearly underestimated the scale of the restoration since in June, Thomas Alen (brother of Sir John, lord chancellor), coordinator of the project, informed the deputy, Sir Edward Bellingham, that the number of carts and labourers for the work on the site was insufficient. In addition to the fifteen carts and 120 labourers already employed, Alen required a further thirty carts and sixty labourers to complete the work, which he envisaged would take another six weeks.[129]

In March 1551, a lease of the manor of Monasterevin was granted to Captain Francis Agard of Grangegorman in Dublin for a term of twenty-one years. This lease stipulated that any lord deputy who might be in the vicinity in the service of the crown should have the use of the house and ought to be provided with victuals and supplies for himself and his retinue. In March 1554, Mary I and her husband Philip, issued the lord deputy, Sir Thomas Radcliffe,

---

127 'Confession of Donogh O'Carroll', 1520 (*S.P. Hen. VIII*, ii, p. 45). 128 Fitzgerald, 'The proprietors of the manor of Monasterevin', p. 80. Fitzgerald's account challenges those of Archdall and Harris who claim that the abbey and its possessions were granted to George Audley who assigned them to Sir Adam, Viscount Loftus of Ely. In the light of its later history, Fitzgerald's interpretation appears the more accurate. See also *Extents Ir. mon. possessions*, p. 286. 129 Thomas Alen to Lord Deputy Bellingham, 21 June 1549 (*Cal. S.P. Ire., 1509-73*, p. 104).

earl of Sussex, with instructions that Monasterevin manor 'shall always be and remain to the use of the ... deputy at such times as it shall like him to resort unto the same, either for his pleasure and recreation, or for defence of the [neighbouring Gaelic] countries, punishment of malefactors, or ministration of justice.[130] This arrangement survived down to at least the 1590s as, in 1596, Elizabeth I confirmed the deputy's right to enjoy the use of the house and its stable 'whenever he chose to lie there'.[131] The dissolved abbey at Monasterevin, like many of the other houses lying in the marches of Kildare, proved a valuable strategic acquisition for the Dublin administration. While the real cost of repairs to the manor was undoubtedly higher than originally envisaged by government officials, it was cheaper than the cost of constructing an entirely new defence outpost. Monasterevin Abbey thus became one of the 'goodly garrisons already built' bordering on O'Connor territory which John Alen had suggested in a general way might be converted for strategic purposes.

VI

While the dissolution of the monasteries had a cataclysmic impact on late medieval monasticism and although clerics such as Richard Weston and Walter Wellesley were to the fore in campaigning for individual houses to be exempted from suppression, in the event, there was no resistance to the suppression commissioners in Kildare for a combination of reasons. Firstly, as we have seen, several houses, particularly in the march areas, were already dissolved or only fit for dissolution. Timolin Nunnery had already been suppressed in 1530 and its property was largely overrun by the O'Mores; it had no personnel to whom pensions were owed or who had to be re-located. Moreover the occupant of the property, Edmund Eustace, was insufficiently influential to pose a serious challenge to those who were invested with the dissolved nunnery's property. In Cloncurry, there was no house and therefore no religious. All of the buildings belonging to the Dominican house of Friars Preachers in Athy were burned by the O'Mores, and the Franciscan friary and Carmelite priory in Kildare town were left with only their churches and fragments of their buildings as a result of raids by O'Connor. Likewise, St John's Hospital in Castledermot was uninhabited and ruinous in 1540 having 'serveth of no purpose' since 1536. Given the decrepit state of their houses, the wasted condition of their lands and the conse-

130 'Instructions given by the king and queen to the earl of Sussex', 20 Mar. 1557 (*Cal. Carew MSS, 1515-74*, pp 272-3); Fitzgerald, 'The house and demesne of Monasterevin', p. 256. 131 *Cal. pat. rolls, Ire., Hen. VIII- Eliz.*, p. 429.

quent reduction in their income, the prospects for the ordinary religious of these houses in 1540 were bleak. Since their valuations tended to be very modest, in the case of the Carmelite priory in Kildare town as little as 8*s.*, it is unlikely that they received pensions of any substance, if indeed at all. In Athy, Castledermot and Kildare town, these were generally entrusted to local worthies, some of whom already held property from the monasteries prior to their dissolution. This helped to minimise the amount of disruption caused by the 'transfer' of monastic holdings from religious to secular hands.

In general, the superiors of the county's large houses eventually secured very favourable terms for themselves and in some cases, their communities, which undoubtedly blunted their potential resistance to the closure of their houses. Pensions granted to these heads of houses ranged from £16 and £15 given to Walinton, last preceptor of Tully and sub-prior of Kilmainham and Hugh Dempsey, last prior of Monasterevin Abbey respectively, to £4 donated to the late prioress of Graney. In other instances, pensions were accompanied by additional special terms. Richard Weston, late prior of St Wolstan's, was, as we have seen, to be provided with comfortable lodgings, food, fuel and a constant income at his dissolved house for the duration of his life. The abbot of Baltinglass was granted a pension of £10 which he was to hold until such time as he might be promoted to a benefice worth twenty marks. Robert Wellesley, the last prior of Connall, only surrendered his house having secured the promise of a grant of a yearly pension of £13 6*s.* 8*d.* and a lease of a vicarage. In the cases of Kildare's largest monastic houses, therefore, potential resistance to suppression was preempted and dissipated by the generosity of the pensions and the special terms of accommodation arranged for their superiors.

Although it is difficult to estimate the impact of the dissolution of these houses on their rank and file religious, Bradshaw's contention that the monks were 'not cast off so much as phased out' appears to have some application in the context of Kildare and explains the lack of any active resistance to the suppression campaign. In several instances when substantial houses were immediately suppressed, for example the Augustinian Hospital of St John's in Naas or the priory at Connall, members of their communities were provided with pensions. In Naas, one friar received 40*s.* while in Connall, two monks received pensions of 40*s.*, two received 26*s.* 8*d.* and three others received 20*s.* each.[132] There is anecdotal evidence to suggest that some of the redundant religious from Kildare houses secured benefices for themselves soon after the suppression of their houses. Hugh Doyne, one of those who had received a pension of 40*s.* following the closure of Connall Priory, was presented by the

132 *Fiants Ire., Hen. VIII*, no. 148.

king to the perpetual vicarage of St Fintan in the diocese of Leighlin in August 1541 and he duly surrendered his pension.[133] In exercising the crown's right of presentation to vicarages and rectories in Kildare in the Henrician era, the king generally only appointed a candidate to a benefice when it had fallen vacant owing to the death or retirement of the previous incumbent.[134] In the absence of any solid evidence concerning the post-dissolution fate of religious from Kildare houses, it can only be presumed that they gradually disappeared by a similar process of attrition.

Several Kildare communities, notably those at New Abbey, Clane, and Monasterevin appear to have been afforded an unofficial stay of execution which lasted at least down to the end of Henry's reign. This protracted period of adjustment and, in the case of New Abbey, the continued patronage of Viscount Baltinglass, necessarily blunted the impact of suppression on their religious. The attempts mounted by members of the dissolved house at New Abbey to re-open their monastery under the Marian regime prove that peaceful acquiescence to the suppression campaign in 1539-41 did not denote acceptance of their fate. In general, however, the fate of the property of Kildare's dissolved mendicant houses conformed to the wider trend whereby new owners firmly entrenched themselves on those sites, precluding the possibility of a general return of the disbanded friars to their old houses. In this way, the Alens, Suttons, Aylmers and Eustaces in particular, all of whom were members of the most politically dynamic elements in county society, made permanent the expropriation of monastic property effected by the suppression commissioners in 1539-40.

There is no evidence to suggest active resistance to the suppression of the monasteries from members of the laity in Kildare. For the peasants who worked the land of these monastic properties, the changeover in ownership if indeed that even occurred would have had a negligible impact on their lives. The dissolution of Connall Priory may have caused the greatest upset to the laity in its vicinity since its religious were said to have educated 'both gentlemen['s] children and others'.[135] However, this was the only house in Kildare for which Lord Leonard Grey was prepared to make a case for exemption from suppression. As in the case of the priories in Aghmacart in Leix, Cahir and Fethard in Tipperary, those of Connall Priory and Baltinglass Abbey served as parochial churches and there are no reports to suggest that these churches were destroyed or that this practice ceased at the time of the dissolu-

---

133 *Cal. pat. rolls, Ire., Hen. VIII-Eliz.*, p. 66.   **134** Ibid., pp 15, 26, 71, 73, 92, 118, 145.   **135** The lord deputy and council to Cromwell, 21 May 1539 (*S.P. Hen. VIII*, iii, p. 130; *L. & P. Hen. VIII*, xiv, no. 1005).

tion campaign.[136] However, it is not possible to ascertain whether they continued to serve as parochial churches following the impropriation of the dissolved monastic property, though it is highly probable that they did. It is likely that the local people continued to resort to the monasteries' cemeteries as burial places since this was certainly the case with members of the gentry and nobility of Kildare throughout the sixteenth century. G.E. Hamilton estimated that approximately seventy per cent of county Kildare's parish rectories were appropriated to monastic houses both within and outside of the county.[137] Following the suppression of the monasteries, the king assumed the right of presentation to virtually all of these benefices; only in isolated cases were laymen or local clergy invested with advowson rights.[138] The dearth of source material precludes any decisive conclusions being drawn regarding the impact of the suppression of the monasteries on the lower strata of the laity of Kildare. What little evidence there is suggests that the interchange between the monastic communities and the local people was limited or, in the cases of Timolin, Cloncurry, and St John's Hospital in Castledermot, non-existent. Besides, the gentry of Kildare were the only figures with the potential to stage opposition to the monastic suppressions. Given their vested financial interest in the county's monastic properties and their hopes for acquisition of additional holdings, these gentlemen were unlikely to resist a favourable tide of change.

VII

The Geraldine revolt served to highlight zones of weakness in the defence structures of the marches of the Pale. Monasteries situated on the borders but also in the towns of Louth, Meath and Dublin all had parcels of their lands wasted by the O'Hanlons, the O'Neills, the McGwynns, the O'Hales, the MacGeoghegans, the O'Connors, the O'Mores, the O'Tooles and the Kavanaghs.[139] Given that it had been the scene for the rebellion and subsequent Gaelic raids, what remained of county Kildare's marchland defences necessitated particularly urgent attention. As this survey has illustrated, all three stages of the campaign for the suppression of the county's monastic houses were clearly guided by an overriding concern to capitalise on the removal of the earls of Kildare by gaining maximum political capital from the distribution

---

136 *Extents Ir. mon. possessions*, pp 126, 157, 329, 331, 333. **137** G.E. Hamilton, 'The names of the baronies and parishes in County Kildare', in *Kildare Arch. Soc. Jn.*, viii (1915-17); ix (1918-21), p. 252. **138** See *Extents Ir. mon. possessions*, pp 43, 91. **139** Ibid., pp 63, 71, 95, 97- 98, 110-12, 216, 220, 231, 235, 237, 251, 309.

of the dissolved properties. The monasteries at Graney, Baltinglass, Timolin, Monasterevin, New Abbey, Athy and Castledermot were earmarked as valuable strategic outposts to be acquired by the Dublin administration. Consequently, each was entrusted to hand-picked officials, soldiers or local gentlemen with a view to establishing more effective royal control on the fringes of the maghery and in the marches of the Pale.

In contrast with the monasteries in outlying regions of county Kildare, there was little need to convert either St Wolstan's Priory in Celbridge, Cloncurry Friary or houses in Naas and Clane into defence outposts for several reasons. The town of Naas already had defence structures in place. The earls of Kildare had been removed from their base in Maynooth for the time being and their former supporters were said to have been in a very subdued state. Thomas Eustace was based at Kilcullen, just south of Naas. David Sutton was based in Tully, due southwest of Naas, and both had been entrusted with supervising defence in their respective areas. Apart from Sir Thomas Luttrell, it was members of the Alen, Aylmer, and Sutton families in particular who were amongst the main beneficiaries in the distribution of the dissolved monastic properties in Naas which in all cases served to significantly consolidate their foothold in the northeast. The distribution of these monastic properties within the bounds of the maghery was therefore determined by speculative and political concerns rather than purely urgent strategic considerations. The investing of dissolved monastic possessions in Naas and Clane to Sir Thomas Luttrell who resided in Dublin illustrates the government's confidence in the security of both. The whole gamut of categories of recipients of dissolved monastic properties – noblemen, lord deputies, 'New English' Pale administrators, native Pale administrators, county gentry, soldiers, and local farmers – was represented among the beneficiaries of the spoils of Kildare's houses. Coming as it did in the immediate wake of the Kildare revolt, the suppression of the county's monasteries was successfully tailored to facilitate the extension of the king's writ throughout and beyond the four English shires. As such it helped to lay the foundations for the advance of St Leger's political programme for establishing order in Leinster in the 1540s.

Sir Patrick Finglas was the first Palesman to introduce the notion of colonization in the context of the distribution of Ireland's dissolved monastic properties. In 1534 he proposed that a number of monasteries on the borders of the territory of the MacMurroughs in Leinster should be suppressed and their lands given to young 'lords and gents out of England' who would infiltrate the Gaelic-occupied outlying districts of the Pale marches.[140] As this study has

140 Bradshaw, *Dissolution of religious orders*, p. 44.

shown, there was only a very slight colonial dimension to the distribution of Kildare's monastic lands as defined by Finglas. A handful of Englishmen came to Kildare in the 1530s and 1540s, namely Sir John Alen, the St Legers, Lord Leonard Grey, and four soldiers, namely Francis Cosby, Francis Herbert, Captain Robert Browne and Captain Henry Colley. Of these only Alen, Cosby, Herbert, and Colley can definitely be said to have settled permanently in Kildare, joining the ranks of the gentry. However, each of these English-born settlers owed their establishment in the county to their receipt of monastic property, or confiscated land belonging to the Kildares or their supporters, or both, and as such they based themselves in areas which were already subject to some degree of English control. While Cosby and Herbert were actively involved in efforts to plant Leix and Offaly in the mid-1550s and again in the 1560s, Oliver Sutton was the only Kildare gentleman personally involved in an attempted colonization of part of the O'Dempseys' territory in Leix in 1548.

In general it was lesser aristocratic and gentry families in Kildare who acquired both monastic property and Geraldine estates and those of their supporters. Thus St Leger sought to establish loyal and strong English landowners and soldiers such as Eustace, Pelles, and Bermingham along the borders of the Leinster septs in the hope that they would exert a restraining influence on lawlessness while at the same time acting as a leaven of loyalty. The effectiveness of this policy was most evident in the case of Sir William Bermingham who kept the neighbouring O'Connor clan under close surveillance. It was not until after the plantation of Leix and Offaly in the mid-1550s that Kildare's borders with neighbouring Gaelic countries were colonised to a significant degree by an influx of English-born soldier-settlers.[141]

---

141 Carey, *Surviving the Tudors.*

4

The Impact of the Distribution of Kildare's Monastic Properties on the County's Lesser Aristocracy and Gentry, 1536–47

The gentlemen of the county of Kildare are the most sorriest afraid men in the world; for they think, that they shall be taken, one after another of them, as Sir James Fitzgerald was, and his brethren.

Francis Herbert to Cromwell, 21 Mar. 1536
(*S.P. Hen. VIII*, ii, p. 308).

Behind the anonymity of recurring references to 'the gentlemen' of Kildare in contemporary reports, there existed a strong comital aristocracy and landed gentry comprised of long established Anglo-Norman and closely interrelated families. The earls of Kildare had to contend with approximately twenty lesser aristocratic and gentry families in exercising their lordship over Kildare. These and the upper echelons of Kildare's gentry society were comprised of the Fitzgeralds, and the long-standing comital families of Eustace, Saint Michael, barons of Rheban, the Wellesleys, barons of Norragh, and the Aylmers, Wogans, Suttons and the Berminghams of Carbury. The Kerdiffs, Sherlocks, Longs, Creffs, Trotts, Wales, Penkistons, and Flatisburys were the principal members of the humbler ranks of the county gentry. During the reigns of Richard III and Henry VII, and in the years following 1534, at least a dozen families were of sufficient standing to serve as county sheriff. Five other families supplied escheators and among these were the Synnaghs of Oldtown, the Eustaces of Mullaghcash and the Birts of Donavale.

Apart from the fluctuations in the political fortunes of the house of Kildare, it was these lesser aristocratic and gentry families who provided Kildare's representatives in the lordship's parliament. They oversaw the administration of justice at local level and by virtue of owning large estates in the marches, they fulfilled a vital role in providing defence against Gaelic raids throughout the fifteenth and sixteenth centuries, thereby supplementing the chain of Geraldine fortifications. In 1496, for example, a commission for erecting ditches and dikes in the Kildare marches was directed to Edmund Lane, bishop of Kildare, the prior of Connall, Richard Eustace of Kilgone, Thomas Eustace, the sovereign of Naas and Bartholomew Aylmer, sheriff of Kildare. It was from the ranks of these families that many of the county's most influential religious were drawn, notably Edmund Lane and Walter Wellesley, bishops of Kildare, and Elizabeth Wale, prioress of Graney nunnery. Although the earls of Kildare may have been jealous of the amount of autonomy enjoyed by the gentry, they were clearly aware that they could not afford to alienate them. This is evidenced by the ninth earl's custom of giving gifts of horses to heads of the county's families, some of whom had declined in importance by the early sixteenth century, notably the Penkistons and the Creffs. Of course Kildare also had a practical motive in doing so: those horses were intended to serve in the defence of the county's marches.[1]

In this section attention will be focused on the composition of Kildare's aristocratic and gentry society in the pre-Reformation and early Reformation period. The impact of the closure of the county's monastic houses on the county's peers and gentlemen will be assessed and it will be shown that a significant change occurred in the composition of both strata of county society. Kildare's gentry became less homogeneous as a result of the arrival and social ascent of individuals such as John Alen, Francis Herbert and Martin Pelles, each of whom owed their initial establishment as gentry, resident in Kildare, exclusively to their receipt of dissolved monastic properties. This admission of elevated soldiers and government officials into the ranks of the county gentry constituted the most significant long-term social impact of the Reformation in Kildare from the late 1530s onwards. The distribution of parcels of the confiscated estates of the Kildares and their supporters will also be discussed in order to provide a fuller insight into the dynamics of change which worked in favour of the advancement of certain members of the county's aristocracy and gentry during this period.

I

Apart from the immediate family of the earls of Kildare, seated at Maynooth, there existed an intricate network of collateral branches of the Fitzgerald family throughout county Kildare. In the sixteenth century, these cadet branches resided at Kildare, Kilkea, Rathangan, Allen, Ballyshannon, Belan, Birtown, Blackhall near Clane, Duneany, Glassealy, Kilrush, Grangemellon, Lackagh, Mullaghmoyne, Narraghbeg, Osbertstown, Puncher's Grange, Timahoe, Dullardstown, Walterstown and Drinanstown, Ballymore, Killeigh and

---

1 Michael Devitt, 'Old proprietors in Straffan and Irishtown', in *Kildare Arch. Soc. Jn.*, x (1922-8), pp 272-300; Ellis, *Tudor frontiers and noble power*, pp 140-1.

Beloagh, Cloncurry, Leixlip and Castletown in Kildrought.[2] The extended Fitzgerald family thus had a foothold in each quarter of the county. In several cases their estates lay in areas which had been marchlands prior to the English recovery in the late fifteenth century. Thomas Fitzmaurice Fitzgerald, the ninth earl's cousin, held 1,700 acres of land in the county, his most important possessions being the manors of Kildare and Kilkea in central and southern Kildare. Gerald, the ninth earl, clearly regarded Fitzmaurice as a valuable ally as in 1526 he conferred the captainship of Old Ross and the administration of his Wexford estates on Fitzmaurice, as well as granting him custody of the duke of Norfolk's properties in the region.

James Fitzgerald of Osbertstown in northeast Kildare was also influential: he held a lease of the manor of Morrett from the ninth earl. He was entrusted with custody of Lea and Morett rent-free in return for providing defence on the western frontier of Kildare in the aftermath of the 1534-5 rebellion which testifies to his proven loyalty and already considerable resources. Moreover, the eighth earl pursued a deliberate policy of entrusting many of the Leinster marchlands which he recovered from Gaelic neighbours to the charge of his younger brothers. To Oliver he granted land in Westmeath and Annaly and he granted the manors of Powerscourt, Fassaghroe and Crevagh along with other land in Fercullen to Richard. James appears to have received an earlier grant of the manors of Hollywood and Three Castles and other lands in the surrounding districts and Kildare's other brother, John, is also likely to have been catered for in this regard.

Among the strongest of these collateral branches in the late fifteenth and early sixteenth centuries were the Fitzgeralds of Lackagh, situated due west of Kildare town, bordering on O'Connor country. The head of this branch in the late fifteenth century was Sir Thomas Fitzgerald, son of the seventh earl of Kildare, and he was one of the richest gentlemen in the lordship, enjoying an annual income of 400 marks from land which he owned in Ireland and England.[3] He played a prominent role in the political life of the lordship in the 1480s, being appointed lord chancellor of Ireland in 1484 for the duration of his life. Given the resources and calibre of these cadet branches, Steven Ellis has observed that the ninth earl's relatives were formidable marchers in their own right and therefore needed an overlord of Kildare's standing and influence to control them.[4] After Maynooth, the most lucrative of all of the

---

2 *Crown surveys*, pp 146, 150, 151, 152, 206, 260, 334, 351; Walter Fitzgerald, 'The principal gentry of the county of Kildare in the year 1600', in *Kildare Arch. Soc. Jn.*, iii (1899-1902), p. 120 (hereafter Fitzgerald, 'The principal gentry'). 3 Ellis, *Reform and revival*, p. 8. 4 Ellis, *Tudor frontiers and noble power*, p. 134.

Geraldine properties was the Leixlip estate which was entailed to the eighth earl's sons by his second wife, Elizabeth St John. James Fitzgerald of Leixlip was imprisoned and attainted on grounds of complicity in the revolt of 1534-5 and was executed in 1537 along with his brothers and his nephew, Thomas.

In addition to being able to harness the independent resources of his kinsmen, the earl of Kildare's extended family provided him with a constant retinue of deputies and military captains. Maurice Fitzgerald of Lackagh was appointed justice by his kinsman, Gerald, ninth earl of Kildare, when the earl was summoned to court in 1519.[5] Sir Gerald Shanesson, who was based in Cloncurry in the north of the county, served as one of the ninth earl's chief advisers.[6] Gerald's brother, Thomas of Leixlip, and his son, Thomas, Lord Offaly, also deputised for the earl during his enforced absences in the late 1520s and early 1530s. While the ninth earl was frequently faced with a degree of opposition from cadet branches upon his return from detention at the court in the 1520s and early 1530s, the Leinster Geraldines generally displayed a striking cohesion. For example, during Kildare's detention at court and following his dismissal from the governorship in 1520, his relatives were reported to be virtually uncontrollable and resistance was such that no government subsidy could be levied in the county. During his term of office as lord deputy (1522), the earl of Ormond complained that Kildare's kinsmen would do nothing for the king's service, not even defend their own county, and he requested Kildare's return in order that he might resolve their disputes.

In the late 1520s the ninth earl's two brothers, James and Thomas, posed serious problems for the Dublin administration. However Cardinal Wolsey, realizing the potential influence of the wealthy Leixlip branch, eventually succeeded in isolating both men from Gerald in the late 1520s and early 1530s to the extent that Henry VIII could rely on occasionally securing the support of that branch against the earl. Propitious marital alliances of the eighth and ninth earls also served to bolster the Geraldine infiltration not only of Kildare gentry society but also of Gaelic Ireland. Apart from intermarriage within the extended family, the Fitzgeralds were also married into the Eustace, Aylmer and Wogan families. Beyond Kildare, their alliances were with the O'Connors, the O'Ferralls, the Shanes of Ballymore, the Hopes and the Tyrrells from modern county Westmeath, as well as with the Darcys, the Keatings, the Walshes of Moyvalley and the Delahides.[7]

5 See Walter Fitzgerald, 'The Fitzgeralds of Lackagh', in *Kildare Arch. Soc. Jn.*, i (1891-95), pp 245-64; Ellis, *Tudor frontiers and noble power*, p. 132; Ellis, *Tudor Ireland*, p. 327. 6 Ellis, *Tudor frontiers and noble power*, p. 134. 7 Nicholls, 'The Geraldines of Allen', in *The Irish Genealogist*, iv, nos 2-3 (1969-70), pp 93-109, 194-200; idem, 'The descendants of Oliver Fitzgeralds of Belagh', in *The Irish Genealogist*, iv (1968-73), pp 2-9.

While the execution of five senior members of the family and the capture of three other had a predictably deleterious effect on the Geraldine hold in the county, not all of those convicted had participated in, or indeed even supported, the rebellion. Silken Thomas's uncles, Sir James, Walter and Richard Fitzgerald, did not take part in the revolt but were nevertheless taken prisoner while attending a banquet at Kilmainham and were subsequently executed. The other leading members of the family, Oliver and John, were also apprehended before they had even learned of their brothers' capture.[8] Some of the properties of the earls and of the senior collateral branches passed to the gentry. The manors of Leixlip, Donadea, Kilcock, and Kilkea all passed to local gentlemen, to Lord Leonard Grey and to the earl of Ormond.[9] Individuals including Walter Peppard of Dublin, Francis Cosby, John Alen of Alenscourt and Rayney Bell, a soldier in the king's retinue, received leases to sections of the former Kildare estate during the mid-1540s.[10]

Likewise Francis Herbert, a young gallant who came to Ireland with Lord Leonard Grey's army, received a grant of the Coghlanstown estate of Christopher Eustace who was attainted and executed for his involvement in the Geraldine rebellion. He and his family subsequently became established as members of the county gentry.[11] That said, however, there is little evidence to suggest that a wholesale transfer of ownership or occupation of their property during the Henrician period followed the execution of Kildare and his uncles. Following their attainder, both Richard's and Walter's property was taken into the king's hands. This, combined with the sheer size·and geographical dispersal of the cadet branches of the family, served to cushion the impact of the removal of Kildare and his uncles on county society to a significant extent. The suppression of the shire's monastic houses yielded such paltry dividends to the family as to have a negligible impact on their standing.

Only one member of the extended Fitzgerald family, namely Sir Gerald Fitzgerald of Croyboy in modern Westmeath, both actively participated in and benefited from the suppression of monastic houses in his locality.[12] Otherwise, only two members of the family were involved in the compilation of the monastic extents, namely Thomas Fitzgarret of Dullardstown and James Fitzgarret of Grangemellon in south Kildare, both of whom presided as extent

8 'The copy of the curse given Thomas Fitzgerald and others, for killing of the archbishop of Dublin', 1534 (*S.P. Hen. VIII*, ii, pp 217-19); Hen. VIII to Skeffington, 1535 (*S.P. Hen. VIII*, ii, p. 291; *L. & P. Hen. VIII*, ix, no. 731); *S.P. Hen. VIII*, ii, p. 293 n.; Fitzgerald, *The earls of Kildare*, p. 173. 9 Carey, *Surviving the Tudors*. 10 *Fiants Ire., Hen. VIII*, nos 464, 478, 515. See also Carey, *Surviving the Tudors*. 11 *Fiants Ire., Hen. VIII*, no. 439; Fitzgerald, 'The principal gentry', p. 120; Bradshaw, *Dissolution of religious orders*, pp 56-7. 12 *Extents Ir. mon. possessions*, pp 37, 261, 269, 281f., 287, 290-3, 295-8.

jurors at Kilkea in November 1540.[13] The Fitzgeralds therefore gained little directly from the distribution of the county's monastic properties. However, as a result of their extensive marital connections, the collateral branches indirectly came into possession of former monastic properties which were granted to such families as the Aylmers and the Eustaces.

In spite of the fall of their principal house of Maynooth, the confiscation of the earl's extensive manors and their exclusion from receipt of dissolved monastic properties, the extended Fitzgerald family, on the strength of their size and their already substantial estates, remained by far the most powerful landed family in sixteenth-century Kildare. This is evidenced by the fact that throughout the sixteenth century, various members of the extended family participated at the highest level in county judicial administration. In 1536 James Fitzgerald of Osberstown was high sheriff of Kildare and in 1541 James Fitzgerald of Ballyshannon held the post. No member of the family appears to have held either position until after the restoration of Gerald, the eleventh earl, in 1554; in the interim, the office of high sheriff was held by members of old stock county gentry, chiefly the Wogans, Aylmers, Eustaces and Suttons.

After 1554, however, the pattern of Fitzgerald participation resumed; in 1558, Redmund Fitzgerald of Rathangan was sheriff and four years later, Sir Maurice Fitzgerald, head of the Lackagh branch, held the post. Moreover, on at least twelve further occasions in the second half of the sixteenth century various members of the Fitzgerald family filled the position of county sheriff, which testifies to their recovery from and survival of the dynastic and monastic upheavals of the 1530s.[14]

The Eustace family ranked second in size and importance in county Kildare during this period. Their association with Kildare had originated in the early fourteenth century when Castlemartin Castle, located on a meander of the river Liffey, west of Kilcullen, became the family's principal seat.[15] By the early sixteenth century the extended family estates stretched from Confey in the extreme northeast of Kildare, beyond the county boundary in the east and southeast, and incorporated an extensive area of the south of the county ranging from the foothills of the Dublin and Wicklow mountains in the east to the town of Athy in the extreme southwest. Within these parameters, one triangular area bounded by Naas, Ballymore Eustace and Old Kilcullen constituted an almost exclusively Eustace-owned estate referred to as 'Criche-Eustace' or 'Cry-Eustace'.

---

13 Ibid., pp 23, 61, 172. 14 John Ribton Garstin, 'The high sheriffs of the County Kildare', in *Kildare Arch. Soc. Jn.*, ii (1896-9), pp 259-60. 15 Tickell, 'Eustace family', pp 270-87, 307-41, 364-413.

In contrast with other long-established Kildare families such as the Aylmers, the Eustaces had already attained an ascendant position in the fifteenth century, being to the forefront in the governance both of Kildare and of the lordship. Several family members held the positions of lord chancellor, keeper of the rolls, baron of the exchequer, lord treasurer and on occasion, the lord deputyship during the fifteenth century. Despite the conspicuous lapse in their appointment to such senior governmental posts in the sixteenth century, the Eustaces continued to play a very influential role in county affairs, through securing regular appointment to the offices of high sheriff and sheriff of the county and also contableships of marchland castles such as Kilkea in the southwest and Ballymore Eustace. Furthermore, they exercised influence through their membership of parliament and in their service as county jurors.[16]

Like the cadet branches of the Fitzgerald family, the Eustaces played a vital role in the provision of defence along the western boundary of the maghery of the Pale. Their strategically located castles stretching from Confey to Donadea, Clongowes Wood, Blackhall, Kilashee, Mullaghcash, Castlemartin, Harristown, Blackrath, Colbinstown and Ballymore Eustace, formed a buffer against raids by the O'Connors, the O'Dempseys and the O'Tooles. In addition, they were members of the Fraternity of St George which was founded in 1474: Sir Roland Eustace was a prominent figure in its institution and he held the position of captain and second-in-command to its leader, Thomas, seventh earl of Kildare. Sir Robert Eustace of Ballymore Eustace, was also a founding member of the Brethren of St George.[17] Though this body is regarded as having been too short-lived to have had any real impact in the provision of adequate defence for the English colony, its very creation provides evidence of an independent drive undertaken by local gentlemen and members of the lesser aristocracy with a view to strengthening the defences within their districts.

Sir Roland, like the eighth earl, took steps to strengthen the Pale's inadequate existing defence structures by his construction (or possible renovation) of Harristown Castle which lay just on the Pale boundary between Old Kilcullen and Ballymore Eustace. He also had a castle built in the vicinity of Baltinglass Abbey in west Wicklow. Like their Fitzgerald counterparts, the Eustaces were thus in an ideal position to defend their own estates while providing inexpensive and constant protection for the western and southwestern boundary of the maghery of the Pale.

---

16 County Dublin exchequer inquisitions, Hen. VIII, no. 36 (N.A.I.).   17 Ellis, *Tudor Ireland*, pp 58-9; Lennon, *Sixteenth-century Ireland*, pp 72-3; Ellis, *Tudor frontiers and noble power*, pp 114-15.

Since the fourteenth century, the Eustaces had built up a closely woven network of extended family marriages, in addition to deliberately cultivating advantageous marital connections with other leading Pale families. The most prestigious of these unions were with the Plunkets, barons of Dunsany; the Fitzpatricks, barons of Ossory; Sir Gerald Aylmer, baronet of Donadea; Joan, daughter of James Butler, eighth lord of Dunboyne; and Edmund Butler, second son of the ninth earl of Ormond. The three Viscounts Baltinglass intermarried with the Talbots of Malahide, the Suttons, the Fitzgeralds of Osbertstown and Ballyshannon, the Burnells and the Travers of Monkstown. Apart from these marriages with very prominent Pale aristocracy and gentry, the cadet branches of the Eustace family intermarried with the Fitzgeralds, the Wogans, the Barnewalls, the Delahides, the Flemings and Gaydons and, to a lesser extent, the Archbolds of Timolin, the Wellesleys, barons of Norragh, the Luttrells and the Chevers of Macetown.[18]

As a result of their peripheral location, members of certain collateral branches were more closely related to Gaelic families than the senior branches in northeastern Kildare and in this respect they resembled the extended Fitzgerald family. For example, in the district of Athy, in the south-western marches of Kildare, a member of the Eustace family married Dorothy O'More of Leix in 1542. Eustace's sister, Ann, married one of the O'Tooles of Imail in county Wicklow with whom the Fitzgeralds of Leixlip were also intermarried. Later in the sixteenth century, another Eustace married James MacKadagh O'More who was chief of Leix during the period 1578-84. These unions were clearly strategic, a means whereby the Eustaces could appease those troublesome Gaelic elements whose countries were adjacent to the family estates. Such cases were on the whole exceptional, their alliances as we have seen being almost invariably with the gentry and aristocracy of counties Kildare, Meath, Dublin and the Ormond patrimony.[19]

The range of these connections was further extended by the fact that certain family members married several times, though the Eustaces were by no means unique in this regard. As might be expected, these marriages brought decisive fluctuations in the influence and social standing both of the Eustaces themselves and the families with whom they became allied. Sir Roland, Lord Portlester, married three times, in each case to a partner of established Pale gentry stock. His first wife was Elizabeth Brune and his second marriage was to Joanna, widow of Christopher Plunket, first Lord Killeen. His third wife was Margaret, the widow of John Dowdall and also of Thomas Barnewall.

---

18 See Tickell, 'Eustace family'. **19** Kingston, 'Catholic families of the Pale', pp 236-56, 245-56; Tickell, 'Eustace family'; Fitzgerald, *The earls of Kildare*, p. 79.

Subsequent generations of the family further expanded the family estates by marrying several times. A particularly striking case is that of William Eustace of Castlemartin (*c.*1574-1635) who married four times, giving rise to connections with the Nugents, barons of Delvin, the Cusacks of Lismullen, the St Lawrences, barons of Howth and the family of Black Tom, earl of Ormond.[20]

Female members of the Baron Portlester's family in particular played a decisive role in consolidating and advancing the social standing and influence of their family in the late medieval period, especially since Portlester's two sons had predeceased him. Alison married Gerald, the eighth earl of Kildare, and her sisters married the baron of Skreen, the second baron of Dunsany, Sir Maurice Eustace of Coghlanstown in southeast Kildare, Sir John Plunket of Bewley, county Louth and Sir Walter Delahide of Moyglare in Meath. Moreover, certain branches of the family owed their genesis to propitious marriages: the line of Blackhall, near Punchestown, in northeast Kildare, of whom William was head in 1535, owed its origins to his marriage to an heiress, Catherine Archdeacon.[21]

The Castlemartin branch of the family was in the ascendant during the early fifteenth century. However, it was the Harristown line which assumed dominance from the mid-fifteenth century down to the Baltinglass revolt of 1580 as it was from this branch that the Baron Portlester and three successive Viscounts Baltinglass originated. Unlike other more humble members of the county gentry such as Philip Flatisbury of Clane, who owed his position to the sponsorship of the earls of Kildare, Sir Roland Eustace achieved political prominence prior to, and largely independently of, the Fitzgeralds. By 1454 he had been appointed chief clerk to the king's bench and keeper of the rolls. In that same year he was appointed lord treasurer, a post which he held for thirty-eight years. He was knighted in 1459 and created Baron Portlester by Edward IV three years later. In 1463 he was nominated as lord deputy to the absent viceroy, the duke of Clarence. He held the post of lord chancellor from 1472 to 1480 and again from 1486 to 1492. Portlester's alliance with the earls of Kildare initially hinged upon their shared support for the Yorkist faction. As early as 1467 his association with the Kildares came under royal scrutiny; in that year his life was threatened when he was charged with treason for having helped Kildare to break free of his arrest, but he was subsequently exonerated by parliament.

It was not until the ascendancy of Gerald, the eighth earl, that Portlester became particularly dependent upon and closely allied with the Geraldine party, an alliance which was copperfastened by the marriage of his daughter,

20 See Tickell, 'Eustace family'. 21 Ibid.

Alison, with the earl. Kildare's esteem for this old ally of his father who had such considerable experience in the governance of the lordship is evidenced both in this marital alliance and also in his protection and patronage of Portlester throughout the remainder of his career. During the 1470s and 1480s, Eustace's Yorkist loyalties again brought him into direct confrontation with the crown. In spite of his refusal to recognise the king's representative, Lord Henry Grey, in 1478, his overt support of Lambert Simnel, and his participation alongside Thomas Fitzgerald in the battle of Stoke in support of the Yorkist claim, Portlester, like Kildare, received a royal pardon. Henry VII confirmed him as lord treasurer and as lord chancellor. His loyalty to both the Yorkist and the Kildare factions had been tested on these occasions at a time when Kildare's authority was paramount and his favour was of more immediate value to members of the Dublin administration than that of the king originating from either house.

Portlester's close association with the Geraldine interest therefore yielded personal returns in terms of security both of his office and of his life. That alliance between the two families proved durable since, although the Eustaces were divided in their stance vis-à-vis the 1534-5 rebellion, some leading members of the family actively supported Offaly's defiance, most notably Janet, the daughter of Portlester, who was married to Sir Walter Delahide of Moyglare in Meath. She and her two sons, James and John, along with Thomas Eustace, her nephew, were accused of inciting Offaly to rebel. By early February 1535, Janet and the countess of Kildare's former lady-in-waiting, Rose Eustace, were imprisoned in Dublin Castle. Janet was alleged to have been in close collusion with the earl of Kildare and was said to have 'provided for the furnishing and victualling of Maynooth' during the revolt. She was regarded by certain contemporaries as 'the best hostage, except Thomas himself' and she was fingered as 'the chief councillor, and stirrer of this inordinate rebellion', particularly since it was believed that 'when the traitor [Thomas] was discomforted, he fled to [Janet] at [Delahide's] Ballina castle'.[22]

Certain individual members of the Eustace family continued to support the Fitzgerald cause even after the suppression of the revolt, with Roland Eustace

22 John Alen to Cromwell, 16 Feb. 1535 (*S.P. Hen. VIII*, ii, p. 228); Note of persons attainted, 1535 (*S.P. Hen. VIII*, ii, p. 315); Draft bill of attainder against Gerald, earl of Kildare, deceased (*L. & P. Hen. VIII*, vii, no. 1382); 'The rebellion of Thomas Fitzgerald', 21 Jan. 1535 (*L. & P. Hen. VIII*, viii, no. 82); Edward Beck to Cromwell, 10 Feb. 1535 (*L. & P. Hen. VIII*, viii, no. 193); John Alen to Cromwell, 16 Feb. 1535 (*L. & P. Hen. VIII*, viii, no. 226); Richard Stanihurst, 'A history of the reign of Henry VIII' in Raphael Holinshed (ed.), *Chronicles*, i, pt iii, FLv-H5 p. 99 quoted in Fitzgerald, *The earls of Kildare*, pp 146-7, 315-18; Tickell, 'Eustace family', p. 279.

of Mullaghcash and his wife, the lady of Slane, secretly contriving to send a saffron shirt and 20s. to the young Gerald, later eleventh earl of Kildare, during his period of hiding in Tyrconnell in 1539.[23] Others who were implicated in the revolt, including James Eustace of Tipperkevin, Thomas of Kerdiffstown and Christopher of Coghlanstown, lost their estates and Christopher was executed in 1537. However, the deleterious effect of this confiscation on the collective Eustace estates was mitigated by the fact that substantial tracts of that land were redistributed among other members of the family. This was certainly true in the case of Christopher's very extensive estate which lay due west of Ballymore Eustace and south of the river Liffey. In addition, parcels of Christopher's estate in Naas, Donadea, Coghlanstown and Ballymore were occupied by members of his extended family and, since these are unlikely to have been evicted following confiscation of the estate, their continued occupation would have cushioned the Eustaces somewhat against the blow dealt the Coghlanstown branch.[24]

As already noted, Portlester's association with the Kildares had proven beneficial for the Eustaces in the late fifteenth century and certain members of the extended family remained firm in their adherence to the Geraldines. However, a number of heads of other branches managed to enhance their individual holdings at the expense of family members who were implicated with the vanquished Kildares, as a result of their abstention from the revolt or through their active opposition to it. By far the most impressive instance of self-aggrandisement arising from a show of opposition to the revolt was that of the baron of Portlester's nephew and heir, Sir Thomas Eustace, later Viscount Baltinglass. Sensitive to the shifting sands of power in the Tudor government regime, Thomas threw in his lot with the Dublin administration and raised troops to help to crush the rebellion. He served as a juror appointed to supervise the seizure of the ninth earl's property in the districts of Kilkea and Castledermot.[25] He also publicly distanced himself from the Coghlanstown branch by presiding as a senior juror over the seizure and assessment of Christopher's estate, though he was not the only member of the family to do so.[26]

His display of loyalty as the leader of the county's second most formidable family at a critical time was lavishly rewarded in grants of dissolved monastic lands and his elevation to a title which ensured his line's dominance down to 1580.[27] The defiant stance of these members of the extended Eustace family and particularly that of Portlester's heir provides a telling insight into the

23 'The confession of Connor More O'Connor', 17 Apr. 1539 (*S.P. Hen. VIII*, iii, p. 140; *L. & P. Hen. VIII*, xiv, no. 1245); Fitzgerald, *The earls of Kildare*, p. 189.   24 *Crown surveys*, pp 219, 221-2.   25 Ibid., pp 161, 173.   26 Ibid., p. 220.   27 Kingston, 'Catholic families', p. 248.

Kildares' relations with this senior gentry family, and highlights the self-interest which motivated both the earls' and Portlester's maintenance of amicable relations. It also shows that in spite of close family ties, certain members of the Eustace family, like the Leixlip branch of the Fitzgeralds, were prepared to put self-interest ahead of loyalty to the Kildares. The dramatic change in the tenor of the Kildares' relations with the senior Eustace line over these two generations provides proof of the finely-tuned and fickle nature of the relationship between the earls and this powerful landed family whose support they had to constantly foster.

In addition to the transfer of ownership of property which resulted from the implication of individual family members in the Kildare revolt, the suppression of the county's monasteries was of great importance in enabling certain branches of the Eustace family to secure their hold on extensive and valuable monastic possessions. In the case of Sir Thomas Eustace, Viscount Baltinglass, the distribution of dissolved monastic properties served to expand his existing holdings greatly. Unlike the Fitzgeralds or the Wogans, the Eustaces were represented on numerous juries charged with compiling extents of the monastic possessions in their districts in late 1540, with three family members on each of the juries of Coghlanstown, Ballymore and Naas, and one member serving on the Kilkea jury. Their involvement in the procedure for overseeing the dissolution of the county's monastic houses was only to be expected in view of their existing occupation of monastic properties in the east and south of the county. The Eustaces' involvement therefore stemmed from their overt determination to secure their existing substantial vested interests in the county's monastic properties, as well as to fight off competition to acquire additional lands in the distribution of those spoils. Many of the monastic lands held by the Eustaces in 1540 in areas such as Brannockstown, Kilcullen, Naas and Coghlanstown which skirted the rampart of the Pale in the east of the county, were particularly valuable because they were adjacent to the Eustace estates.[28]

Like many of their astute contemporaries in Pale aristocratic and gentry circles, the Eustaces moved fast to secure preferential grants to monastic properties in which they had a particularly keen interest. In the case of Sir Thomas, lord of Kilcullen, this strategy paid handsome dividends as virtually all of his preferential grants were ratified. Less successful in his endeavours was Edmund Eustace. Since 1538 he had been authorised to hold the nunnery of Timolin and its properties in southeast Kildare for a period of twenty-one years at a rent of 106*s.* 8*d*.[29] In spite of this preemptive manoeuvre Edmund

28 *Extents Ir. mon. possessions*, pp 130, 133, 124, 159, 165-6, 173. **29** Ibid., p. 165; Bradshaw,

ultimately failed to secure possession of the property, which instead became fragmented by piecemeal grants issued in the early 1540s to individuals such as Richard Brasier and John Goldsmith.

In addition, the cadet branches of the Eustace family learned that in spite of their prominence in both county and Pale society, they could not compete with speculators drawn from the ranks of the Dublin administration. In 1540 a sizeable proportion of the land and revenues of the nunnery of Graney on the Kildare-Carlow border lay in the possession of several members of the Eustace family, namely Thomas, William, Edmund, John, Sir Thomas, Maurice and Robert. Yet the family failed to secure outright ownership of the dissolved nunnery's estate. Graney, by virtue of its border location, was the object of attention from some of the most influential political figures in the Dublin administration, including Sir Anthony St Leger, and Lord Leonard Grey, whose military background was a consideration favouring his suit for the dissolved monastery.[30] Clearly, the Eustaces were unable to compete with such influential contenders for the property.

At the time of the dissolution of the monasteries in November 1540, Sir Thomas Eustace, then lord of Kilcullen, had substantial interests in houses in Kilcullen, Naas, Connall and Rathergett as well as certain property belonging to Baltinglass Abbey. He received quit rents from property owned by the priory of Connall; from land in the town of Naas which was owned by the Austin friars and he shared the returns from a quit rent with Patrick Barnewall, lord of Trimleston, from land also owned by the Dominicans in Naas. Eustace was said to have occupied the house and all the premises of the Franciscan house of New Abbey in Kilcullen in November 1540. He also received a chief rent for land which he leased to the abbot of Baltinglass Abbey in Westown. In Rathergett, Duncreevan and Cannycourt near Gilltown in east Kildare, he held a total of 206 acres.[31]

Eustace's career prior to the Geraldine rebellion had been impressive though relatively unremarkable: in 1523 he had served as high sheriff of the county and he was knighted at some point between 1528 and 1533. He clearly had immense resources at his disposal in terms of land and military forces and the ninth earl of Kildare viewed him as a formidable figure as is evident in his presentation of gifts of horses to Eustace during the period 1516-17.[32] He was heavily criticised by another member of the county gentry, David Sutton, for imposing 'coign and livery upon the king's tenants as well as upon other gen-

Dissolution of religious orders, p. 76.   **30** Bradshaw, *Dissolution of religious orders*, pp 76, 193; *Extents Ir. mon. possessions*, p.125.   **31** *Extents Ir. mon. possessions*, pp 131-3, 159,165-6, 172. **32** Ellis, *Tudor frontiers and noble power*, p. 138.

tlemen's lands, for he is not able to keep half the men he hath upon his own lands and there is no man in the country that hath men of war but he in effect for the defence of the country'.[33]

Eustace's opposition to the rebellion greatly boosted the English administration's efforts to contain and crush the insurgence. His part in the campaign against the Fitzgeralds and later against O'Neill in the mid- to late 1530s resulted in his elevation to the dignity of baron of Kilcullen in 1535 and, in 1541, to the title Viscount Baltinglass.[34] It also resulted in his being invested with the former Geraldine manor of Kilcock and several grants of lucrative monastic properties.[35] Bradshaw has emphasised that the receipt of monastic property by members of the local gentry was symptomatic rather than a cause of their political influence, and this was certainly true in the case of Sir Thomas, as the following outline of his principal acquisitions illustrates.[36]

Sir Thomas was one of the assessors who oversaw the dissolution of the county's monastic houses and, as already mentioned, he took shrewd preemptive steps to ensure an uncontested transfer of ownership in his favour when the suppression campaign would be finally set in train.[37] In 1538 he secured a preferential grant of the Franciscan house of New Abbey in Kilcullen, and in the process fended off a serious challenge posed by Archbishop George Browne of Dublin. That achievement bore testimony to the Dublin government's estimation of Eustace as a powerful and strategically valuable ally to their interests.[38] In that same year he received a grant by indenture of castles, messuages and other properties of Baltinglass Abbey in Duncreevan, Cannycourt, Castlegrange, Kilmacow and in the Growe in county Kildare (some of which he already held prior to dissolution) as well as three rectories.[39]

In 1541 he was granted the very extensive possessions of Baltinglass Abbey, again with definite strategic interests at the forefront of the minds of the Dublin administrators.[40] Following the suppression of St Patrick's Cathedral in Dublin in 1546, Sir Thomas received a grant of the demesne and large parish of Kilberry, located north of Athy, and also the advowson rights to the

33 Hore and Graves (eds), *Southern and eastern counties*, p. 163.   **34** Ossory to Cowley, June 1535 (*S.P. Hen. VIII*, ii, p. 252; *L. & P. Hen. VIII*, viii, no. 881); Aylmer and Alen to Cromwell, 21 Aug. 1535 (*S.P. Hen. VIII*, ii, pp 263-4; *L. & P. Hen. VIII*, ix, no. 147); *Fiants Ire., Hen. VIII*, no. 211; *Liber mun. pub. Hib.*, pts 1-2, pp 19, 27; Tickell, 'Eustace family', p. 282; Fitzgerald, 'Baltinglass Abbey', p. 394. Sir Thomas is generally styled 'lord of Kilcullen'.   **35** Carey, *Surviving the Tudors*.   **36** Bradshaw, *Dissolution of religious orders*, p. 202.   **37** *Extents Ir. mon. possessions*, p. 177.   **38** Archbishop Browne to Cromwell, 21 May 1538 (*S.P. Hen. VIII*, iii, p. 10; *L. & P. Hen. VIII*, xiv, no. 1006).   **39** *Extents Irish mon. possessions*, p. 132.   **40** *Fiants Ire., Hen. VIII*, no. 211; Fitzgerald, 'Baltinglass Abbey', p. 394.

parish.[41] By this stage, he appears to have owned a very substantial estate in west Wicklow in addition to his other properties in counties Kildare and Meath. He was therefore one of the many lesser aristocrats and landed gentlemen of the Pale, such as the Barnewalls and Cusacks of Meath, who expanded their existing holdings by astutely annexing dissolved monastic lands contiguous to their original estates.

The fact that no definitive evidence exists to indicate the degree to which Sir Thomas Eustace accepted Reformation teaching is not unusual since he died in 1549, only two years into Edward VI's reign. However, the fact that the friars were only officially expelled from New Abbey in Kilcullen in 1547 and that he died two years later in the abbey where the sick were still being tended by the friars stirs suspicion that the impact of the Reformation on Sir Thomas, while substantial in terms of material acquisitions, was negligible with respect to his ecclesiastical patronage or personal religious beliefs. In this, Eustace was by no means unique. His son Patrick strongly opposed the act of uniformity in 1558 and his overtly Catholic stance resulted in an order for his arrest and conveyance to England in 1567. Sir Thomas's career and those of his successors, Roland, second viscount and James, third viscount, also lend weight to the impression that the Protestant faith failed to take root in the ascendant Harristown branch of the Eustace family. This was also the case with the offspring of Sir Thomas's contemporaries such as Sir Thomas Cusack of Lismullen in county Meath.

Although the majority of the extended Eustace family adhered to Catholicism throughout the sixteenth century, the founding branch of the family, based at Castlemartin, converted to Protestantism in the mid-sixteenth century during the lifetime of Maurice Eustace. Yet, even within this line of the Eustaces, some members such as Maurice's grandson and namesake remained Catholic and became implicated in the Baltinglass rebellion in 1580.[42] The impact of the Henrician Reformation on the extended Eustace family was therefore largely restricted to their receipt of substantial grants of dissolved monastic properties within the county. However, that sharing out of the spoils had an impact on only a handful of senior family members and, even in the cases of beneficiaries such as Sir Thomas, this failed to induce them or their families to adopt the Protestant faith on a long-term basis.

Throughout the second half of the sixteenth century the Eustaces continued to maintain a high level of participation in county judicial administration, with several members of the family filling the post of high sheriff along with

---

41 *Fiants Ire., Hen. VIII*, no. 90; Tickell, 'Eustace family', pp 282, 365.   42 Tickell, 'Eustace family', pp 308-17.

serving as justices of the peace, commissioners and MPs for Kildare.[43] While the Geraldine rebellion and the dissolution of the monasteries had brought a change in the dynastic fortunes of several branches of the family, especially the Coghlanstown and Harristown branches, the Baltinglass rebellion replicated for the Eustaces the crisis experienced by the Fitzgeralds in the 1530s. On this occasion, the property of the viscount of Baltinglass passed to an English captain, Sir Henry Harrington.[44] Thus, Sir Thomas Eustace's Harristown branch was deposed from its status as principal line of the extended Eustace family.

The cases of Sir Thomas Eustace and Sir William Bermingham of Carbury in northwest Kildare are remarkably similar. Both were conferred with titles and received grants of monastic lands in gratitude for services rendered and as inducements to oversee the defence of the Pale marches in their respective spheres of influence. And yet their family histories were diametrically opposed since, unlike old-stock county families such as the Eustaces or the Aylmers, the Berminghams had largely lapsed in their allegiance to the crown from the mid-fourteenth century down to the 1530s. As late as 1534, Sir William Bermingham, the head of the principal branch of the family, was still regarded by David Sutton as a close ally of the O'Connors.[45] As we have seen, the mid- to late 1530s were marked by the Dublin administration's concerted attempts at establishing a firmer foothold in the extreme marches of the Pale. The fall of the Kildares and the subsequent closure of the Pale's monasteries dovetailed to facilitate the implementation of a policy designed to reap the maximum gains from the opportune circumstances then obtaining in county Kildare.

Bermingham territory in northwest Kildare was, therefore, a prime target of this policy, and the appeasement of this family who had been long-standing opponents of the Dublin administration was greatly assisted by the inducement of acquiring dissolved monastic properties. In 1537, therefore, William Bermingham of Dunfierth was identified by Robert Cowley as one of those march lord, who were considered 'most worthy, for their truth, power, and ability of any in that land [who could be] put in such places and marches of danger'.[46] In spite of Sutton's mistrust of him, by the 1530s William Bermingham had gained a favourable reputation in Dublin administration circles, evidenced by Sir John Alen's recommendation in 1537 that 'because of his activity', Bermingham should have a large section of O'Connor's territory restored to him since his family had a lapsed claim to that district. Alen also

43 Ibid. **44** Fitzgerald, 'Baltinglass Abbey', pp 395-401. **45** Hore and Graves (eds), *Southern and eastern counties*, pp 163-5. **46** Robert Cowley to Cromwell, 1537 (*S.P. Hen. VIII*, ii, p. 446).

suggested that Bermingham be recognised as lord of this area and that he be created a lord of parliament.[47] Both Cowley and Alen, two of the keenest observers and advisers on the course of action to be taken in the lordship in the late 1530s, counselled Henry VIII to bring the apparently benign Bermingham fully into the fold with enticements of grants of land and a title.

This was, of course, an overtly calculated manoeuvre designed to neutralise the extended Bermingham family threat by entrusting William with responsibility for the safe-keeping of the western marches of the Pale. And it succeeded. The senior branches of the Bermingham family detached themselves from their former allies the O'Connors, though this brought swift reprisals from the chief of the Gaelic sept who in 1540 'with a great number of horsemen, galloglases, and kerne, burned the Bermingham country'. However, William's newly established alliance with the Dublin administration immediately proved effective. At the time of O'Connor's attack, the lord chancellor, Sir John Alen and the treasurer were in Kildare and 'seeing ... Bermingham's country afire' they went with as many men as they had with them into O'Connor's country. There they burned several towns and drove off cattle and this campaign caused O'Connor to abandon his raid on Bermingham's property and return home.[48] William continued to act in a compliant manner, serving as a juror on several panels which oversaw the dissolution of the monasteries in the northwestern region of Kildare in November 1540. In return he received £20 from lands belonging to the dissolved houses of Ballyboggan and Clonard, along with a lease of several rectories which were affiliated to the abbey at Clonard.[49]

In 1540 Bermingham was high sheriff of county Kildare and at a time when many Gaelic lords were being incorporated as titled subjects into the newly-instituted kingdom of Ireland, the rehabilitation of the Berminghams as loyal English subjects was copperfastened in June 1541. 'In consideration of the acceptable services of William Bermingham, knight, and of his circumspection, courage and fidelity', he was elevated to the rank of baron of Carbury, with the remainder to his male heirs.[50] Sir William assisted at solemn high Mass on Corpus Christi, then rode in the procession to the parliament house and attended the parliamentary session in his capacity as

---

47 Sir John Alen to St Leger, 1537 (*S.P. Hen. VIII*, ii, p. 485).   **48** Brereton to Essex, 17 May 1540 (*S.P. Hen. VIII*, iii, p. 205).   **49** Lord deputy and council to Hen. VIII, 30 Dec. 1540 (*L. & P. Hen. VIII*, xv, no. 367); *Fiants Ire., Hen. VIII*, no. 191.   **50** Sir William died on 17 July 1548. At the time, his only son, Edward, second baron of Carbury, was just two years old. Edward died without male issue and the lands granted by patent to Sir William reverted to the crown while the manor of Dunfierth in the north of the county devolved on Walter Birmingham of Mylerstown in county Kildare.

baron of Carbury, voting with his peers for the abolition of papal jurisdiction in the newly established kingdom.[51] In support of the dignity conferred upon him and as part of the administration's policy of pacifying this quarter of Kildare, William received a grant of the site of priory of Ballyboggan and the former abbey of Clonard with all adjacent messuages. In addition, he was invested with all of the manors, lands and liberties pertaining to these monasteries which lay in county Meath.[52] Sir William fostered ties with leading Pale families through his two marriages, his first wife being Rose the daughter of Gerald Fitzgerald of Blackwood and his second being Anne, the daughter of Sir John Plunket of Beaulieu in Louth. During the 1540s his service as arbitrator between Bernard O'Connor and Cahir O'Connor, his brother, provides a clear example of the Dublin administration's use of Bermingham's former alliance with the Gaelic clan in order to quell unrest in the Pale marches. He was also involved in mediation in a dispute among the O'Neills in Ulster.[53]

Although Bermingham supported the royal supremacy and received grants of lucrative dissolved monastic properties, he appears to have maintained his adherence to Catholic beliefs and religious practices. His tombstone bears decidedly Catholic features including representations of the twelve apostles and a crucifixion scene fashioned in a characteristically Renaissance style.[54] This adherence is hardly surprising given that Sir William, like Sir Thomas Eustace, died in the early years of Edward VI's reign, and also given his remoteness from the archdiocese of Dublin, which during his lifetime, was the only jurisdiction in which efforts to propagate Reformation teaching were being pursued, however, intermittently, with any real vigour.[55] The case of the Berminghams clearly illustrates the manner in which the campaign for the suppression of the monasteries was deliberately geared towards realizing political and strategic ends, successfully neutralizing as it did the long-standing threat posed by this Gaelicised family to the security of the Pale. The high regard in which Bermingham was held by the Dublin administration is evident in one of the articles presented against Lord Leonard Grey in 1540, which claimed that while Sir Thomas Eustace and Sir William Bermingham were in

51 St Leger to Hen. VIII, 26 June 1541 (*S.P. Hen. VIII*, iii, p. 304). 52 *Cal. pat. rolls, Ire., Hen. VIII-Eliz.*, p. 85. 53 'Bernard O'Connor', 16 Aug. 1541 (*S.P. Hen. VIII*, iii, p. 316; *L. & P. Hen. VIII*, xv, no. 1101); Devitt, 'Carbury', pp 108-9. 54 Walter Fitzgerald, 'Stone effigies in the county', in *Kildare Arch. Soc. Jn.*, i (1891-95), p. 207 (hereafter Fitzgerald, 'Stone effigies'); idem, 'Parish of Carbury: Dunfierth churchyard', in *Association for the preservation of the memorials of the dead in Ireland Journal*, ii (1892-4), pp 512-14; John Hunt, 'Tomb of Sir Walter Birmingham, obit 1548', in *Kildare Arch. Soc. Jn.*, xv (1971), pp 12-16. 55 *Cal. pat. rolls, Ire., Hen. VIII-Eliz.*, p. 171.

attendance on the lord deputy in Dublin, 'there was no leader left in the country [Kildare]'.[56] The suppression campaign thus proved beneficial to a single member of this large family and he, like Sir Thomas Eustace, died before any real demand for a show of conformity on Protestant doctrinal issues was in question.

The Aylmers of Lyons ranked among the most influential families of Kildare in the early sixteenth century. They were of old Anglo-Norman stock, having settled in Kildare immediately after their arrival in 1169. The senior branch of the family was seated at Lyons on the Kildare-Dublin border from 1300.[57] Since the late fifteenth century, the Aylmers of Lyons had emerged as increasingly prominent members of the county's landed gentry, serving as senior officials in local government and, from the 1530s onwards, as influential officials in the Dublin administration.[58] Initially they held posts in the administration of justice in their vicinity and their standing at that level was significantly boosted when Bartholomew Aylmer of Lyons was appointed high sheriff of county Kildare in 1495. In terms of their involvement in local administrative affairs, the Aylmers were therefore set on an equal footing with members of the extended Fitzgerald and Eustace families.

Bartholomew's son and heir, Richard, also of Lyons, held the post of chief sergeant of the county in 1535.[59] The family continued to play an influential role in county administration throughout the sixteenth century. But it was during the lifetimes of Bartholomew, Richard, Gerald and their offspring that the Aylmers emerged as prominent figures in the Dublin administration and as expanding estate owners through their acquisition of properties in counties Meath and Dublin. Before the end of the century they had established two independent branches at Dollardstown in county Meath and at Donadea in north Kildare.

This advancement in the family's fortunes was significantly facilitated by astute marriage alliances. In the late fifteenth and early sixteenth centuries, the Aylmers were intermarried with the Petit family of Piercetown, county Meath, the Bathes of Dollardstown, the Chevers of Macetown, the Tews of Dublin, the Suttons of Kepok and the Dillons of Kepocke in Fingal. Over the course of the sixteenth century, the family's ascending social standing was manifest in their alliance with other notable Pale gentry families such as the Cusacks of Lismullen in Meath, the Husseys, barons of Galtrim, the Flemings, the

---

56 'Lord Leonard Grey', 1540 (*L. & P. Hen. VIII*, xvi, no. 304). **57** Hans Hendrick Aylmer, 'The Aylmer family', in *Kildare Arch. Soc. Jn.*, i (1891-95), p. 296 (hereafter Aylmer, 'The Aylmer family'). **58** Aylmer, 'The Aylmer family', p. 298; Lodge, *Peerage Ire.* (revised ed. 1789), vii, p. 44; O'Hart, *Irish pedigrees*, ii, p. 28. **59** *Cal. pat. rolls, Ire., Hen. VIII-Eliz.*, pp 15, 19.

Warrens of Navan and the Fitzgeralds of Allen.[60] The widespread trend towards intermarriage between gentry families with shared Catholic connections is also evident in the case of the Aylmers of Kildare, as a social manifestation of growing religious dissent and, from the 1580s onwards, overt recusancy among the Pale gentry.[61] The most prominent member of the Aylmer family in the second half of the sixteenth century was Sir Gerald Aylmer of Donadea. His two marriages also reflect that trend, his wives being Mary Eustace, widow of the attainted Viscount Baltinglass and Julia, the daughter of the fourteenth Lord Delvin who had been imprisoned for his implication in the Baltinglass revolt. Such alliances contributed to the expansion of the Aylmer estates: in 1558, Richard Aylmer of Lyons owed his acquisition of the Donadea estate to his wife's kinsman, the earl of Ormond, and this facilitated the establishment of the Donadea branch of the Aylmer family later in the sixteenth century.

The head of the Lyons branch in the 1530s was Richard, who held the posts of chief sergeant of Kildare in 1535 and high sheriff in 1543.[62] He owed his advancement as a landowner and figure of authority in local administration to the fall of the Kildares rather than to any significant gains arising from the dissolution of the county's monasteries. His appointment to this senior position while Kildare was still in the throes of the Geraldine rebellion is indicative of the Dublin administration's certainty of his loyalty, in return for which he was handsomely rewarded by a grant of the earl of Kildare's manor of Donadea. Richard was thus admitted to the interest group which had been formed by Lord Leonard Grey and whose membership was comprised of figures such as Sir Thomas Eustace, lord of Kilcullen, who had received the earl's manor of Kilcock; James, earl of Ormond, who was granted the earl's manor of Kilkea; Thomas Cusack who received the manor of Ardmulghan; and of course, Grey himself, who had secured possession of the lucrative manor of Maynooth.[63]

In Richard's case, the suppression of the monasteries proved a beneficial means of consolidating the Lyons estate at a purely local level. When the county's monastic properties were surveyed, he held forty-six acres in the

---

60 Lodge, *Peerage Ire.* (revised ed.), pp 44-67. **61** For a discussion of the alienation of the local èlite from the Dublin administration from the 1550s onwards see N.P. Canny, *The formation of the Old English élite* (Dublin, 1975); Brendan Bradshaw, *The Irish constitutional revolution of the sixteenth century* (Cambridge, 1979); Colm Lennon, *Richard Stanihurst the Dubliner, 1547-1618* (Dublin, 1981); Ciaran Brady, 'Conservative subversives: the community of the Pale and the Dublin administration 1556-86', in P.J. Corish (ed.), *Radicals, rebels and establishments* (Belfast, 1985), pp 11-32; Colm Lennon, *The lords of Dublin in the age of reformation* (Dublin, 1989). **62** *Cal. pat. rolls, Ire., Hen. VIII-Eliz.*, p. 29. **63** Carey, *Surviving the Tudors.*

immediate vicinity of Lyons, which was the property of the glebe of Oughterard rectory from the abbot of Thomas Court Abbey, Dublin. He also held three gardens in Kill and the tithes of Fenaghes in the parish of Cloncurry which were the property of Thomas Court Abbey.[64] He was in receipt of tithes from the rectory of Whitechurch as well as holding its glebe land. Both were the property of St John's Hospital, Naas, and he and David Sutton jointly held them in 1540.[65] The dissolution of the monasteries facilitated the consolidation of his estates through his continued occupancy of these parcels of dissolved monastic properties which were adjacent to his core estate lands. However, Richard did not rank among the recipients of the county's more substantial monastic holdings. His only acquisition of monastic buildings was his purchase of the church, chancel and superfluous buildings of the Dominican house in Naas for the sum of £4 66s. 8d.[66] Even these remained only temporarily in his possession: in June 1542 Robert Eustace received a grant of property for the use of Thomas Luttrell of Luttrellstown, part of which comprised the site of the Dominican house in Naas along with its holdings in county Kildare.[67]

Altogether different was the case of Richard's younger brother, Gerald. In the mid-1520s, the ninth earl of Kildare recognised Gerald as a gentleman of some standing, presenting him with gifts of horses.[68] He began his political ascent in the late 1520s when, being 'bred to the law', he was appointed to the post of second justice of the common bench in 1528. He became justice of the common pleas in 1532, chief baron of the exchequer in 1534, chief justice of the common pleas in 1535 and eventually chief justice of the king's bench.[69] Unlike Sir Thomas Eustace whose advancement stemmed from his position as a powerful county magnate who opposed Kildare, it was Gerald Aylmer's senior rank in the Dublin administration which empowered him to head the military campaign to suppress the revolt. Aylmer served as one of the commanders of the force which burned the village of Maynooth in 1534.[70] He was subsequently dispatched by Sir William Skeffington to England in charge of Offaly and his five uncles, a clear indication of the Dublin administration's confidence in him. In 1539 he attended Lord Deputy Grey in his northern expedition against O'Neill. Later that year, he was appointed as one of the commissioners sent to treat with O'Neill on the borders of Ulster.

Like Sir Thomas Eustace, Gerald Aylmer was richly rewarded for his services during the Geraldine crisis and for his role in the expedition against

---

64 *Extents Ir. mon. possessions*, pp 37, 39, 41. **65** Ibid., p. 156. **66** Ibid., p. 166. **67** *Fiants Ire., Hen VIII*, no. 313. **68** *Crown surveys*, p. 341. **69** *Cal. pat. rolls, Ire., Hen. VIII-Eliz.*, pp 12, 16; *Fiants Ire., Hen. VIII*, nos 25, 30, 38; Lodge, *Peerage Ire.* (revised ed.), vii, p. 59. **70** 'Ireland', 1535 (*L. & P. Hen. VIII*, viii, no. 449).

O'Neill. In the course of the Ulster campaign he was knighted on the battle-field for his valour and services. Soon after, in September 1539, he was granted the manor and lordship of Dollardstown in county Meath along with other lands which formerly comprised the estate of William Bathe who had been attainted owing to his implication in the Geraldine revolt.[71] In 1540 he was found in possession of several properties and incomes in Kildare, Dublin and Louth; he managed to retain his Kildare interests in the aftermath of the suppression campaign. He was in receipt of the tithes of Swordlestown near Naas, property of Thomas Court Abbey, Dublin and he also secured receipt in the future of the tithes of the rectory of Naas, property of the Hospital of St John of Jerusalem in Dublin. In 1540 these were held for life by indenture by a widow, Margaret Fleming, with reversion to Sir Gerald. He also enjoyed receipt of two-thirds of the tithes and altarages of the rectory of Bodenstown in northeast Kildare, property of the priory of Connall, and these were leased to him for a fixed term.[72]

Sir Gerald was very actively involved as a juror in surveying dissolved monastic properties, especially in county Meath, and he also served as a juror in the assessment of the crown's ancient demesne lands and those of the ninth earl of Kildare's kinsman, Oliver Fitzgerald, in the early 1540s.[73] Sir Gerald's continued loyal service to the Tudors was further rewarded throughout the 1540s and 1550s both in terms of career advancement and the expansion of his estate. In 1542 and again in 1547, he was appointed a privy councillor. In 1543 he was granted the site of the monastery of Friars Minor of Drogheda and its properties in Louth, Meath and Dublin.[74] Under the Edwardian regime, Aylmer's career continued its ascent. In 1547 he was appointed chief justice of the king's bench in which capacity he was nominated as a commissioner to oversee the granting of leases of all the king's castles and properties.[75] His career reached its zenith in his tenure of the joint governorship of Ireland along with Sir Thomas Cusack during the period December 1552 to November 1553.[76] During this period he participated in the campaign for the reduction of O'Connor and his allies and in the assault on O'Neill near Dundalk. Aylmer's service outlasted a second Tudor monarch and Queen Mary appointed him chief justice of the queen's bench soon after her accession to the throne in 1553.[77]

The longevity of Aylmer's career, in spite of the vicissitudes of changing monarchs and factional alliances, suggests that down to the early years of the

71 *Cal. pat. rolls, Ire., Hen. VIII-Eliz.*, pp 37-8; *Fiants Ire., Hen. VIII*, no. 66. **72** *Extents Ir. mon. possessions*, pp 48, 94, 160. **73** *Crown surveys*, pp 61-2, 70, 211. **74** *Fiants Ire., Hen. VIII*, p. 66. **75** *Cal. pat. rolls, Ire., Hen. VIII-Eliz.*, pp 150-1. **76** Ellis, *Tudor Ireland*, p. 329. **77** Lodge, *Peerage Ire.* (revised ed.), vii, p. 60; Ellis, *Tudor Ireland*, pp 232, 328.

Marian regime, no discriminatory policy was adopted by the crown, by the royal secretary or by the senior figures on the Dublin administration with respect to the appointment of Englishmen in Ireland to senior government positions. However, the opposite was true in the case of the political climate which prevailed during the career of Gerald's nephew and namesake. Gerald, third son of Richard of Lyons, spearheaded a campaign from the 1580s down to the 1610s to represent and defend the rights and privileges of his peers, both of which he regarded as being jeopardised by the arbitrary imposition of cess by the Dublin administration and by the forcible imposition of Protestantism. On several occasions Gerald was imprisoned while he made his representations to the court and he was clearly viewed as a dangerous subversive recusant. In 1592, for example, his keepers were ordered to treat him as 'a close prisoner [so] that he might have no conference with any priests, seminaries or evil affected subjects to the state'.[78] Gerald's funerary monument at Donadea in northeast Kildare also testifies to survivalism in the Aylmer family as it bears many of the hallmarks of Catholicism.[79]

In the case of the Aylmers of Kildare, the Protestant Reformation had a very limited impact both during the reign of Henry VIII and in the following generation. Sir Gerald of Dollardstown alone reaped substantial benefits from the suppression campaign and from the confiscation of the estate of a Geraldine supporter. His brother, Richard, made substantial gains from the removal of the Kildares in terms of his acquisition of Geraldine land and his career advancement. But while the Lyons branch did receive very modest grants of monastic properties in their vicinity, the greatest impact of the dissolution campaign as far as they were concerned was the regularization of their continued occupancy of monastic lands. This merely served to consolidate the Aylmers' already strong position as a senior landed family. In the later sixteenth century, this family's continued adherence to Catholicism was manifest in the marital ties of the descendants of Sir Richard Aylmer of Lyons, which were mainly with Catholic families and also in Sir Gerald Aylmer of Donadea's funerary monument. In short, the government's attempts to introduce Protestantism ultimately had a reverse effect on the Aylmer family of Kildare with Sir Gerald of Donadea, like the Barnewalls of Meath, adopting a very public stance of recusancy in a campaign for religious toleration in the late sixteenth and early seventeenth centuries.

---

78 Fenton Aylmer, 'Sir Gerald Aylmer, knight and baronet', in *Kildare Arch. Soc. Jn.*, xi (1930-33), p. 376 (hereafter Aylmer, 'Sir Gerald Aylmer'). See also Aylmer, 'The Aylmer family', p. 301.   **79** Aylmer, 'Sir Gerald Aylmer', pp 384-5; Walter Fitzgerald, 'Donadea church', in *Association for the preservation of the memorials of the dead in Ireland Journal*, vi, no. 1, pts 1-2 (1904), pp 93-7; idem, 'Stone effigies', p. 207.

Unlike the Wogan and Wellesley families, the Suttons of Kildare were in the ascendant in the early sixteenth century, especially the Richardstown, Tully and Tipper branches.[80] In the short term in particular, the heads of these branches of the family reaped sizeable gains from the transfer of ownership of monastic properties in northeast and central Kildare. The extended family's estates were located in the districts of Clane, Rathbride, Kilcock, Naas, Richardstown, Tipper, Castletown and Tully. The principal members of the extended family in this period were John, Gerald, and David Sutton and the latter's two sons, Gerald and Oliver. As in the case of the Eustaces, the Suttons were divided along political lines; John Sutton, the head of the Tipper branch, was on favourable terms with the earls of Kildare and the senior members of the extended Fitzgerald family. At the time of the outbreak of the rebellion, he held land to the use of Richard Fitzgerald who was attainted, and legal possession of this property which extended over south Dublin and north Wicklow was assumed by the crown. In addition he was seized of the manor of Hollywood with all its properties to the use of James Fitzgerald.[81] The head of the Richardstown branch, Gerald Sutton, also appears to have had at least a functional relationship with the ninth earl who leased him the tithes of Clane in 1519.[82]

By contrast, David Sutton of Rathbride and later styled of Tully actively supported the Dublin government in its bid to suppress the Kildare revolt in 1534-5.[83] It was he who, in September 1537, made the presentment to the commissioners on the subject of the late ninth earl's illegal exactions on the county of Kildare. Sutton's harsh criticism of the ninth earl is ironic since he had served as Kildare's estate receiver prior to 1534. Evidently sensitive to the shifting sands in the political arena, David Sutton deserted the Geraldine cause and threw in his lot with the Dublin administration and was almost immediately rewarded through career and financial advancement. Robert Cowley, writing to the duke of Norfolk in 1540, testified to David Sutton's loyal service to the crown during the crisis of the 1530s, describing him as 'a good gentleman ... who keepeth at his [own] charge diverse horsemen and footmen' and who at one stage held the constableship of Kildare Castle.[84]

David Sutton had a strong vested interest in the distribution of dissolved monastic properties in east Kildare, given his existing occupancy of monastic

80 Hore and Graves (eds), *Southern and eastern counties*, p. 157. See also Walter Fitzgerald, 'Castletown and its owners' in *Kildare Arch. Soc. Jn.*, ii (1896-9), pp 367; O'Hart, *Irish pedigrees*, ii, p. 402.   **81** *Calendar of inquisitions*, pp 66-9, 106.   **82** *Crown surveys*, pp 250-52.   **83** *Cal. pat. rolls, Ire., Hen. VIII-Eliz.*, pp 9, 17; Hore and Graves (eds), *Southern and eastern counties*, p. 158.   **84** Hore and Graves (eds), *Southern and eastern counties*, p. 158.

land. In 1540, he and Edward Sutton held the manor and rectory of Killy-beggs, property of the Hospital of St John of Jerusalem, by a grant from the prior for a fixed term. He was also in receipt of the tithes and profits of the glebe land of the rectory of Ballynafagh, near Clane. Sutton and Sir Thomas Russell jointly held the rectory of Clonshanbo and his most valuable posses-sion was the preceptory of Tully, property of the Hospital of St John of Jerusalem at Kilmainham, which he held in 1540 from the priory for a fixed term. In 1540 he and Richard Aylmer received the income from the tithes and glebe land of the rectory of Whitechurch, property of St John's Hospital in Naas, and he was an occupier of some of the property of the Franciscan house of Clane. This, combined with the fact that he was favoured in the Dublin administration and that he served as an assessor in the dissolution of the monasteries, augured well for his securing lucrative gains from the dissolution of the monastic properties in Kildare.[85]

As already noted, he was granted leases to the commandery at Tully, to the Franciscan friary at Clane and to the dissolved property of the friars minor and the Carmelite priory in Kildare town and he also managed to retain his right to receive tithe payments.[86] In 1540-1 he served as a juror in the sur-veying of crown lands in Kildare.[87] In reward for his 'very acceptable ser-vice', he was granted leases to parcels of the forfeited Kildare manor of Kilkea and was created mayor of Dublin in 1543. In the following year, he was recommended by the Dublin administration for appointment as a member of the privy council and for the right to purchase substantial former Kildare and monastic lands to which he held leases.[88] Sutton thus managed to hold onto the monastic and Kildare properties which he had acquired and when he died in the late 1540s, his sons, Gerald, and Oliver of Richardstown, suc-ceeded to his estate.[89] David Sutton was not the only beneficiary in the extended family: Gerald Sutton of the Castletown branch of the family also benefited greatly from the dissolution of the county's monasteries, receiving Connall Priory and its possessions in the early Edwardian period.[90]

In the words of Hore and Graves, 'the office of belling the cat' subse-quently passed to David Sutton's son, Oliver of Richardstown, who 'bravely during the displeasure of the [eleventh] earl of Kildare' presented several memorials to Elizabeth I recounting the 'enormities' of the earl. Like David Sutton of Rathbride, Oliver's ascent to prominence in Kildare had resulted

---

85 *Extents Ir. mon. possessions*, pp 92-3, 95, 97, 156, 165, 177.   **86** *Cal. pat. rolls, Ire., Hen. VIII-Eliz.*, p. 113; *Fiants Hen. VIII*, nos 174, 345.   **87** *Crown surveys*, pp 10, 99, 144, 149, 152, 155, 156, 161, 171, 173, 206, 214, 219, 220.   **88** Hore and Graves (eds), *Southern and eastern counties*, p. 158.   **89** *Extents Ir. mon. possessions*, pp 119, 165, 167.   **90** *Fiants Ire., Edw. VI*, no. 405.

from the political vacuum created by the Geraldine collapse in 1537. Oliver was a late beneficiary of confiscated Kildare lands. He had served in the campaign against the O'Mores, the O'Connors and the 'bastard Geraldines' in 1546 in his capacity as county sheriff and in 1548 he held the post of high sheriff of Kildare. Sutton evidently spoke Gaelic and worked as an interpreter with Sir Anthony St Leger during his campaign in Ulster.[91] Like the Alens, the Suttons of Rathbride-Tully and those of Richardstown feared the restoration of the earldom of Kildare and mounted a defence in the early 1560s. With the lord lieutenant's backing, Oliver Sutton led the Kildare gentry in their presentments against the exaction of coign and livery. In 1565 he sent a document to the queen in which he opposed Kildare's imposition of military exaction, and complained that he had been compelled by the earl to forsake his ploughing and had been obliged to reside either in Dublin or in England for the safety of his life.[92]

However, following the departure of Lord Lieutenant Sussex from Ireland in 1564, the Kildare faction gained the ascendant position in the Dublin administration. This brought a sharp halt to Sutton's advance and Elizabeth reproved him for writing 'books of disorders' which, in her view, 'too directly touch the earl of Kildare'. Oliver Sutton's enmity towards the eleventh earl of Kildare brought him personal hardship and expense. In the late 1560s he complained of having suffered a loss of £2,000 at the hands of the earl and claimed that his life was in continual danger on account of his having reported Kildare's disorders.[93] However, the restoration of the eleventh earl did not involve friction between Kildare and all branches of the Sutton family. In 1557, for example, the eleventh earl requested confirmation by parliament of an assurance concerning the manor of Castletown in Kildrought, which he gave to 'his servant Gerald Sutton' and his assigns for ever.

David Sutton's opposition to the Kildare revolt thus paid rich dividends in terms of his acquisition of Geraldine and monastic properties and his continued career advancement. His son, too, was handsomely rewarded for his defiance of the Kildares. Their receipt of these properties in the 1540s was symptomatic of both men's political influence. The fall of the Kildares and the closure of the county's monasteries therefore directly served to expand the estates of the Suttons of Rathbride-Tully and Richardstown and, in the process, greatly boosted their standing as members of the county gentry. However, after David's death, the political climate began to take on a new character with the prospect of the imminent reinstatement of the eleventh earl of Kildare. The

91 Carey, *Surviving the Tudors*.   **92** Ibid.   **93** Hore and Graves (eds), *Southern and eastern counties*, pp 167-7, 176, 190.

fragility of the Suttons' recently elevated standing was exposed when Oliver Sutton was left in a vulnerable position at the hands of the earl.

Like the Aylmers and the Wogans, the Wellesleys were another long-established Kildare family who were influential at county level throughout the fifteenth and sixteenth centuries. Their associations with Kildare dated back to the late thirteenth century. In the early fourteenth century their principal holdings were concentrated in the districts of Kineagh, Pollardstown and Galmorestown.[94] However, in 1422 the family acquired large possessions in county Meath and settled at Dangan, which became the principal Meath branch of the family. The Wellesleys had emerged in importance in landed gentry circles in the Kildare-Meath area from the mid-fifteenth century onwards and their standing was greatly enhanced when, following the death of Elizabeth Calf, baroness of the Norragh in 1445, they acquired her estates in Kildare.[95] By the sixteenth century the holdings of the Kildare branch of the family had expanded to encompass a large quarter of the southeast and south central area of the county, with the manor of Norragh forming the focal point. The Eustaces of Moone, Clongowes Wood, Blackrath, Newland, and Baltinglass and the Fitzgeralds of Allen were the chief lessors of the family's property.

The Wellesleys forged close marital links with some of the county's senior gentry families and those of the neighbouring counties, including the Eustaces and the Fitzgeralds.[96] They also played an important role in ecclesiastical circles in the early sixteenth century with the Kildare and Meath branches both providing religious who served in Kildare and Dublin. Among these were Walter Wellesley, bishop of Kildare and prior of Connall; Robert Wellesley, the last prior of Connall and David Wellesley who was archdeacon of Kildare in the early 1530s. During the 1550s, William Wellesley served as archdeacon of Dublin and Robert Wellesley was successively archdeacon of Kildare and of Dublin. At local level too, the Wellesleys continued to provide diocesan clergy in county Kildare throughout the sixteenth century.[97]

In the early sixteenth century James Wellesley, Baron of Norragh, was the head of the Kildare branch of the family and he held his manor from the ninth earl of Kildare by knight's service. He died soon after the outbreak of the Geraldine rebellion and was succeeded by his son, Richard.[98] No member of

94 Walter Fitzgerald, 'Narraghmore and the barons of Norragh', in *Kildare Arch. Soc. Jn.*, vii (1912-14), pp 242-72.   95 Edmund Curtis, 'The barons of Norragh, County Kildare 1171-1600', in *Journal of the Royal Society of Antiquaries of Ireland*, 7th ser., v (1935), p. 99.   96 *Cal. pat. rolls, Ire., Hen. VIII-Eliz.*, p. 100; Fitzgerald, 'Narraghmore and the barons of Norragh', p. 266. 97 *Cal. pat. rolls, Ire., Hen. VIII-Eliz.*, p. 65; *Extents Ir. mon. possessions*, p. 163.   98 *Cal. pat. rolls, Ire., Hen. VIII-Eliz.*, p. 70; Walter Fitzgerald, 'Extracts from a County Dublin exchequer inquisition concerning landholders in the county of Kildare in 1535', in *Kildare Arch. Soc. Jn.*,

the family served as a juror in the surveying of the county's dissolved monastic properties and the extent of their occupancy of monastic properties in the 1530s was virtually negligible. In 1540 Oliver Wellesley held one messuage at Kill and William Wellesley held four gardens in the same district, both of which were formerly the property of St Thomas's Abbey in Dublin and these were held from the king. Oliver also shared possession of a castle and several messuages and cottages and 100 acres of land in Walterstown, formerly the property of St John's Hospital in Naas.[99] Neither James, nor his son, Richard, nor his son in turn participated in the Dublin administration or in local government. Not surprisingly therefore the Wellesleys benefited little by the closure of Kildare's monastic houses.

As already mentioned, the Wellesley estates spanned southeastern and south central Kildare and the religious houses at Connall, Timolin, New Abbey, Kilcullen, and Kilrush were all roughly adjacent to their properties. However, there was very keen competition for the acquisition of these monastic properties amongst influential government officials and stronger county gentry families. Unable to compete with either group, the Wellesleys failed to make any significant gains in monastic properties in the early 1540s. Nonetheless they remained a potent presence in Kildare society in the late sixteenth and early seventeenth centuries when the family had four distinct branches at Bishopscourt, Blackhall, Narraghmore and Painstown. They therefore proved that their position as one of the county's leading landed families was neither indebted to nor enhanced by receipt of dissolved monastic property; nor did it depend upon their active participation in local government or in the Dublin administration.[100]

Like the Wellesleys, the Wogans were a long-standing Kildare family of Anglo-Norman origin whose principal seat was Rathcoffey and whose estates spanned the baronies of Ikeathy and Oughterany in the north of the county. They were intermarried with the extended Fitzgerald family, as well as with the Eustaces, the Flatisburys, the Suttons and the Boices of county Meath.[101] Although the Wogans were prominent landowners in the county and had held the posts of viceroy and chancellor of Ireland in the medieval period, their influence and participation in the Dublin administration had waned prior to the sixteenth century, a bitter internal dispute in the 1450s undoubtedly being a contributory factor.[102] Sir William Wogan of Rathcoffey held the post of high

vi (1901-11), p. 180 (hereafter Fitzgerald, 'Extracts from a County Dublin exchequer inquisition'). **99** *Extents Ir. mon. possessions*, pp 39, 156. **100** Fitzgerald, 'The principal gentry', p. 122. **101** Devitt, 'Rathcoffey', p. 79. **102** *Cal. pat. rolls, Ire., Hen. VIII-Eliz.*, p. 33. See also Devitt, 'Rathcoffey', pp 80-1.

sheriff of county Kildare during the period 1502-4 and he was on favourable terms with the ninth earl of Kildare from whom he received a gift of a bay horse in 1516.[103] Sir William's cousin and heir, Nicholas Wogan, also of Rathcoffey, was high sheriff of the county in 1542.[104] Although the Wogans were intermarried with the Fitzgerald family, the removal of the earls of Kildare clearly exerted no negative impact on their involvement in local administration. However, by the mid-sixteenth century, even their role in local government had faded.

They had virtually no vested interest in the monastic properties in the county and no member of the Kildare family served as a juror in the survey conducted in 1540. Predictably, therefore, the Wogans did not benefit from the campaign for the suppression of Kildare's monastic houses. The family survived very varied fortunes throughout the remainder of the sixteenth century. Several members were implicated in the Baltinglass revolt, Richard and William Wogan being executed in Dublin in 1581-2 along with thirty-six noblemen and gentlemen of the Pale.[105] Throughout the Elizabethan period the Wogans generally adopted a stand of opposition to the Dublin administration, their names frequently appearing in lists of confiscations and pardons.[106] Yet they maintained their substantial estates and their status as one of the county's leading old-stock gentry families as is evidenced by the fact that in 1600 they had four seats at Rathcoffey, Downings, Blackhall and Newhall.[107]

II

Having concluded this survey of the impact of the suppression campaign on the lesser aristocracy and large, long-established gentry families of the county, attention is now turned to its effect upon families of more humble status, notably the Kerdiffs, the Sherlocks, and the Flatisburys. The Kerdiffs of Kildare were a secondary branch of the family who had become established in Ratoath, county Meath, in the fourteenth century. The Kildare branch was always small and their single seat of residence was at Kerdiffstown near Naas with parcels of their estate spanning the neighbouring districts of Castlesize, Rathmore, Bodenstown, and Sherlockstown. Only one family member, Nicholas Kerdiff, served as a juror in the compilation of extents of the county's monastic properties in 1540. Given their small size, their modest means and

---

103 *Crown surveys*, p. 325.   **104** *Cal. pat. rolls, Ire., Hen. VIII-Eliz.*, p. 27; Fitzgerald, 'Extracts from a County Dublin exchequer inquisition', p. 180.   **105** Patrick Woulfe, 'Some martyrs of the Pale', in M.V. Ronan (ed.), *Catholic emancipation centenary record* (Dublin, 1929), p. 34.   **106** Devitt, 'Rathcoffey', p. 81.   **107** Fitzgerald, 'The principal gentry', p. 122.

their non-participation in local government, the Kerdiffs did not stand to gain from the suppression of the nearby monasteries of Clane and Naas though this did not adversely affect their standing since they retained their rank as one of the county's principal gentry families throughout the sixteenth century.[108]

The Sherlocks based at Sherlockstown in northeast Kildare were another of these small gentry families. They were actively involved in the local political and judicial administration in the early fifteenth and late sixteenth centuries. During the period of this study, however, the Kildare branch of the family were overshadowed by their Wexford kinsmen in both fields. The Sherlocks of Kildare served as representatives of the borough of Naas in the 1560s and 1580s and their involvement in local government continued into the early decades of the seventeenth century. Their moderately prosperous standing in the late sixteenth century is evident in the head of the family James Sherlock's possession of two castles, a stone house, thirty-five messuages, 132 acres of arable land, one garden and one water mill, all of which were located in Naas.[109]

However, the Sherlocks owed little to the suppression of monastic houses in their consolidation of their position as county gentry and as rank and file officials of government in the second half of the sixteenth century. Thomas Sherlock, described as a clerk and a chaplain, was the only family member to serve on the juries which examined the monastic properties at Tully, Connall and Kildare town in November 1540. He and Patrick Barnewall held a joint lease of payments of tithes and altarages pertaining to the rectory of Carnalway which were in the gift of the prior of Connall and which were valued at £8.[110] Apart from this lease, the Sherlocks, like the Kerdiffs, were excluded from sharing in the dissolved monastic spoils in the early 1540s.

Another small Kildare gentry family who were similarly exempted from receiving monastic properties and revenues were the Flatisburys, whose association with Kildare dated back to the thirteenth century.[111] Throughout the thirteenth and fourteenth centuries members of the family held local administrative and judicial positions. By the mid-fifteenth century, the family estate had extended to the point of comprising one-third of the barony of Naas. In the early sixteenth century, the Flatisburys were closely affiliated to the house of

---

108 Ibid., p. 121. 109 J.F.M. Ffrench, 'Notes on the family of Sherlock: chiefly gathered from the state papers and other official documents' in *Kildare Arch. Soc. Jn.*, ii (1896-9), p. 46. 110 *Extents Ir. mon. possessions*, pp 157, 160, 163. He also served as a juror in the crown surveys of the estates of Gerald, ninth earl of Kildare and of the duke of Norfolk and Lord Berkeley in 1541. See *Crown surveys*, pp 10, 149. 111 Arthur Vicars, 'The family of Flatesbury of Ballnasculloge and Johnstown, County Kildare' in *Kildare Arch. Soc. Jn.*, iv (1903-5), pp 87-94 (hereafter Vicars, 'The family of Flatesbury').

Kildare. Philip of Johnstown, the son of Christopher Flatisbury and Rose Boice, was employed by the eighth earl of Kildare to compile his 'Red Book', commenced in 1503. According to Richard Stanihurst, Philip Flatisbury was 'a worthy gentleman, and a diligent antiquarian [who] wrote in the Latin tongue'.[112] He was evidently held in high regard by the ninth earl of Kildare and his association with the Fitzgeralds during the period of their ascendancy proved beneficial for him and his family, who obtained leases of properties in Clane and Sallins from the earls.[113] Philip also secured leases to farms at Baronrath, Whitechurch and Baronswood in Kildare. However, neither he nor any other member of the family held monastic land; nor were they in receipt of any income from monastic properties, rectories or vicarages.

The family's importance in the early sixteenth century thus largely hinged upon Philip's services to both the eighth and ninth earls of Kildare which boosted his family's status in social terms as well as consolidating their standing as landowners in county gentry society. Despite the fall of the Kildares, and independently of the distribution of monastic properties, the Flatisburys still maintained their position as one of the county's principal gentry families in the late sixteenth century. By that time they had established a lateral seat at Palmerstown in west Dublin in addition to their original seat at Johnstown in county Kildare.[114] A similar pattern is also evident in the cases of the St Michaels, barons of Rheban, an aristocratic family (whose influence had declined by this period), and also the Longs, the Trotts, the Wales, the Penkistons and the Creffs who ranked amongst the county's gentry but who were at best only negligibly affected by the dissolution of Kildare's monasteries.[115]

III

In short, the most notable impact of the suppression campaign upon the lesser aristocracy and strong county gentry families was to consolidate their existing holdings, the Suttons of Rathbride-Tully enjoying a relatively exceptional degree of aggrandisement through their acquisition of particularly lucrative dissolved monastic properties. Individual figures, notably Sir William Bermingham, Sir Thomas Eustace, Sir Gerald Aylmer, and David Sutton benefited most from the suppression campaign. In the case of Aylmer, Sutton and

---

112 See Vicars, 'The family of Flatesbury', p. 89. 113 *Crown surveys*, p. 291; Vicars, 'The family of Flatesbury', p. 91. 114 Fitzgerald, 'The principal gentry', p. 120. 115 *Extents Ir. mon. possessions*, pp 39-40, 61, 160-61; 'Articles against Lord Leonard Grey', 1540 (*L.&P. Hen. VIII*, xvi, no. 304).

Eustace, these grants were in reward for loyal service rendered during the crisis of the Geraldine revolt and the more general disturbances in the mid- and late 1530s, and they were used to supplement grants of confiscated Geraldine lands. Another key consideration in the selection of Eustace, Bermingham and Sutton, in particular, was the strengthening of the county's defences. The men for this project were handpicked. David Sutton, whom St Leger commended for his services in searching out treason and defending the northeast of the county during the 1530s, was installed in the dissolved pre- ceptory of Tully in central Kildare. Eustace, Viscount Baltinglass, was assigned the dissolved abbey at Baltinglass to secure the southeastern quarter of the county's marches while Lord Deputy St Leger and his brother, Robert, presided in the South Kildare-North Carlow area, occupying the nunnery of Graney and the former preceptory of Killerig respectively in the early 1540s.

The case of Bermingham especially exemplifies the success of this defen- sive dimension to the suppression campaign, weakening as it did the tradi- tional ties between the extended Bermingham family and the O'Connors, and thereby helping to neutralise the threat posed to the Dublin administration from this quarter of Kildare. While Thomas Eustace, Viscount Baltinglass made very substantial gains in his holdings as a direct result of the closure of the county's monasteries, those gains were soon lost again with the confisca- tion of Eustace land following the Baltinglass revolt of 1580. The Kerdiffs, the Sherlocks and the Flatisburys along with the Longs, the Trotts, and the Creffs received little or none of the monastic spoils. Their size, their limited holdings and wealth, their possession of little or no monastic holdings prior to the dis- solution campaign, and their lacking positions of influence in the Dublin administration all resulted in their failure to gain from the suppression of the monasteries in their immediate vicinity. In the keen competition for the prop- erties in Clane, Naas, and Connall, these low-ranking gentry were superseded by members of more prominent families with political influence, namely, David Sutton, Richard Aylmer, Sir John and Thomas Alen. As such the shar- ing out of the spoils facilitated the entrenchment of Kildare's already strong landed families in their ascendant positions.

Yet several of the county's minor gentry families managed, in spite of the vicissitudes of confiscation of Kildare lands and monastic suppressions, to retain possession of their existing holdings and in some individual cases to extend them, ranking among the county's principal gentry in 1600. While the balance of power remained constant within the ranks of the lesser aristocracy and the gentry of Kildare society, the composition of the latter underwent a significant change as a direct result of the distribution of the county's monas- tic properties and simultaneous leasing of parcels of the former Kildare estate from the mid-1530s onwards. This came about as a result of the arrival of English-born officials such as Sir John Alen, and as a consequence of the self-advancement which leases and grants of land in the county afforded individuals such as Martin Pelles, Francis Herbert, Captain Henry Colley, and a handful of others.

Sir John Alen owed his establishment as a member of Kildare gentry society entirely to his gains from the dissolution of the county's monasteries and from the fall of the senior comital dynasty. His establishment of his seat at Alenscourt in Kildare brought a change in the very composition of the county gentry, he being the first of several English-born servants of the crown who acquired property in the county in subsequent decades. However, in the Henrician era the arrival of individuals such as Alen in Kildare was still a rarity. Sir John Alen left his home in Cotteshall in Norfolk in order to serve as secretary to his cousin and namesake, John Alen, archbishop of Dublin. Both Sir John Alen and Sir Gerald Aylmer soon became products of Thomas Cromwell's efforts to reform the administration of the lordship prior to the fall of the Kildares and both gained substantially from the post-rebellion settlements and from the dissolution of Kildare's monasteries.[116] Through diligent service in the Dublin administration Sir John was quickly promoted to senior government posts, including clerk of parliament, master of the rolls, and chancellor of the exchequer. He was involved, on Cromwell's instruction, in drafting the Dublin administration's bill against the Kildares at some stage between August and September 1535.

His career advancement was greatly aided by the removal of the Kildares. From the mid-1530s onwards he established a near monopoly on the offices of keeper of the seal and later, the chancellorship, a position which he held down to 1550. In 1540 he and his brother, Thomas, were granted the offices of constable of Maynooth Castle, seneschal of the court and surveyor of Maynooth manor and keeper of the park of Maynooth.[117] Like many of his contemporaries such as William Brabazon, Thomas Luttrell and Thomas Cusack, whose careers were in the ascendant, John Alen reaped substantial personal gains as a result of the dissolution of the monasteries, being richly rewarded with the grant of a substantial estate arising from the exceptional suppression of St Wolstan's priory. He also benefited from the widespread suppressions of 1540-1 having played a leading role in the commission established to oversee this campaign. Moreover, Alen capitalised on the removal of Kildare and his uncles by securing a lease to the castle and manor of Leixlip in 1546.[118] The

---

116 Carey, *Surviving the Tudors*.   117 *Cal. pat. rolls, Ire., Hen. VIII-Eliz.*, pp 16, 34, 41, 164; *Fiants Ire., Hen. VIII*, nos 41, 160; Ellis, *Tudor Ireland*, p. 331.   118 *Fiants Ire., Hen. VIII*, no.

extent of the properties which he had amassed by the early 1550s is evident in the substantial holdings in northeast Kildare and in west Dublin which he alienated to Christopher Barnewall and others, and testifies to his success in establishing a very sizeable estate in a period of just twenty years.[119]

Sir John's brother, Thomas, accompanied him to Ireland. Thomas also carved out a successful career for himself in the Dublin administration, though not so illustrious as that of his brother. In 1535 he was appointed clerk of the hanaper and head chamberlain of the exchequer.[120] Thomas served as constable of Rathmore in east Kildare and oversaw the reparation of Athy castle in the mid- to late 1530s. In 1540 he and his brother were appointed to the constableship of Maynooth Castle.[121] In 1547 he was granted the office of constable of Wicklow Castle, a post which he was to hold for life.[122] Thomas Alen had a vested interest in certain monastic houses prior to their dissolution, most notably the preceptory of Kilteel which, as we have seen, he managed to secure for himself by negotiating a conveyance with the prior of the hospital of St John of Jerusalem prior to its dissolution. In 1543 he was granted a lease of this and other properties in Dublin which belonged to the former hospital.[123] He received grants of the dissolved property of St John's Hospital in Naas and leases of the possessions of the monastery of the order of Preachers by the mote in Naas. He also received the manorial estate of the dissolved abbey of Thomas Court at Kill along with leases of tithes and parcels of land belonging to the former prebendary of Finglas in north Dublin.[124] As late as 1550 he was still in receipt of ecclesiastical property, when he was granted a lease of the parsonage of the Norragh in southeast Kildare.[125]

Although he lived in Dublin, Thomas, like his brother, certainly made substantial gains as a result of the dissolution of Kildare's monasteries which facilitated his establishment as a landed gentleman and which complemented his standing as a favoured figure in the Dublin administration. His acquisition of Kilteel preceptory provides a clear illustration of the practice whereby members of the gentry capitalised on family connections in order to fully avail of the opportunities presented by the dissolution of the monasteries. Thomas's wife, Mary Rawson, was a relative of Sir John Rawson, the last prior of the hospital of St John of Jerusalem at Kilmainham, who made the preferential grant of the property to Alen and his wife. Thomas's brother, Sir John, was, at

478. This lease was to take effect from 1558 for a period of twenty-one years. **119** *Fiants Ire., Edw. VI*, no. 1095. **120** *Cal. pat. rolls, Ire., Hen. VIII-Eliz.*, p. 16; *Fiants Ire., Hen. VIII*, no. 42. **121** *Cal. pat. rolls, Ire., Hen. VIII-Eliz.*, p. 34; *Fiants Ire., Hen. VIII*, no. 160. **122** *Fiants Ire., Edw. VI*, no. 138. **123** *Cal. pat. rolls, Ire., Hen. VIII-Eliz.*, pp 76, 92; *Extents Ir. mon. possessions*, p. 91; *Calendar of inquisitions*, p. 90. **124** *Fiants Ire., Hen. VIII*, nos 80, 245; *Fiants Ire., Edw. VI*, no. 62. **125** *Cal. pat. rolls, Ire., Hen. VIII-Eliz.*, p. 217.

that time, keeper of the great seal, and he ratified this rather dubious arrangement.

Sir John and Thomas both owed their political advancement to the removal of the Kildares, and Sir John owed a substantial section of his estate to the attainder of James Fitzgerald of Leixlip. It is therefore hardly surprising that both men were fearful for their positions and vigorously resisted the restoration of the eleventh earl in the early 1550s.[126] Sir John had no son to succeed him and so Thomas's son, also named John, inherited his uncle's estate of Alenscourt and ensured the establishment of the Alen family within the ranks of the Pale gentry beyond this first generation.[127] However, during the sixteenth and early seventeenth centuries the Alens did not integrate with county Kildare's existing gentry; instead they married the daughters of Dublin and Meath families.[128]

At the other end of the social scale, Martin Pelles managed to elevate himself to the status of a county gentleman as a direct result of his acquisition of dissolved monastic property and parcels of the former Kildare estate. However, Pelles's acquired status only lasted during his lifetime and his family name failed to appear among the principal gentry of Kildare in 1600. In 1543 Captain Robert Browne was granted a lease of a parcel of the dissolved property of Baltinglass Abbey.[129] Other individuals, including a yeoman named John Lye of Ballina in Kildare and Captain Henry Colley, received leases of Walter Delahide's county Kildare possessions arising from his attainder for his implication in the Geraldine revolt.[130] However, unlike Pelles and Browne, both Lye and Colley ensured that their successors became firmly established as members of the county gentry.[131]

IV

In essence, therefore, the impact of the suppression campaign in Kildare (the most effectively implemented aspect of the Henrician Reformation in Ireland) was to boost the estates and the social standing of individual members of the

---

126 For a detailed discussion of the Alens' reaction to the restoration of the eleventh earl of Kildare see Carey, *Surviving the Tudors*. 127 H.L. Lyster Denny, 'An account of the family of Alen of St Wolstan's, County Kildare', *in Kildare Arch. Soc. Jn.*, iv (1903-05), pp 95-110. 128 Ibid. 129 See Bradshaw, *Dissolution of religious orders*, p. 233. 130 *Fiants Ire.,Hen. VIII*, nos 442, 443. See also Edward O'Leary, 'John Lye, of Clonaugh, County Kildare', in *Kildare Arch. Soc. Jn.*, iii (1899-1902), pp 39-50 and Walter Fitzgerald, 'Two Colley inscriptions in the Castle Carbury churchyard; with notes on the founder of the family', in *Kildare Arch. Soc. Jn.*, viii (1915-17), pp 369-87. 131 Fitzgerald, 'The principal gentry', pp 119, 121.

county's lesser aristocracy and leading gentry families. It also marked the first phase in the introduction of English-born gentlemen and soldiers into Kildare society which changed the composition of the county gentry. The political vacuum caused by the removal of the Kildares and the distribution of some of their manorial estates combined with the dissolution of the county's monasteries provided individual members of the Eustace, Alen, Bermingham, Sutton, and Aylmer families with an unprecedented opportunity for advancement.[132] Having become accustomed to their freedom from the restraining influence of the earl of Kildare throughout the 1540s, those beneficiaries who survived to witness the restoration of the eleventh earl of Kildare fought hard to resist the earl's endeavours to revive his predecessors' authority over them.[133] The eighth and ninth earls of Kildare had been acutely aware of their need to constantly court the support, and to restrain the independence, of county Kildare's aristocracy and gentry. Relations between the ninth earl and the county's gentlemen were said to have been based upon the latter's having formally granted the earl permission 'to have ... the defence of them, and also to spend them ... but at their own pleasure'.

However, as David Sutton wistfully remarked, the gentry only consented to this ostensibly voluntary arrangement since they 'durst not say the contrary'.[134] The reaction of individuals such as Sir Thomas Eustace, Richard Aylmer, Sir Gerald Aylmer and David Sutton to the Geraldine rebellion exposed the frailty of their ties with the senior comital family and provided a telling illustration of their capacity to deploy their independent resources to advance their own interests at the expense of the Kildares. As Sir John and Thomas Alen, and Oliver Sutton, were at pains to impress upon Gerald, the eleventh earl, the Kildare to which he was returning had undergone significant change since the era of his forefathers and they were determined to resist any efforts to cause the shire to revert to being a Geraldine enclave.

---

132 Hore and Graves (eds), *Southern and eastern counties*, pp 160, 168; Ellis, *Tudor frontiers and noble power*, p. 139. 133 Similarly, a new minor nobility emerged in the north of England following the reduction of the Dacre and Percy families by the crown in the 1530s. See Carey, *Surviving the Tudors*. 134 For a detailed discussion of the reaction of the county gentry to the restoration of the eleventh earl of Kildare see Carey, *Surviving the Tudors*.

Conclusion

The period 1470-1547 marks a threshold in the history of the Irish lordship and of county Kildare in particular. Between 1471 when Gearóid Mór Fitzgerald succeeded his father, Thomas, as eighth earl of Kildare and 1519 when Gearóid Óg was summoned to the court of Henry VIII to answer complaints regarding his governance, this dynasty's relations with the crown and their joint roles as county overlords and captains were characteristic of the late medieval era. Successive English monarchs resorted to aristocratic delegation as the most effective if otherwise problematic means of governing outlying areas of the realm, notably the Northern marches of England, the Welsh marches and the lordship of Ireland. Like most noblemen in the medieval era, the Kildares and especially the eighth earl had a direct personal relationship with the monarch. Down to the outbreak of the Geraldine rebellion in 1534 the dynasty had a strong faction within the Irish council. In the era of the seventh and eighth earls, their dynastic and official roles and actions were largely indistinguishable. The revival of the medieval liberty of Kildare in the early 1500s was wholly in line with a medieval style of government and served as recognition of loyal service rendered by this nobleman to the crown. The earls of Kildare and the county gentry embraced the trappings of decadent medieval piety and were munificent patrons of the church. They actively intervened in ecclesiastical affairs and Edmund Lane, bishop of Kildare between 1480 and 1522/3, was a close ally and friend of both the eighth and ninth earls.

At county level, Thomas, the seventh earl, had been responsible for reviving the Kildare dynasty from its abeyance during the period 1432-c.1453. During his lifetime and particularly in the period following his appointment as justiciar of the lordship in 1454, Thomas devoted his energies to restoring his wasted dynastic inheritance and to establishing the basis of the Kildare ascendancy in the government of Ireland. Together, Thomas, Sir Edward FitzEustace and later, Sir Roland, baron of Portlester, successfully arrested and reversed Gaelic incursions of the colony's marchlands in county Kildare, a task continued by Thomas's successor, Gearóid Mór. At the turn of the cen-

tury, the combination of the Gearóid Mór's unrivalled position as governor of
the lordship and Bishop Lane's episcopacy in the diocese of Kildare brought
about stability in both church and society in Kildare.

At the height of their ascendancy, the eighth and ninth earls, at once overlords of twenty manors in the county and captains of the Pale's defences, dominated both the secular and ecclesiastical spheres of Kildare society, their
influence percolating down to virtually every locality throughout the county.
Their authority was boosted by Henry VIII's grant of liberty jurisdiction to the
shire in the mid-1510s and down to the outbreak of rebellion in 1534, they
succeeded in checking the ambitions and supplanting the lurking opposition
of the county's lesser aristocracy and gentry.

Signs of the onset of a change in the political arena in the lordship first
became manifest in the late 1510s but more especially in the 1520s and early
1530s. Increasingly a coterie of Palesmen, joined by Ossory and his supporters, as well as Cardinal Wolsey, Thomas Cromwell and prominent ecclesiastics including John Alen, archbishop of Dublin and Walter Wellesley, bishop
of Kildare, highlighted the distinction between Kildare's pursuit of dynastic
and official roles and accused him of maladministration. The divorce issue and
the break with Rome in the early 1530s necessitated the introduction of a more
bureaucratic centralised approach to governing the sovereign Tudor state. The
medieval style of aristocratic, semi-autonomous governance to which the earls
of Kildare were accustomed was incompatible with Thomas Cromwell's
'Ordinances for the government of Ireland' as were liberties such as that conferred on county Kildare, and the refusal of the ninth earl of countenance a
compromise of his position resulted in an infamous stance of defiance. The
year 1534 indeed marked a decisive transition in the strategy for governing the
lordship which dispensed with a medieval style of government based on aristocratic rule and replaced it with a more modern bureaucratic regime, headed
by an English-born lord deputy, backed by a standing English army.

In the aftermath of the Geraldine rebellion, almost at once county Kildare
underwent cataclysmic changes. It lost its principal dynasty. It was stripped of
its liberty status. Its monastic houses were suppressed. It was left in a partially
wasted state as a result of the Geraldine rebellion and subsequent raids
mounted by neighbouring Gaelic elements. And, as a result of the removal of
the earls of Kildare and the closure of the monasteries, it witnessed the emer-
gence of a strong, independent-minded county gentry, some of whom were to
fiercely oppose the restoration of the eleventh earl of Kildare in the early
1550s.

Though the gentlemen of the county were collectively described as 'the
most sorriest afraid men in the world' in 1536, individuals such as Thomas

Eustace, David Sutton, Richard and Gerald Aylmer and William Bermingham, were poised to reap the rewards for their show of loyalty to the crown during the crisis. For the first time in three generations, the restraining grip of the earls of Kildare had been removed from the county's peers and gentlemen who, according to David Sutton, had only ever grudgingly acquiesced to the ninth earl's authority. While they could no longer depend on the earl's protection, they were freed from their obligation to tolerate his uncertain exactions, his costly hostings, his sporadic and often viscious surprise attacks as in the case of Castledermot and his alleged abuse of legal codes in the pursuit of his own interests. With the Kildares gone, Ossory had less reason to mount attacks on their former lordship. The suppression of the county's liberty once again opened the shire to the Dublin administration and provided county gentlemen with local government and judicial positions. The Kildares having been ousted as the county's premier magnates, individuals such as Sir Thomas Eustace and Sir William Bermingham were promoted to the most senior ranks in the county's aristocracy, the two men being regarded as the most influential figures on the county in the wake of the Kildare rebellion.

The removal of the earls from their dominant position in the Dublin administration directly facilitated the career advancement of county gentlemen including Sir Gerald and Richard Aylmer, David and Oliver Sutton and that of English-born officials such as Sir John Alen and his brother, Thomas. Most importantly of all, the distribution of confiscated land belonging to the earl and his supporters among the county's aristocracy and gentry greatly strengthened the position of these individuals, and provided others such as Sir John Alen, Captain Henry Colley, and Francis Herbert with a seat in the county. Members of the clergy, especially Walter Wellesley, bishop of Kildare, were also relieved by the removal of the ninth earl. During the early 1540s, these lesser aristocrats and strong gentry consolidated their positions and became accustomed to their new-found freedom in the wake of the attainder of the Kildares. Not surprisingly, they were loath to surrender their land, their independence, their political influence, and their role in local government and judicial affairs in the event of the restoration of the eleventh earl of Kildare. Consequently, throughout the 1550s and 1560s, Oliver Sutton and the Alen brothers did their utmost to preserve the newly-acquired, though still rather tenuous position, which the lesser aristocracy and the gentlemen of Kildare had established for themselves.

The Henrician Reformation provided the second major dynamic for change in county Kildare in the 1530s and 1540s and as this study has shown, the dissolution of the county's monastic houses was the only element of the Henrician Reformation which had a real impact in the county. Coming as it did in the immediate aftermath of the Kildare rebellion, the suppression campaign served to consolidate the positions of the county's aristocracy and gentry just as it had done in England, and was deliberately tailored to facilitate the extension of effective royal authority throughout Kildare and beyond the four shires of the colony.[1] While the earls of Kildare overshadowed the county's political, social, economic and ecclesiastical life down to their demise in 1534, its aristocracy and gentry embraced the fall of the county's leading magnates and the closure of its monasteries, turned both to their advantage, and poised themselves to resist any attempts on the part of the eleventh earl of Kildare to undermine the new order established in Kildare during the Geraldine abeyance.

1 See Christopher Kitching, 'The disposal of monastic and chantry lands', in Felicity Heal and Rosemary O'Day (eds), *Church and society in England: Henry VIII to James I* (London, 1977), pp 119-36.

Appendix: The Monastic Houses of County Kildare, *c*.1530

A. *Independent,* * *isolated religious houses in county Kildare*

Priory of Connall
Baltinglass Abbey
Graney Nunnery
Monasterevin Abbey
St Wolstan's Priory
Timolin Nunnery
New Abbey, Kilcullen
Cloncurry Friary

B. *Independent monastic houses based in the towns and villages of county Kildare*

Naas
 St John's Hospital
 Dominican priory
 Austin friary

Athy
 St John's Hospital
 Dominican priory

Castledermot
 St John's Hospital
 Franciscan friary

Kildare
 Franciscan friary
 Brigittine nunnery
 Carmelite priory

Clane
 Franciscan friary

C. *Cell and preceptories located in county Kildare and affiliated to external houses*

Kilrush (cell of Cartmel Priory, England)
Tully (preceptory of St John's Hospital, Kilmainham)
Kilteel (preceptory of St John's Hospital, Kilmainham)
Killybeggs (preceptory of St John's Hospital, Kilmainham)

* Monasteries not affiliated to parent houses located outside of county Kildare

186

Bibliography

GUIDES TO SOURCES

GUIDES TO ARCHIVAL MATERIAL

Edwards, Robin Dudley and O'Dowd, Mary, *Sources for modern Irish history, 1534-1641* (Cambridge, 1985).

Wood, Herbert, *A guide to the records deposited in the Public Record Office of Ireland* (Dublin, 1919).

GUIDES TO MISCELLANEOUS MANUSCRIPT MATERIAL

Harris: 'Collectanea de rebus Hibernicus', ed. Charles McNeill, in *Analecta Hibernica*, no. 6 (1934), pp 248-50.

Hayes, R.J., *The manuscript sources for the history of Irish civilization* (11 vols, Boston, Mass., 1965).

O'Grady, S.H., *Catalogue of Irish manuscripts in the British Museum* (3 vols, London, 1926-53).

GUIDES TO PRINTED BOOKS AND ARTICLES

Eager, A.R., *A guide to Irish bibliographical material* (London, 1964).

Hayes, R.J., *Sources for the history of Irish civilization: articles in periodicals* (9 vols, Boston, Mass., 1970).

ORIGINAL SOURCES

MANUSCRIPT MATERIAL

Dublin

National Archives of Ireland, Bishop St.

    County Kildare exchequer inquisitions, Hen. VIII-Jas. I.

    County Dublin exchequer inquisitions, Hen. VIII-Eliz. I.

National Library of Ireland

    MS 5769. Photostat copy of the Red Book of the earls of Kildare.

Trinity College

    MS 566 Valor of Irish ecclesiastical benefices from 20 Hen. VIII to 1591.

    MS 584 (E.3.22). Chronica Hiberniae by Philip Flatisbury.

PRINTED AND CALENDARED MATERIAL

Accounts of sums realised by sale of chattels of some suppressed Irish monasteries, ed. Charles McNeill, in *Journal of the Royal Society of Antiquaries of Ireland*, lii (1922), pp 11-37.

A statute of the fortieth year of King Edward III, enacted in a parliament held in Kilkenny, AD 1367. Before Lionel, duke of Clarence, lord lieutenant of Ireland, ed. James Hardiman, in *Tracts relating to Ireland*, ii (Dublin, 1843).

Brevis synopsis provincae Hiberniae FF. Minorum, ed. Brendan Jennings, in *Analecta Hibernica*, vi (1934), pp 139-91.

Calendar of ancient records of Dublin, ed. J.T. Gilbert (18 vols. Dublin, 1889-1922).

Calendar of Archbishop Alen's register, c.1172-1534, ed. Charles McNeill (Dublin, 1950).

Calendar of entries in the papal registers relating to Great Britain and Ireland, xvi, ed. Anne Fuller (Dublin, 1994).

Calendar of fiants, Henry VIII to Elizabeth, in *Report of the Deputy Keeper of the Public Records of Ireland*, 7-22 (Dublin, 1875-90).

Calendar of inquisitions formerly in the office of the chief remembrancer of the exchequer prepared for the MSS of the Irish Record Commission, ed. Margaret Griffith (Dublin, 1991).

Calendar of Ormond deeds, 1172-1350 [etc.], ed. Edmund Curtis (6 vols, Dublin, 1932-43).

Calendar of the Carew manuscripts preserved in the archiepiscopal library at Lambeth, 1515-1624 (6 vols, London, 1867-73).

Calendar of the patent and close rolls of chancery in Ireland of the reigns of Henry VIII, Edward VI, Mary, and Elizabeth, ed. James Morrin. i (1514-75); ii (1576-1603) (Dublin, 1861-63).

Calendar of the state papers relating to Ireland, 1509-1625 (16 vols, London, 1860-61).

Collections on Irish church history from the MSS of ... Laurence F. Renehan, ed. Daniel McCarthy (2 vols, Dublin, 1861-74).

Crown surveys of lands, 1540-41 with the Kildare rental begun in 1518, ed. Gearóid MacNiocaill (Dublin, 1992).

De annatis Hiberniae, eds M.A. Costello and Ambrose Coleman (Dundalk, 1909).

Extents of Irish monastic possessions, 1540-1541, from manuscripts in the Public Record Office, London, ed. N.B. White (Dublin, 1943).

Letters and papers, foreign and domestic, Henry VIII (21 vols, London, 1862-1932).

Letters and papers illustrative of the reigns of Richard III and Henry VII, ed. James Gairdner (2 vols, Nendeln, 1965 reprint).

Liber munerum publicorum Hiberniae, ab. an. 1152 usque ad. an. 1827; or, the establishments of Ireland ... report, ed. Rowley Lascelles (7 vols, London, 1824).

Obligationes pro annatis diocesis Darensis, 1413-1521, ed. Ambrose Coleman, in *Archivium Hibernicum*, ii (1913), pp 39-72.

Obligationes pro annatis diocesis Dublinensis, 1421-1520, ed. Ambrose Coleman, in *Archivium Hibernicum*, ii (1913), pp 1-37.

Original letters and papers in illustration of the history of the Church of Ireland during the reigns of Edward VI, Mary and Elizabeth, ed. E.P. Shirley (London, 1851).

Registrum de Kilmainham, ed. Charles McNeill (Dublin, 1932).

State papers, Henry VIII (11 vols, London, 1830-52).

The bills and statutes of the Irish parliaments of Henry VII and Henry VIII, ed. D.B. Quinn, in *Analecta Hibernica*, no. 10 (1941), pp 71-169.

The book of obits and martyrology of the cathedral church of the Holy Trinity, ed. John Clarke Crosthwaite (Dublin, 1845).

The 'dignitas decani' of St Patrick's Cathedral, Dublin, ed. N.B. White (Dublin, 1957).

The Kildare rental book, ed. duke of Leinster, in Historical Manuscripts Commission, *Ninth Report, Part II, Appendix* (London, 1884).

The Red Book of the earls of Kildare, ed. Gearóid MacNiocaill (Dublin, 1964).

The registers of Christ Church Cathedral, Dublin, ed. Raymond Refaussé and Colm Lennon (Dublin, 1998).

The rental book of Gerald Fitzgerald, ninth earl of Kildare, begun in the year 1518, ed. H.F. Hore, in *Journal of the Royal Society of Antiquaries of Ireland*, 2nd ser., ii (1858-9), pp 266-80, 301-13; iv (1862-3), pp 110-37; v (1864-6), pp 501-18, 525-46.

The reportorium viride of John Alen, archbishop of Dublin, 1533, ed. N.B. White, in *Analecta Hibernica*, no. 10 (1941), pp 173-222.

The social state of the southern and eastern counties of Ireland in the sixteenth century: being the presentments of the gentlemen, commonalty and citizens of Carlow, Cork, Kilkenny, Tipperary, Waterford, and Wexford, made in the reigns of Henry VIII and Elizabeth, ed. H.F. Hore and James Graves (Dublin, 1870).

Valor beneficiorum ecclesiasticorum in Hiberniae: or the first fruits of all the kingdom of Ireland (Dublin, 1741; reprint 1780).

PRINTED CONTEMPORARY OR NEAR CONTEMPORARY CHRONICLES AND ACCOUNTS

Annála Connacht: the annals of Connacht, AD 1224-1544, ed. A.M. Freeman (Dublin, 1944; reprint 1970).

Annála ríoghachta Éireann: annals of the kingdom of Ireland by the Four Masters, from the earliest period to the year 1616, ed. John O'Donovan (7 vols, Dublin, 1851).

Annála Uladh: annals of Ulster ... : a chronicle of Irish affairs ... ,431 to 1541, ed. W.M. Hennessy and Bartholomew MacCarthy (4 vols, Dublin, 1887-1901).

Campion, Edmund, *A historie of Ireland, written in the year 1571* (Dublin, 1809 ed.).

Chronicles of England, Scotland and Ireland, ed. Raphael Holinshed (6 vols, London, 1577).

Davies, John, *A discovery of the true causes why Ireland was never entirely subdued ... until ... his majesty's happy reign* (facsimile reprint, Shannon, 1969).

Spenser, Edmund, *A view of the present state of Ireland* (Dublin, 1763).

Stanihurst, Richard, 'A plain and perfect description of Ireland', in *Chronicles of England ...*, ed. Raphael Holinshed.

——. 'A history of the reign of Henry VIII', in *Chronicles of England ...*, ed. Raphael Holinshed.

The whole works of Sir James Ware concerning Ireland, ed. Walter Harris (2 vols, Dublin, 1764).

Vergil, Polydore, *The Anglica historia ... AD 1485-1537*, ed. and trans. Denys Hay (London, 1950).

Ware, James, *The antiquities and history of Ireland* (Dublin, 1705).

MODERN WORKS

PUBLISHED WORKS

Anonymous, *Old Kilcullen, with notes and sketches and a short bibliography* (n.p., 1977).

Archdall, Mervyn, *Monasticon Hibernicum: or, a history of the abbeys, priories, and other religious houses in Ireland*, ed. P.F. Moran (2 vols, incomplete revised ed. Dublin, 1873-6).

Aylmer, Fenton, 'Sir Gerald Aylmer, knight and baronet', in *Kildare Arch. Soc. Jn.*, xi (1930-33), pp 367-85.

Aylmer, Henrick, 'The Aylmer family', in *Kildare Arch. Soc. Jn.*, i (1891-95), pp 295-307.

——. 'Rathangan', in *Kildare Arch. Soc. Jn.*, iii (1899-1902), pp 372-81.

Bagwell, Richard, *Ireland under the Tudors* (3 vols, London, 1885-90; reprint, 1962).

Bottingheimer, Karl, 'The failure of the Reformation: une question bien posée', in *Journal of Ecclesiastical History*, xxxvi, no. 2 (Apr. 1985), pp 196-207.

Blacker, George, *A record of the history of Maynooth church, but principally of the prebendaries of Maynooth and the vicars of Laraghbryan* (Dublin, 1867).

Bradley, John, 'The chantry college, Ardee', in *Louth Arch. Soc. Jn.*, xxii, 1 (1989), pp 16-19.

Bradshaw, Brendan, *The dissolution of the religious orders in Ireland under Henry VIII* (Cambridge, 1974).

——, 'Cromwellian reform and the origins of the Kildare rebellion, 1533-34', in *Transactions of the Royal Historical Society*, 5th ser., xxvii (1977), pp 69-93.

——, 'Sword, word and strategy in the Reformation in Ireland', in *Historical Journal*, xxi, no. 3 (1978), pp 475-502.

——, *The Irish constitutional revolution of the sixteenth century* (Cambridge, 1979).

Brady, Ciaran, 'Conservative subversives: the community of the Pale and the Dublin administration 1556-86', in P.J. Corish (ed.), *Radicals, rebels and establishments* (Belfast, 1985), pp 11-32.

Brady, John, 'The medieval diocese of Meath', in *Ríocht na Midhe*, i, no. 3 (1957), pp 34-40.

Brady, W.M., *The Irish Reformation, or the alleged conversion of the Irish bishops* (5th ed., London, 1867).

——, *The episcopal succession in England, Scotland, and Ireland, AD 1400 to 1875* (3 vols, Rome, 1876-7; reprint, with a new introduction by A.F. Allison, Farnborough, 1971. ii. Ireland).

Bryan, Donough, *Gerald Fitzgerald, the great earl of Kildare, 1456-1513* (Dublin, 1933).

Canny, N.P., *The formation of the Old English élite in Ireland* (Dublin, 1975).

——, 'Why the Reformation failed in Ireland: une question malposée', in *Journal of Ecclesiastical History*, xxx (1979), pp 423-50.

——, *From Reformation to Restoration: Ireland, 1534-1660* (Dublin, 1987).

Carroll, James, 'Remains in Athy and neighbourhood', in *Kildare Arch. Soc. Jn.*, i (1891-95), pp 102-12.

Clark, Mary and Refaussé (eds), *Directory of historic Dublin guilds* (Dublin, 1993).

Comerford, Michael, *Collections relating to the dioceses of Kildare and Leighlin* (3 vols, Dublin, 1883-6).

——, ' "The ford of Ae": some historical notes on the town of Athy', in *Kildare Arch. Soc. Jn.*, i (1891-95), pp 57-70.

——, 'Castledermot: its history and antiquities', in *Kildare Arch. Soc. Jn.*, i (1891-95), pp 361-78.

Cosgrove, Art and McCartney, Donal (eds), *Studies in Irish history presented to R. Dudley Edwards* (Dublin, 1979).

Cosgrove, Art, *Late medieval Ireland, 1370-1541* (Dublin, 1981).

——. (ed.), *A new history of Ireland, ii. Medieval Ireland, 1169-1534* (Oxford, 1987).

Cotton, Henry, *Fasti ecclesiae Hibernicae* (6 vols, Dublin, 1848-78).

Curtis, Edmund, A *history of medieval Ireland from 1086 to 1513* (London, 1923; 2nd ed., 1938; reprint, 1968).

——, 'The barons of Norragh, Co Kildare, 1171-1660', in *Journal of the Royal Society of Antiquaries of Ireland*, lxv (1935), pp 84-101.

——, *History of Ireland* (London, 1936; 6th ed., 1950).

Cusack, Pearse, 'The Cusacks of Killeen, Co Meath', in *Ríocht na Midhe*, vii, no. 4 (1980-81), pp 3-35.

De Burgh, T.J., 'Ancient Naas', in *Kildare Arch. Soc. Jn.*, i (1891-95), pp 184-201, 265-80, 318-36.

De La Poer, Edmund, 'James de Poher, Count. FitzEustace or Eustace of Baltinglass', in *Waterford Arch. Soc. Jn.*, v (1899), pp 190-5.

Devitt, Michael, 'Carbury and the Birminghams' country', in *Kildare Arch. Soc. Jn.*, ii (1896-9), pp 85-110.

——, 'Rathcoffey', in *Kildare Arch. Soc. Jn.*, iii (1899-1902), pp 79-98.

——, 'The rampart of the Pale', in *Kildare Arch. Soc. Jn.*, iii (1899-1902), pp 284-8.

——, 'The see lands of Kildare', in *Kildare Arch. Soc. Jn.*, ix (1903), pp 358-65, 416-29.

——, 'Old proprietors in Straffan and Irishtown', in *Kildare Arch. Soc. Jn.*, x (1922-8), pp 272-300.

Dickens, A.G., *The English Reformation* (14th ed. Glasgow, 1988).

Duffy, Eamon, *The stripping of the altars: traditional religion in England, 1400-1580* (New Haven, 1992).

Dudley Edwards, Robin, 'Venerable John Travers and the rebellion of Silken Thomas', in *Studies*, xxiii, no. 92 (1934), pp 687-99.

——, *Church and state in Tudor Ireland* (Dublin, 1936; reprint, 1972).

Ellis, Steven, 'The Kildare rebellion and the early Henrician Reformation', in *Historical Journal*, xix (1976), pp 807-30.

——, 'Tudor policy and the Kildare ascendancy in the lordship of Ireland, 1496-1534', in *Irish Historical Studies*, xx, no. 79 (Mar. 1977), pp 235-71.

——, 'Parliaments and great councils, 1483-99; *addenda et corrigenda*', in *Analecta Hibernica*, no. 29 (1980), pp 96-111.

——, 'Thomas Cromwell and Ireland, 1532-40', in *Historical Journal*, xxiii (1980), pp 497-519.

——, 'Henry VII and Ireland, 1491-1496', in James Lydon (ed.), *England and Ireland in the later middle ages in honour of Jocelyn Otway-Ruthven*, pp 237-54.

——, 'Henry VIII, rebellion and the rule of law', in *Historical Journal*, xxiv, no. 3 (1981), pp 513-31.

——, 'The destruction of the liberties: some further evidence', in *Bulletin of the Institute of Historical Research*, liv (1981), pp 150-61.

——, *Tudor Ireland: crown, community and the conflict of cultures, 1470-1603* (London, 1985).

——, *Reform and revival: English government in Ireland, 1470-1534* (London, 1986).

——, 'Economic problems of the church: why the Reformation failed in Ireland', in *Irish Economic and Social History*, xli, no. 2 (1990), pp 257-69.

——, *Tudor frontiers and noble power: the making of the British state* (Oxford, 1995).

Fitzgerald, Brian, *The Geraldines: an experiment in Irish government, 1169-1601* (London, 1951).

Fitzgerald, C.W., *The earls of Kildare and their ancestors from 1057 to 1773* (Dublin, 1858).

Fitzgerald, Walter, 'Stone effigies in the county', in *Kildare Arch. Soc. Jn.*, i (1891-95), p. 207.

——, 'The Fitzgeralds of Lackagh', in *Kildare Arch. Soc. Jn.*, i (1891-95), pp 245-64.

——, 'Queries', in *Kildare Arch. Soc. Jn.*, i (1891-95), p. 407.

——, 'Parish of Carbury – Dunfierth churchyard', in *Association for the preservation of the memorials of the dead in Ireland Journal*, ii (1892-4), pp 512-14.

——, 'Cathedral of St Brigid', in *Association for the preservation of the memorials of the dead in Ireland Journal*, ii, no. 2 (1893), pp 321-23.

——, 'Kilkea Castle', in *Kildare Arch. Soc. Jn.*, ii (1896-9), pp 3-32.

——, 'Castle Rheban', in *Kildare Arch. Soc. Jn.*, ii (1896-9), pp 167-78.

——, 'Great Connell Abbey, Co Kildare', in *Kildare Arch. Soc. Jn.*, ii (1896-9), pp 304-14.

——, 'Castletown and its owners', in *Kildare Arch. Soc. Jn.*, ii (1896-9), pp 361-78.

——, 'Leixlip Castle', in *Kildare Arch. Soc. Jn.*, ii (1896-9), pp 393-406.

——, 'Timolin', in *Kildare Arch. Soc. Jn.*, ii (1896-9), pp 413-25.

——, 'The principal gentry of the county of Kildare in the year 1600', in *Kildare Arch. Soc. Jn.*, iii (1899-1902), pp 118-22.

——, 'New Abbey of Kilcullen', in *Kildare Arch. Soc. Jn.*, iii (1899-1902), pp 301-17.

——, 'Ballymore Eustace and its neighbouring antiquities', in *Kildare Arch. Soc. Jn.*, iii (1899-1902), pp 343-60.

——, 'Members of parliament for the County Kildare in 1560 and 1585', in *Kildare Arch. Soc. Jn.*, iv (1903-05), pp 167-8.

——, 'The members of the Eustace family on the inquisition jury in 1537', in *Kildare Arch. Soc. Jn.*, iv (1903-05), p. 255.

——, 'The house and demesne of Monasterevin', in *Kildare Arch. Soc. Jn.*, iv (1903-5), pp 256-7.

——, 'Donadea church', in *Association for the preservation of the memorials of the dead in Ireland Journal*, vi, no. 1, pts 1-2 (1904), pp 93-7.

——, 'Baltinglass Abbey, its possessions, and their post-Reformation proprietors', in *Kildare Arch. Soc. Jn.*, v (1906-08), pp 379-405.

——, 'Extracts from a County Dublin exchequer inquisition concerning landholders in the county of Kildare in 1535', in *Kildare Arch. Soc. Jn.*, vi (1909-11), pp 179-80.

——, 'The Kerdiffs of Kerdiffstown, County Kildare', in *Kildare Arch. Soc. Jn.*, vii (1912-14), pp 182-6.

——, 'Norraghmore and the barons of Norragh', in *Kildare Arch. Soc. Jn.*, vii (1912-14), pp 242-72.

——, 'The parish of Yago, and the townland of Gaganstown', in *Kildare Arch. Soc. Jn.*, vii (1912-14), pp 336-7.

——, 'The priory or nunnery of Graney, County Kildare', in *Kildare Arch. Soc. Jn.*, vii (1912-14), pp 373-81.

——, 'The preceptory or commandery of Kilteel, County Kildare', in *Kildare Arch. Soc. Jn.*, viii (1915-17), pp 267-75.

——, 'Two Colley inscriptions in the Castle Carbury churchyard; with notes on the founder of the family', in *Kildare Arch. Soc. Jn.*, viii (1915-17), pp 369-87.

——, 'The earl of Kildare's manor of Geashill in the King's County, with notes on Killeigh in the parish of Geashill', in *Kildare Arch. Soc. Jn.*, ix (1918-21), pp 3-33.

——, 'The proprietors of the manor of Monasterevin', in *Kildare Arch. Soc. Jn.*, ix (1918-21), pp 80-82.

Flanagan, M.T,. 'Henry II and kingdom of Uí Fáeláin', in John Bradley (ed.). *Settlement and society in medieval Ireland: studies presented to F.X. Martin, O.S.A.* (Kilkenny, 1988), pp 312-24.

Ffrench, J.F.M., 'Notes on the family of Sherlock: chiefly gathered from the state papers and other official documents', in *Kildare Arch. Soc. Jn.*, ii (1896-9), pp 39-47.

Garstin, John Ribton, 'The high sheriffs of the County Kildare', in *Kildare Arch. Soc. Jn.*, ii (1896-9), pp 253-61.

Gilbert, J.T., *A history of the city of Dublin* (3 vols, Dublin, 1854-9; reprint with index 1861; abridged ed., by R.M. Gilbert, Dublin, 1903).

Grattan Flood, W.H., 'The episcopal succession of Kildare, 1206-1577', in *Irish Ecclesiastical Record*, 5th ser., xxi (1923), pp 154-63.

Gwynn, Aubrey, *The medieval province of Armagh, 1470-1545* (Dundalk, 1946).

——, *Anglo-Irish church life: fourteenth and fifteenth centuries* (Dublin, 1968.

—— and Hadcock, R., *Medieval religious houses: Ireland with an appendix to early sites* (London, 1970).

Hamilton, Bernard, *Religion in the medieval west* (London, 1986).

Haigh, Christopher (ed.), *The English Reformation revised* (Cambridge, 1987).

——, *English Reformations: religion, politics and society under the Tudors* (Oxford, 1993).

Hamilton, Gustavus, 'The names of the baronies and parishes in County Kildare', in *Kildare Arch. Soc. Jn.*, viii (1915-17), pp 241-66, 425-45; ix (1918-21), pp 110-23, 246-57.

Hand, Geoffrey, 'The medieval chapter of St Mary's Cathedral, Limerick', in Watt, Morrall and Martin (eds), *Medieval studies presented to Aubrey Gwynn*, pp 74-89.

Hannan, T.J., 'St John's Friary, Athy', in *Kildare Arch. Soc. Jn.*, i (1891-95), pp 113-14.

Harper-Bill, Christopher, *The pre-Reformation church in England, 1400-1530* (London, 1989).

Hayden, Mary, 'Lambert Simnel in Ireland', in *Studies*, iv (1915), pp 622-36.

Hayden, Tadhg, *Castledermot: its history and traditions* (Carlow, 1953).

Heal, Felicity and O'Day, Rosemary (eds), *Church and society in England: Henry VIII to James I* (London, 1977).

Heal, Felicity, 'Economic problems of the clergy', in Heal and O'Day (eds), *Church and society in England: Henry VIII to James I*, pp 99-118 .

Healy, John, 'The college of the Blessed Virgin Mary of Maynooth, County Kildare', in *Irish Ecclesiastical Record*, 3rd ser., i (1880), pp 537-48.

Heath, Peter, *The English parish clergy on the eve of the Reformation* (London, 1969).

Hunt, John, *Irish medieval figure sculpture, 1200-1600: a study of Irish tombs, with notes on costume and armour* (2 vols, Dublin, 1974).

——, 'Tomb of Sir Walter Bermingham, obit. 1548', in *Kildare Arch. Soc. Jn.*, xv (1971-6), pp 12-16.

Hutton, Ronald, 'The local impact of the Tudor Reformations', in Christopher Haigh (ed.), *The English Reformation revised*, pp 114-38.

Jefferies, Henry, 'The church courts of Armagh on the eve of the Reformation', in *Seanchas Ardmhacha*, xv (1993), pp 1-38.

——, 'Diocesan synods and convocation in Armagh on the eve of the Tudor Reformations', in *Seanchas Ardmhacha*, xvi (1995), pp 120-32.

——, 'The laity in the parishes of Armagh *inter Anglicos* on the eve of the Reformation', in *Archivium Hibernicum*, lii (forthcoming)

——, *Priests and prelates of Armagh in the age of Reformations, 1518-1558* (Dublin, 1997).

Kingston, John, 'The Catholic families of the Pale', in *Reportorium Novum*, i, nos 1-2 (1955-6), pp 76-90; ii, nos 1-2 (1957-6), pp 88-108, 236-56.

Kirkpatrick, W.T., 'Donacomper church', in *Kildare Arch. Soc. Jn.*, ii (1896-9), pp 277-82.

Kitching, Christopher, 'The disposal of monastic and chantry lands', in Heal and O'Day (eds), *Church and society in England: Henry VIII to James I*, pp 119-36.

Leask, H.G., *Irish churches and monastic buildings* (3 vols, Dundalk, 1955-60).

Leinster, duke of, 'Maynooth Castle', in *Kildare Arch. Soc. Jn.*, i (1891-95), pp 223-39.

Lennon, Colm, *Richard Stanihurst, the Dubliner, 1547-1618* (Dublin, 1981).

——, *The lords of Dublin in the age of Reformation* (Dublin, 1989).

——, 'The chantries of the Irish Reformation: the case of St Anne's Guild, Dublin, 1550-1630', in R.V. Comerford, Mary Cullen, J.R. Hill and Colm Lennon (eds), *Religion, conflict and coexistence in Ireland: essays presented to Monsignor Patrick J. Corish* (Dublin, 1990), pp 6-25.

——, *Sixteenth-century Ireland: the incomplete conquest* (Dublin, 1994).

Lodge, John, *The peerage of Ireland* (4 vols, Dublin, 1754; revised by Mervyn Archdall, 7 vols, Dublin, 1789).

Luxton, Imogen, 'The Reformation and popular culture', in O'Day and Heal (eds), *Church and society in England Henry VIII to James I*, pp 57- 77.

Lydon, James, *Ireland in the later middles ages* (Dublin, 1973).

—— (ed.), *England and Ireland in the later middle ages in honour of Jocelyn Otway-Ruthven* (Dublin, 1981).

—— (ed.), *The English in medieval Ireland* (Dublin, 1984).

Lynch, Anthony, 'Religion in late medieval Ireland', in *Archivium Hibernicum*, xxxvi (1981), pp 3-15.

Lyons, Mary Ann, 'Revolt and reaction: the Geraldine rebellion and monastic confiscation in County Kildare, 1535-1540', in *Kildare Arch. Soc. Jn.*, xviii (1992-3), pp 39-60.

——, 'The foundation of the Geraldine college of the Blessed Virgin Mary, Maynooth 1518', in *Kildare Arch. Soc. Jn.*, xviii, pt 2 (1994-5), pp 134-50.

——, *Gearóid Óg Fitzgerald, ninth earl of Kildare* (Dundalk, 1998).

Lyster Denny, H.L., 'An account of the family of Alen, of St Wolstan's, Co Kildare', in *Kildare Arch. Soc. Jn.*, iv (1903-05), pp 95-110.

MacCurtain, Margaret, *Tudor and Stuart Ireland* (Dublin, 1972).

MacSweeney, M.T., 'The parish of Maynooth, AD 1040 –1614', in *Irish Ecclesiastical Record*, 5th ser., lvi (July-Dec. 1940), pp 305-20, 412-28, 497-509.

Martin, F.X., 'Confusion abounding: Bernard O'Higgins, OSA, bishop of Elphin, 1542-1561', in Cosgrove and McCartney (eds), *Studies in Irish history*, pp 38-84.

Marshall, Peter, *The Catholic priesthood and the English Reformation* (Oxford, 1994).

Martin, Geoffrey, 'Plantation boroughs in medieval Ireland, with a handlist of boroughs to c.1500', in David Harkness and Mary O'Dowd (eds), *The town in Ireland. Historical Studies XIII* (Belfast, 1981), pp 23-53.

Mason, W.M., *The history and antiquities of the collegiate and cathedral church of St Patrick near Dublin, from its foundation in 1190 to the year 1819* (Dublin, 1820).

McCorristine, Laurence, *The revolt of Silken Thomas: a challenge to Henry VIII* (Dublin, 1987).

McRoberts, David (ed.), *Essays on the Scottish Reformation, 1513-1625* (Glasgow, 1962).

Meigs, Samantha, *The Reformations in Ireland: tradition and confessionalism, 1400-1690* (Dublin, 1997).

Moeller, Bernd, 'Piety in Germany around 1500', in Steven Ozment, *The Reformation in medieval perspective* (Chicago, 1971).

Moody, T.W., Martin, F.X. and Byrne, F.J. (eds), *A new history of Ireland, iii. Early modern Ireland, 1534-1691* (Oxford, 1971).

——, *A new history of Ireland, ix. Maps, genealogies, lists* (Oxford, 1984).

Mooney, Canice, *The church in Gaelic Ireland: thirteenth to fifteenth centuries* (Dublin, 1969).

Murphy, Denis, 'The Eustaces of Co Kildare', in *Kildare Arch. Soc. Jn.*, i (1891-95), pp 115-30.

——, 'Kildare: its history and antiquities', in *Kildare Arch. Soc. Jn.*, ii (1896-9), pp 289-302.

——, 'The Pale', in *Kildare Arch. Soc. Jn.*, ii (1896-9), pp 48-58.

Murray, James, 'Archbishop Alen, Tudor reform and the Kildare rebellion', in *Proceedings of the Royal Irish Academy*, lxxxix, sect. C (1989), pp 1-16.

——, 'The sources of clerical income in the Tudor diocese of Dublin, c.1530-1600', in *Archivium Hibernicum*, xlv (1990), pp 139-60.

Murray, L.P., 'The ancient chantries of County Louth', in *Louth Arch. Soc. Jn.*, ix, no. 3 (1989), pp 181-208.

Nicholls, K.W., 'The descendants of Oliver Fitzgerald of Belagh', in *The Irish Genealogist*, v (1968-73), pp 2-9.

——, 'The Geraldines of Allen', in *The Irish Genealogist*, iv (1968-73), pp 93-108, 194-200.

——, *Gaelic and gaelicised Ireland in the middle ages* (Dublin, 1972).

——, 'Medieval Irish cathedral chapters', in *Archivium Hibernicum*, xxxi (1973), pp 102-11.

O'Day, Rosemary and Heal, Felicity (eds), *Of princes and paupers in the English church, 1500-1800* (Leicester, 1981).

O'Hanlon, John, O'Leary, Edward, *History of the Queen's County* (2 vols, Dublin, 1907-14).

O'Hart, John, *Irish pedigrees*, 4th ed. (2 vols, Dublin, 1887-8).

O'Leary, Edward, 'John Lye, of Clonaugh, County Kildare', in *Kildare Arch. Soc. Jn.*, iii (1899-1902), pp 39-50.

Ó Lochlainn, Colm (ed.), *Irish men of learning: studies by Fr Paul Walsh* (Dublin, 1947).

O Murethi, 'Castlemartin', in *Kildare Arch. Soc. Jn.*, iii (1899-1902), pp 319-24.

——, 'The white castle of Athy and its sculptured stones', in *Kildare Arch. Soc. Jn.*, iv (1903-05), pp 47-62.

O'Reilly, Matthew, 'The Barnwalls', in *Ríocht na Midhe*, i, no. 3 (1957), pp 64-8.

O'Sullivan, Harold, 'The landed gentry of the county of Louth in the age of the Tudors', in *Louth Arch. Soc. Jn.*, xxii, no. 1 (1989), pp 67-81.

Otway-Ruthven, Jocelyn, 'The medieval county of Kildare', in *Irish Historical Studies*, xi, no. 43 (Mar. 1959), pp 181-99.

——, 'The medieval church lands of Co Dublin', in Watt, Morrall and Martin (eds), *Medieval Studies presented to Aubrey Gwynn*, pp 54-73.

——, *A history of medieval Ireland* (London, 1968; 2nd ed. London, 1980).

Palliser, D.M., 'Popular reactions to the Reformation during the years of uncertainty, 1530-70', in Haigh (ed.), *The English Reformation revised*, pp 94-113.

Ponsonby, Gerald, 'Bishopscourt and its owners', in *Kildare Arch. Soc. Jn.*, viii (1915-17), pp 3-29.

Pontfarcy, Yolande de, 'Pre-Reformation pilgrimages to St Patrick's Purgatory', in *Ulster Local Studies*, xv, no. 2 (Winter 1993), pp 7-21.

Pigott, H.T., 'The family of Eustace', in *The Irish Builder*, xi, no. 914 (Jan. 1898), p. 16.

Quinn, D.B., 'Anglo-Irish local government, 1485-1534', in *Irish Historical Studies*, i, no. 4 (Sept. 1939), pp 354-81.

——, 'Parliaments and great councils in Ireland, 1461-1568', in *Irish Historical Studies*, iii, no. 9 (Mar. 1942), pp 60-77.

——, 'Henry VIII and Ireland, 1509-34', in *Irish Historical Studies*, xii, no. 48 (Sept. 1961), pp 318-44.

—— and Nicholls, K.W., 'Ireland in 1534', in Moody, Martin and Byrne (eds), *A new history of Ireland, iii. Early modern Ireland*, pp 1-38.

Rae, Edwin, 'The tomb of Bishop Walter Wellesley of Great Connell Priory, County Kildare', in *Kildare Arch. Soc. Jn.*, xv (1970), pp 544-63.

Ronan, M.V., *The Reformation in Dublin, 1536-58* (London, 1926).

——, 'Anglo-Norman Dublin and diocese', in *Irish Ecclesiastical Record*, 5th ser., xlv (1935), pp 148-64, 274-91, 485-504, 576-95; xlvi (1935), pp 11-30, 154-71, 257-75, 377-93, 490-510, 577-96; xlvii (1936), pp 28-44, 144-63, 459-68; xlviii (1936), pp 170-93, 378-96; xlix (1937), pp 155-64.

Russell, C.W., 'On an agreement in Irish between Gerald, ninth earl of Kildare, and the MacRannals, executed at Maynooth', in *Proceedings of the Royal Irish Academy*, x (1869), pp 480-9.

Sadleir, T.U., 'Kildare members of parliament, 1559-1800', in *Kildare Arch. Soc. Jn.*, vi (1909-11), pp 398-406, 425.

Scribner, R.W., 'Ritual and popular religion in Catholic Germany at the time of the Reformation', in *Journal of Ecclesiastical History*, xxxv (1985), pp 47-77.

Sherlock, William, *Some account of St Brigid and of the see of Kildare with its bishops, and of the cathedral, now restored* (Dublin, 1896).

——, 'Donadea and the Aylmer family', in *Kildare Arch. Soc. Jn.*, iii (1899-1902), pp 169-78.

——, 'The original Anglo-Norman settlers in County Kildare', in *Kildare Arch. Soc. Jn.*, iii (1899-1902), pp 290-19.

——, 'Further notes on the history and antiquities of the parish of Clane', in *Kildare Arch. Soc. Jn.*, iv (1903-5), pp 35-46.

——, 'Knights Hospitallers in Co Kildare', in *Kildare Arch. Soc. Jn.*, vi (1909-11), pp 89-95.

Simms, Anngret and Andrews, J.H. (eds), *Irish country towns* (Cork, 1994).

Stokes, Margaret, 'Old Kilcullen', in *Kildare Arch. Soc. Jn.*, ii (1896-9), pp 431-46.

Stokes, George, 'Clane Abbey', in *Kildare Arch. Soc. Jn.*, iii (1899-1902), pp 101-6.

Swanson, R.N., *Church and society in late medieval England* (Oxford, 1989).

Thomas, Avril, *The walled towns of Ireland* (2 vols, Dublin, 1992).

Tickell, E.F., 'The Eustace family and their lands in County Kildare', in *Kildare Arch. Soc. Jn.*, xiii, no. 6 (1955), pp 270-87; no. 7 (1958), pp 307-41; no. 8 (1960), pp 364-413.

Valkenburg, Augustine, 'A study in diplomacy: Gerald, eleventh earl of Kildare, 1525-85', in *Kildare Arch. Soc. Jn.*, xiv, no. 3 (1968), pp 293-315.

——, 'Walter Wellesley, bishop of Kildare, 147?-1539', in *Kildare Arch. Soc. Jn.*, xiv, no. 3 (1968), pp 518-43.

Vandeleur, W.E., *Notes on the history of Castledermot* (Carlow, n.d).

Vicars, Arthur, 'The family of Flatesbury, of Ballynsculloge and Johnstown, Co Kildare', in *Kildare Arch. Soc. Jn.*, iv (1903-05), pp 87-94.

Watt, J.A., Morrall, J.B. and Martin, F.X. (eds), *Medieval studies presented to Aubrey Gwynn* (Dublin, 1961).

Watt, J.A., *The church and the two nations in medieval Ireland* (Cambridge, 1970).

——, *The church in medieval Ireland* (Dublin, 1972).

——, 'The church and two nations in late medieval Armagh', in W.J. Sheils and Diana Wood (eds), *The churches, Ireland and the Irish* (Oxford, 1989), pp 37-54.

Whiting, Robert, *The blind devotion of the people* (Cambridge, 1989).

Williams, Glanmor, *The Welsh church from conquest to Reformation* (Cardiff, 1962).

——, *Recovery, reorientation and Reformation: Wales, c.1415-1642* (Oxford, 1987).

Wood, Anthony. *Athenae Oxonienses: an exact history of all the writers and bishops who have had their education in the university of Oxford*, ed. Philip Bliss (4 vols, London, 1813-20).

Wood-Legh, K.L., 'Some aspects of the history of chantries in the later middle ages', in *Transactions of the Royal Historical Society*, 4th ser., xxviii (1946), pp 47-60.

Woulfe, Patrick, 'Some martyrs of the Pale', in M.V. Ronan (ed.), *Catholic emancipation centenary record* (Dublin, 1929), pp 30-5.

Young Cowell, George, 'St Brigid and the cathedral church of Kildare', in *Kildare Arch. Soc. Jn.*, ii (1896-9), pp 235-52.

UNPUBLISHED WORKS

Carey, Vincent, *Surviving the Tudors* (forthcoming monograph).

Lennon, Colm, The Reformation in the Pale (seminar paper).

Murray, James, The Tudor diocese of Dublin: episcopal government, ecclesiastical politics and enforcement of the Reformation, *c.*1534-1590 (Ph.D. thesis, University of Dublin, 1997).

Index